CHALK HILL WINERY

Sommelier Guide

to Restaurants in America

FEATURING 800 OF THE COUNTRY'S BEST RESTAURANTS
AND ULTIMATE FOOD AND WINE PAIRINGS

YVES SAUBOUA · RONN WIEGAND, M.W., M.S.

2003 EDITION

ACKNOWLEDGEMENTS

Chalk Hill Winery Sommelier Guide to Restaurants in America,
2003 Edition

Published by Chalk Hill Press, Healdsburg, California
Produced and printed by Diablo Custom Publishing, Walnut Creek,
California
ISBN: 1-891267-53-1
All rights reserved.

Special thanks to authors and contributors Catherine Fallis, M.S.;
Yves Sauboua, Chalk Hill Estate Sommelier; Ronn Wiegand, M.S.,
M.W.; Jean L. Arnold; Erica Valentine; Annemarie Jones, Marie Clary
and Joanne Peterson of Chalk Hill Estate Vineyards & Winery.

Illustrations: Patricia Healey
Cover and inside front cover photographs: Lenny Siegel
Inside back cover vineyard photograph: Thomas Heinser

Although the publisher, authors and editors have done exhaustive
research to assure accuracy of the information presented here, we
assume no responsibility for any errors and omissions. We will make
every effort to update the sommelier and restaurant information in
future editions. Updated and new information may be sent to:

Chalk Hill Press
10300 Chalk Hill Road
Healdsburg, CA 95448
jpeterson@chalkhill.com

2003 Edition

CHALK HILL WINERY

Sommelier Guide

to Restaurants in America

FEATURING 800 OF THE COUNTRY'S BEST RESTAURANTS
AND ULTIMATE FOOD AND WINE PAIRINGS

Contents

Professional sommeliers and wine managers can make the dining experience a brilliant adventure for diners new to wine as well as for seasoned wine enthusiasts. As producers of wine, we have tremendous respect for the depth of knowledge, style of presentation, as well as the creativity and sense of adventure that these wine professionals bring to dining in restaurants both in America and abroad.

The Chalk Hill Winery Sommelier Guide to Restaurants in America acknowledges the important contribution that the sommelier profession provides in educating the public about the pleasure wine brings to a meal and the wonderful results of their guidance in selecting ultimate food and wine combinations. We are pleased to offer this guide for discerning diners who want to choose a restaurant for both its menu and its wine selection.

Those of us in the winemaking profession understand the rigors and demands as well as the depth of education required to become a professional sommelier. Many diners are eager to learn more about this proud tradition. Thus, we hope the Chalk Hill Winery Sommelier Guide to Restaurants in America is educational as well as inspirational and will be a useful resource for those interested in joining the sommelier profession.

In 2003 the United States is hosting the "Best Sommelier in the World" competition. In this book you will find profiles of some of the brightest and best sommeliers in America. These professionals will most certainly have a significant impact upon the global contest, and we eagerly await the results.

Wishing you many wonderful experiences with wine in America's best restaurants,

Atalon, Cambria, Chalk Hill Estate, Hanzell Vineyards, Hartford Family Wines, Jordan Vineyards, Rudd Estate, Silver Oak, Stature, Stonestreet, Vérité

January 2003

Dear Fellow Sommeliers,

Finally a volume that brings together wine professionals from restaurants throughout the United States. Thank you, Yves Sauboua, Ronn Wiegand and Chalk Hill Winery for highlighting the role of the sommelier in American restaurants.

As an organization seeking to create a community of sommeliers that promotes our role in the hospitality industry, the American Sommelier Association is pleased to welcome Chalk Hill's ground-breaking guide. This innovative publication puts faces and personalities alongside the names of people who work in our country's restaurants and recognizes the contributions which sommeliers make as curators of the wine and food experience.

Never before has the sommelier been more important to the continued growth and success of the nation's hospitality industry. With each vintage, more wines are available from around the world, and we sommeliers have the opportunity to act as guides and ambassadors in the customer's exploration of exciting and emerging wines and their proper role at the table.

In our effort to maintain the spotlight on the sommelier, in 2003 ASA will host the Concours de Meilleur Sommelier du Monde (World's Best Sommelier Competition) for the first time in the United States. Forty member nations will send their best sommeliers to compete to be the best of the best. The co-host for this competition is the Association de la Sommellerie Internationale (A.S.I.). Join us and be a part of this powerful movement that is changing the way Americans look at food and wine.

À votre santé,

ANDREW F. BELL
PRESIDENT-CEO
AMERICAN SOMMELIER ASSOCIATION
580 BROADWAY
SUITE 716
NEW YORK, NEW YORK 10012
212-226-6805
WWW.AMERICANSOMMELIER.COM

AMERICAN
SOMMELIER
ASSOCIATION

We are pleased to present the 2003 edition of the Chalk Hill Winery Sommelier Guide to Restaurants in America. We thank the Furths of Chalk Hill Winery and the other sponsoring wineries for their support in promoting the sommelier profession. We hope you find this guide helpful in several ways:

- Finding restaurants with great wine programs throughout the United States
- Learning about sommeliers and professional wine service in restaurants
- Insights on the world of wine and food from some of America's leading wine professionals
- Resources for learning more about wine for the wine professional as well as new wine enthusiasts

How to use this guide:

This guide to restaurants is organized:
- Alphabetically by state, and by region within certain states
- Featured sommeliers are listed first, alphabetically by restaurant
- Additional restaurants are listed alphabetically after the featured section

Highlights to look for:
- Ultimate wine and food pairing suggestions
- Types of wine programs and selections offered by featured restaurants
- Profiles on sponsoring wineries and their contact information for visits

We invite you to enjoy this guide and we wish you the best of wine and dining experiences!

Cheers! À votre santé!

Ronn Wiegand
MASTER OF WINE,
MASTER SOMMELIER
Editor, *Restaurant Wine*
P.O. Box 222
Napa, California 94559-0222
707-224-4777 • 707-224-6740 Fax
ronn-w@pacbell.net

Yves Sauboua
ESTATE SOMMELIER
*Chalk Hill Estate Vineyards
& Winery*
10300 Chalk Hill Road
Healdsburg, California 95448
707-838-4306 • 707-838-9687 Fax
boiteajaja@aol.com

Chapter One
The Sommelier

by Catherine Fallis, M.S.

The Sommelier

In today's exciting restaurant scene, sommeliers are considered the beverage experts—those people who preside over and recommend everything from cocktails, aperitifs, wines and cognacs to coffees and teas. In short, a sommelier is usually knowledgeable, adventurous and agreeable on all beverage fronts.

1. What is a Sommelier?

Few Americans know what a sommelier (summel-YAY) is, or just exactly what the job entails. The sommelier's primary role is to help guests select wine, to make sure it is sound and then to refill glasses throughout the meal. The best sommeliers in the world are also able to answer questions about production methods of wines and spirits, wine regions, grape varieties and the pairing of food and wine. Knowledge of waters, coffees, teas, liquors, liqueurs, brandies, ports and cigars is also required. A good sommelier is a showman on the floor; the act of decanting a bottle of wine, for example, or pouring wine with a flourish can add an air of drama and entertainment to the dining experience.

Some may think that, before working in the dining room, sommeliers sit around and drink wine all day. The much less glamorous reality is that they regularly meet with sales representatives to taste through many wines to find those they believe are best for their restaurant. They must taste and spit constantly. Their palate is the restaurant's guinea pig, and it is constantly on call. Each vintage, from all reaches of the planet, needs to be tasted for quality, style and its price-value ratio. At the same time, sommeliers must decide if a particular wine will marry well with what is coming out of the kitchen, if it matches the image of the restaurant and, most important, if it will satisfy guests. They must also negotiate with suppliers for the best deals, try to lower pouring costs, increase sales volume, turn inventory quickly and improve service standards. Sommeliers stock the wines, lift cases and often climb up and down eight-foot ladders to place bottles in their racks. They regularly take physical inventory and oversee staff training, and they are responsible for running a profitable wine program.

But wine management and service are only part of a sommelier's job. Off duty, they read stacks of wine publications, regularly visit wine regions and try new foods and wines to hone their pairing skills, always striving to improve the wine and dining experience for their customers.

II. History of the Sommelier

According to the Robert French Language History Dictionary, The name "sommelier," meaning wine waiter in English, stemmed from the old French words "sommerier," "somier," and "bête de somme." In this old French language, a "bête de somme" was a "beast of burden" and the "sommelier" was its herdsman.

Chalk Hill Estate sommelier Yves Sauboua adds, "Since the Belle Époque in Europe, the sommelier has worn a short black jacket, a black apron and a symbolic golden grape. In those times, his responsibility was as important as that of the chef. The sommelier's origin dates far back in the history of mankind. We find traces of Ganymede pouring wines for the gods of Olympia. And the Merovingian and Carolingian kings had servants whose sole job was to pour wines for them."

Around 1690, in the royal court, the word sommelier came to be used for the person who laid the table and prepared the wine for a meal. This definition replaced all earlier meanings. Today, that definition has developed to refer to the person responsible for wine and beverages in a restaurant.

Larousse Gastronomique defines a sommelier as (1) [an] employee charged with the care of the cellars, (2) a member of a religious order concerned with the convent plates, linen, bread and wine. A sommellerie is either a group of persons engaged in looking after cellars and drinks in a royal household, or the place where the work of the sommelier is done, notably in monasteries and convents.

III. The French Sommelier

In France, the sommelier is as indispensable as the chef. It is not unusual for a sommelier to begin his or her career at 16. By the time sommeliers in France are 21, they may have moved beyond the regional Ruinart Champagne competition to the title of French Master Sommelier, sanctioned by the Union de la Sommellerie Française. Later, they may sit for the Master Sommelier exams, an internationally recognized program run by the Court of Master Sommeliers in England, or go on to the Grand Prix Sopexa du Sommelier and Le Meilleur Sommelier du Monde en Vins et Spiritueux de France, two internationally recognized competitions sponsored by Food and Wines from France. By age 30, they may have attempted to sit for the toughest competition in the business, the Concours du Meilleur Sommelier du Monde (also called Concours Mondiale, Best Sommelier in the World) sponsored by the Association de la Sommellerie Internationale.

French wine training, discipline and education begin under a mentor's guiding hands. In France, the Union de la Sommellierie Française provides the infrastructure. With 18 chapters across the country, this organization welcomes working sommeliers equally without club politics, and provides the network of mentors, colleagues and role models that all sommeliers need at some point. Colleges and universities also offer extensive sommelier certification programs. The Sommelier Diploma Program, given by the National Education Academy in Bordeaux, for example, bestows the Sommelier Certificate, a title that assures the highest level of professionalism and expertise, to those who successfully complete an intensive, 12-month program. The syllabus, similar to that of the master sommelier program, includes production methods of wines, spirits and beers, international wine laws, harmony of food and wine, wine tasting skills and practical service and salesmanship, including service of liqueurs, brandies, ports and cigars. In a blind tasting examination, candidates must correctly identify the grape varieties, country and region of origin, age and quality of each wine presented.

IV. The North American Sommelier

The best American sommeliers seek out professional training, continue their education and find time to mentor others, either informally in their restaurants or in formal school programs. Though finding educational wine courses here is much more challenging than it is in France, organizations such as the Court of Master Sommeliers and the American Sommelier Association are playing a major role in the renaissance of the professional sommelier. ASA programs, along with those offered under the auspices of the Wine and Spirit Education Trust, offer sophisticated courses taught by leading professionals. (See Resources for more information.)

Here are a few comments from top professionals about the role of a sommelier.

These days there has been a revitalized interest in wine, largely thanks to the growth of the American wine industry. As a result, more and more restaurants are realizing the importance of a well-thought-out wine program that reflects the style of the restaurant and its cuisine. The sommelier is the key. Without an astute buyer and knowledgeable wine stewards to properly place the product, none of this is possible.

—Marnie Old, past education chair of the
American Sommelier Association

The sommelier may be the one person who can help orchestrate and enliven your entire meal. Using a competent sommelier offers two advantages: He or she has tasted the wines on the list more recently than you and also knows how the menu items you ordered are actually being prepared.

—Kevin Zraly, wine educator and author of Windows on the
World Complete Wine Course

It's important for a restaurant to have a sommelier, and the amazing thing is that most of the time when the sommelier introduces a customer to a new wine, properly paired with the food, the customer will fall in love with it and wonder why nobody ever told them anything about it before.

—Andre Rochat, chef-proprietor of Andre's French Restaurant,
Andre's at the Monte Carlo Resort and Alize, in Las Vegas

For the restaurateur, a sommelier can add improved service through guest contact and, of course, improve the bottom line. My experience at Judson Grill is proof! Since my arrival, the average price per bottle sold has increased from $40 to $60, the sales have increased 20 percent and the cost reduced 15 percent. The results speak for themselves.

—Beth von Benz, wine director at New York City's Judson Grill

New American cuisine is based on a wealth of cultural traditions from all over the world. Americans' palates are eagerly evolving and chefs are becoming more wine-savvy, striving to offer wine and food pairings that optimize flavor harmonies and enjoyment for diners.

Master sommelier Larry Stone, in his essay "Wine Service in the U.S." in The Oxford Companion to the Wines of North America, says: "One of the most exciting developments over the last 30 years, especially over the last 10 years, is that regardless of the region or city, having wine with a meal, especially at restaurants, has become more important to a broad range of people from various professional and cultural backgrounds. The enjoyment of wine is no longer restricted to an elite, aging and wealthy upper class."

Modern sommeliers are not only educated, they're warm, friendly and engaging. The best sommeliers today are working to create a refreshingly open and wine-friendly atmosphere. They understand that fostering a fun, exciting wine experience works for the novice and the seasoned connoisseur alike. Most important, they know that the primary focus of their job is to serve their customers in the enjoyment of food and wine.

Chapter Two

The Service of Wine in the Restaurant

BY CATHERINE FALLIS, M.S.

The Service of Wine in the Restaurant

Wine, like food, is a pleasure for
the senses. We use our eyes, our noses
and our palates each time we eat.
Enjoying a glass of wine requires
the exact same tools.

In Europe, wine graces nearly every
table, and this is increasingly so in
America. Yet many of us are untrained
in the understanding and consumption
of wine and the subject of wine service.
Here are a few notes to assist you.

I. To Your Health

Wine tastes good. It enhances the flavor of everything we consume
and tastes delicious in its own right. Sipping wine throughout your
meal enhances your sense of well-being and may even slow the pace
at which you eat. You feel sated earlier on, which could spare hundreds of calories (a 5-ounce glass of wine has only 60 to 80 calories). A sip of wine gets your digestive juices flowing, and primes
your palate by tuning in your sensory receptors. Even America's
medical establishment has acknowledged that wine is a part of a
healthy lifestyle, recommending a glass a day (two for men) with a
meal. So raise your glass in a toast to health. À votre santé! Salute!

II. Ordering Wine in the Restaurant

Wine is food. For centuries, wine has served to enhance the overall
experience of a meal—from casual to sophisticated. Today, with our
melting-pot ethnicity and love of international as well as regional
foods, wine and food pairings inspire us to try new, exciting combinations.

This is where the sommelier can be a great help. Once you and
your dining companions have made your meal selections, ask your
sommelier for wine suggestions. He should be able to accommo-
date any personal preferences and budgets. Even if you know what
you want, it's always fun to compare notes with the experts. After
all, sommeliers are the ones who compose the wine list to accord
with the restaurant's menu.

Prices vary considerably, especially at the ultrapremium level. You may prefer a $25 wine to a $125 wine; only you can determine how much that pleasure is worth. A good rule of thumb is to spend twice as much on a bottle of wine as you do on the entrée. This is not to say that a reserve Cabernet Sauvignon, a classified Bordeaux or a vintage Champagne is not worth the sometimes exorbitant price tag. It is a good practice to ask your sommelier to recommend wines that will best enhance your meal. Don't be afraid to order a moderately priced wine. After all, the sommelier has chosen each wine on the list for a reason.

Corkage fees—what the restaurant charges when you bring in your own bottle—are an attempt to recoup some of the lost profit and are wholly appropriate where professional wine service is offered. Even if you do bring a bottle in, it is good form to order one from the wine list as well.

It is often agreeable to begin with an aperitif such as sparkling wine or Champagne, or a crisp, dry, appetite-stimulating wine such as Sauvignon Blanc, Sancerre or Pouilly-Fumé. Ask for this to be served right away. This can help to break the ice and sets the tone for a convivial table.

Look for older vintages, especially in well-established restaurants with large wine cellars. Unless the restaurant has just acquired them at today's cost, these are hidden values.

With more than four people, you may wish to order a magnum (1.5 liters, which is equal to two 750-milliliter bottles). Magnums are impressive and usually have a good price-value ratio. Plus, you just might get extra attention from your server or sommelier.

Dessert wines are often overlooked. Save room for a small glass of port or a late-harvest Sauvignon Blanc to enjoy with or in lieu of dessert.

III. Presentation and Service

When the sommelier brings the bottle to the table, scrutinize the label. Make sure it is the exact wine that you ordered—vintage, region of origin and varietal, if noted. If the wine steward hands you the cork, smile and politely accept it. Look at it, roll it around in your hands and smell it if you like. This is one of the many traditions surrounding formal wine service. Since you are paying for the bottle, you have a right to watch the opening and cork extraction and to physically examine the closure. Just keep in mind that the only way to tell if your wine is "corked"—tainted by TCA, a random mustiness that sometimes occurs in wine—or "off" due to some other cause is to smell and taste the wine itself. After the sommelier has poured a small taste for you, pick up the glass, take a quick sniff and taste, and just nod your approval so he can move on to his other duties, including filling the glasses of your guests. You are simply assessing the soundness of the wine. If you sense something is wrong, engage the sommelier in a conversation about it, and make a quick decision whether to accept the wine or to request either a second bottle or an alternative choice.

A good sommelier will keep your glasses appropriately filled and will be at the ready with additional bottles. The sommelier should present a new glass to the host with each new bottle, to allow the host to check for soundness. A top-notch sommelier will ask the host if he would like new glasses set around for each bottle, but this is not necessary if the wine is similar.

Sommeliers are usually compensated with a percentage of their sales plus a small base salary. Rarely are they included in the servers' tip pool, though most guests assume they are. A 15-percent tip for service is standard, but use your own best judgment. If you are pleased with the sommelier's service and would like to be sure he is compensated appropriately, you should tip him directly.

Chapter Three
Featured Wineries

ATALON

Atalon

7600 St. Helena Highway
Oakville, California 94562
(800) 224-4090
www.atalon.com
(visit by appointment only)

Atalon is a modern adventure, created to explore the unique soils and flavor profiles of grapes grown on volcanic mountain peaks and those grown on benchland vineyards. This grand exploration of microclimates and sub-appellations is reflected under both a Mountain Estate and Napa Valley designation. Our hand-to-vine philosophy interprets the diverse texture and flavors found within the Napa Valley, from the elegance of the Valley to the intensity of the Mountain. Atalon is a story of comparative revelations. Inspired from the French word étalon meaning "benchmark" or "equestrian standard," Atalon is committed to today's high standard and tomorrow's potential.

First Vintage
The inaugural vintage for Atalon was 1997 with the introduction of Mountain Estate Cabernet Sauvignon and Merlot and Beckstoffer Vineyard Cabernet Sauvignon.

Winemaker
Thomas Peffer

Vineyard Manager
Patty McClain

Wines
Mountain Estate Cabernet Sauvignon and Napa Valley Cabernet Sauvignon
Mountain Estate Merlot and Napa Valley Merlot, Beckstoffer Vineyard Cabernet Sauvignon

Vineyard Sources
Mountain Estate grapes grown on Mt. Veeder, Diamond Mountain, Howell Mountain and Atlas Peak. Napa Valley grapes grown in Beckstoffer (Oakville), Ars Gratia Artis (Rutherford), Stagecoach (Atlas Peak), Ahman (Carneros) and Laird (Dry Creek).

Cambria

Cambria

5475 Chardonnay Lane
Santa Maria, California 93454
(888) 339-9463
cambriawines.com
(tasting room open Sat. and
Sun. 10 a.m.–5 p.m. and
weekdays by appt.)

Cambria creates the ultimate
expression of estate bottled
Santa Barbara County Pinot
Noir, Chardonnay and Syrah
from our family-owned estate vineyard in the heart of the Santa Maria Bench.
The Santa Maria Bench, home to Cambria, is a study in contrasts. There is the
understated beauty of the landscape—the wide-angle vistas of undulating vineyards and gently rolling hills; the cool Pacific breezes that cloak the vineyards in
morning coastal fog. And then there are the wines—head turning, opulent,
larger-than-life affairs that impress with their power and seduce with their texture. At Cambria we celebrate these contrasts, from the restrained beauty of our
land to the bold intensity of our wines.

First Vintage
The inaugural vintage for
Cambria was 1988 with the
introduction of Sur Lees
Chardonnay and Julia's
Vineyard Pinot Noir.

Winemaker
Fred Holloway

Vineyard Manager
Patrick Huguenard

Wines
Chardonnay, Pinot Noir and
Syrah

Vineyard Sources
Cambria Estate Vineyards
Santa Maria Valley

Chalk Hill

Sonoma County
10300 Chalk Hill Road
Healdsburg, California
95448
(707) 838-4306
www.chalkhill.com
(visit by appointment only)

Chalk Hill Estate Vineyards & Winery is family-owned and operated in the Chalk Hill sub-appellation of Russian River Valley in Sonoma County, California. Since 1972 Founders and Proprietors Frederick and Peggy Furth have lived on the 1200-acre estate, 350 acres planted in vineyard. Each one of more than 80 vineyard parcels has been created up and down the hillsides and on the valley floors to grow naturally balanced vines. Winemaking consistently conveys the individuality of each site by using natural, traditional methods. The hallmark of all Chalk Hill wines is the land that sustains the vines and the winemaking that authenticates this incomparable terroir.

First Vintage
The inaugural vintage for Chalk Hill was 1980 with the introduction of Estate Bottled Chardonnay, Cabernet Sauvignon and Sauvignon Blanc.

Winemaker
William Knuttel

Vineyard Manager
Mark Lingenfelder

Proprietors
Frederick & Peggy Furth

Wines
Chardonnay, Sauvignon Blanc, Merlot, Cabernet Sauvignon, Pinot Gris, Botrytised Semillon

Vineyard Source
Chalk Hill Estate, Chalk Hill Valley, Russian River Valley

Hanzell

V I N E Y A R D S

Hanzell Vineyards
18596 Lomita Avenue
Sonoma, California 95476
phone (707) 996-3860
facsimile (707) 996-3862
hanzell.com

Hanzell Vineyards, located in the hills above Sonoma Valley, is a private estate winery and vineyard founded in 1957 by Ambassador J. D. Zellerbach. Zellerbach's passion for the great wines of Burgundy prompted his planting of Chardonnay and Pinot Noir vines and the building of an architectural jewel of a winery inspired by Clos de Vougeot. Hanzell Vineyards is renowned for its innovative introduction (in the 1960s) of stainless steel for fermenting its wines and French oak for barrel aging.

As it has been for the past thirty years, Hanzell Vineyards today, now under President, Jean L. Arnold and Winemaker Daniel Docher's stewardship, is still under Bob Session's watchful eye. His new team continues to live the "Hanzell Way"—absolute commitment to quality, the singular expression of terroir from this land, and honoring the tremendous heritage of this unique estate. Hanzell Vineyards is owned by the de Brye Family and has been since 1975.

First Vintage
In 1953, Ambassador Zellerbach and his wife Hanna planted Chardonnay and Pinot Noir on the Hanzell Estate. The winery's first offering was the 1957 Hanzell Vineyards Chardonnay.

Winemaker
Daniel Docher became the Hanzell Vineyards winemaker in January 2002, after apprenticing for seven years under longtime Hanzell winemaker Bob Sessions.

Vineyard Manager
Jose de Jesus Ramos began working at Hanzell in 1977 and has been Hanzell vineyard manager since 1985.

Wines
Estate grown and produced Chardonnay and Pinot Noir

Vineyard Sources
Since 1962, the Hanzell Estate has been the sole vineyard source.

HARTFORD FAMILY
WINES

Hartford Family Wines

8075 Martinelli Road
Forestville, California 95436
(800) 588-0234
(707) 887-1756
hartfordwines.com
(tasting room open daily
10 a.m.–4:30 p.m.)

Hartford Family Wines produces Pinot Noir, Chardonnay and Old Vine Zinfandels from the Sonoma Coast, Russian River Valley and other nearby coastal-influenced appellations that express personality and distinctive terroir. The case production for our vineyard designated wines ranges from 100 to about 800 cases per wine. Hartford Family Wines also makes three blended vineyard wines; Hartford Sonoma Coast Pinot Noir, Sonoma Coast Chardonnay and Russian River Valley Zinfandel. Our blended vineyard wines are made with the same care and attention to detail that characterizes our vineyard designated wines.

First Vintage
The inaugural vintage for Hartford Family Wines was 1994.

Winemaker
Mike Sullivan

Vineyard Manager
Walt Chavoor

Wines
Hartford–Multi-vineyard Chardonnay, Pinot Noir and Zinfandel; vineyard designated Zinfandel Hartford Court–Vineyard designated Chardonnay and Pinot Noir

Vineyard Sources
Arrendell, Annapolis, Dutton-Sanchietti, Pasternak, Savoy, Carneros Hills, Piner, Marshall, Seascape, Occidental-Bones, Durrell, Martinelli, Ross, Hartford, Fanucchi-Wood Road, Dina's, Chelli, Lytton Springs and Pitts

Jordan

Jordan
1474 Alexander Valley Road
Healdsburg, California 95448
(707) 431-5250
fax: (707) 431-5259
www.jordanwinery.com

Founded in 1972, Jordan Vineyard & Winery has specialized in the production of ultra-premium Cabernet Sauvignon and Chardonnay. Located in Sonoma County's renowned Alexander Valley, the winery stands on an oak-covered knoll overlooking 375 acres of carefully tended hillside and valley floor vineyards. Situated less than twenty miles from the Pacific Ocean, the topography, soil and climate impart a distinctive character to Jordan wines. For over twenty-five years Jordan has consistently produced elegant, balanced wines with the philosophy that winemaking is simply a logical completion of nature's work.

First Vintage
The inaugural vintage for Jordan Cabernet Sauvignon was 1976; the inaugural vintage of Jordan Chardonnay was 1979.

Winemaker
Rob Davis joined Jordan Winery as enologist and assistant to Andre Tchelistcheff in 1976 and was made winemaker in 1977.

Vineyard Manager
Mark Bailey

Wines
Cabernet Sauvignon and Chardonnay

Vineyard Sources
Jordan Estate, Alexander Valley, Russian River Valley and Mendocino County

RUDD

Rudd
500 Oakville Crossroad
Oakville, California 94562
(707) 944-8577
(visit by appointment only)

Rudd winery was established in 1996, when Leslie Rudd purchased the 54-acre estate in Oakville. Since the purchase, Mr. Rudd has made extensive renovations to the property that include a complete replanting of the vineyards to close-spaced, red Bordeaux varietals and the expansion and renovation of the winery, adding custom-designed tanks and a gentle, gravity-flow system. In addition, 22,000 square feet of caves have been dug below the winery to provide ideal aging conditions. In April 2002, Charles Thomas joined the Rudd team as Director of Vineyards & Winemaking. Charles brings to Rudd over 25 years of winemaking and vineyard experience. Rudd uses a blend of tradition and innovation, adhering to a philosophy of continuous improvement, to provide discriminating consumers with an exceptional wine-drinking experience.

First Vintage
The first wines under the Rudd label were released in October 2000. The first estate wine will be released in Fall 2003.

Winemaker
Charles Thomas

Vineyard Manager
Terry Mathison

Wines
Cabernet blend, Sauvignon Blanc, Chardonnay

Vineyard Sources
Oakville, and Russian River Valley

SILVER OAK CELLARS
CABERNET SAUVIGNON

Silver Oak Cellars
(800) 273-8809
www.silveroak.com

Napa Valley
915 Oakville Crossroad
Oakville, California 94562

Alexander Valley
24625 Chianti Road
Geyserville, California 95441

In the early 1970s Silver Oak Cellars emerged as a dream tied to an intrepid idea: to create a Cabernet Sauvignon of fully developed flavors and velvety soft textures on the day it was released for sale.

Silver Oak is consistently the most requested Cabernet Sauvignon in America's finest restaurants. The elegance and finesse of our wines have attracted as zealous a circle of customers as any winery, and we are truly grateful for their allegiance, although we will never relax in our pursuit of perfection. We believe that we have yet to make our best bottle of wine, and we will never stop trying.

First Vintage
The inaugural vintage for Silver Oak was 1972 North Coast Cabernet Sauvignon.

Winemaker
Daniel Baron

Vineyard Manager
Dane Petersen

Wine
Cabernet Sauvignon

Vineyard Sources
Alexander Valley and Napa Valley vineyards

Stature
5007 Fulton Road
Fulton, California 95439
(707) 571-8100

Stature represents the pinnacle of Kendall-Jackson wine-making excellence. Created from only the finest vineyards and handcrafted without compromise, these limited production wines take their respective varieties to new levels of perfection. Within the Stature portfolio, Kendall-Jackson offers the ultimate expressions of wine artistry.

First Vintage
The augural release of Kendall-Jackson's Stature was March 2001 with the 1997 Napa Valley Cabernet Sauvignon, 1998 Santa Maria Valley Chardonnay and the 1998 Russian River Valley Pinot Noir.

Winemaker
Randy Ullom

Winemaster
Randy Ullom

Wines
Napa Valley Cabernet Sauvignon, Carneros Pinot Noir, Santa Maria Valley Chardonnay and North Coast Merlot

Vineyard Sources
Rutherford Bench, Santa Maria Bench, Carneros and Russian River Valley

STONESTREET

Stonestreet
7111 Highway 128
Healdsburg, California 95448
(707) 433-9463
stonestreetwines.com
(tasting room: 337 Healdsburg
Ave., Healdsburg, California
95448, (707) 433-7102)

Located on the outskirts of
Healdsburg at the base of the
Mayacamas Mountains lies
Stonestreet's new winery.
Ideally located, the winery lies minutes from our vineyards at Alexander
Mountain Estate, a 5,000-acre parcel that rises on the crest of the Alexander
Valley appellation of eastern Sonoma County. Its unique mountain terroir is
ideal for producing world-class estate and single-vineyard Cabernet Sauvignon,
Merlot, Sauvignon Blanc and Chardonnay.

First Vintage
The inaugural vintage for
Stonestreet was 1989 with the
introduction of Cabernet
Sauvignon and Merlot. In the
autumn of 1989, Jess Jackson
established and named Stonestreet
in honor of his late father, Jess
Stonestreet Jackson. Mike
Westrick, winemaker since 1996,
continues to build upon the
legacy of producing distinctive
wines to savor, collect and age.

Winemaker
Mike Westrick

Vineyard Manager
Tony Viramontes

Wines
Cabernet Sauvignon, Merlot,
Sauvignon Blanc, Chardonnay,
and Legacy "Meritage"

Vineyard Sources
Alexander Mountain Estate

Vérité

4611 Thomas Road,
Healdsburg, California 95448
(707) 433-9000
www.veritewines.com
(visit by appointment only)

Simply put, but profound in its intent, Vérité is dedicated to producing red wines of style and substance along a traditional model. The winery selects the finest Merlot, Cabernet Sauvignon, Cabernet Franc and Malbec from a handful of outstanding mountain and hillside sites or micro-crus along the Mayacamas Mountain range. Each micro-crus or "vineyard within a vineyard" is based on diverse criteria of soil, climate, and other aspects specifically selected for their potential to express a strong sense of terroir. Our winemaker's approach is to envision a model of the wine he would like to create, then to obtain precisely the fruit needed to express that vision.

First Vintage
The inaugural vintage for Vérité was 1998 with two wines, Vérité, Merlot based, and La Joie, Cabernet Sauvignon based.

Vigneron (Winemaker)
Pierre Seillan

Assistant Vignerons
Charles Gendrot
Olivier Rousset

Wines
La Muse (Merlot, Cabernet Sauvignon), La Joie (Cabernet Sauvignon, Merlot), Le Désir (Merlot, Cabernet Franc, Cabernet Sauvignon)

Vineyard Sources
John Alexander Mountain Estate, Alexander Valley, Mt. Taylor, Bennett Valley, Kellogg, Knights Valley, Diamondback, Chalk Hill

Chapter Four

The Restaurants

Crow's Nest in the Hotel Captain Cook

Fifth and K Streets
Anchorage, Alaska 99501
phone 907-276-6000 fax 907-343-2298
website www.captaincook.com

Randal S. Lindsey
SOMMELIER

WHAT ARE SOME OF YOUR ULTIMATE FOOD AND WINE PAIRINGS?
German Kabinetts or Spätleses with an appetizer such as our horseradish, wakame, soy vinaigrette, "Peeky Toe" crab salad; lobster Thermidor with a Spanish Penedès Chardonnay; 1998 Franken Traminer with a Roquefort cheesecake; a chocolate exposé (five different items) served with a Domaine du Mas Blanc Banyuls.

DESCRIBE YOUR WINE SELECTIONS.
Very diverse. We have 900 different wines on our list from around the world. Our clientele generally prefers California wines, but we have an amazing assortment of the best French wines.

WHAT CATEGORIES OF WINE ARE THE BEST VALUES IN YOUR RESTAURANT?
Australian, Chilean and French country wines.

NAME RECENT WINE DISCOVERIES THAT HAVE EXCITED YOU.
There have been huge improvements everywhere, particularly in Italy, Spain, South America, South Africa and New Zealand. Pinotage from South Africa is unique; it's getting better and an international style is emerging.

WHAT IS YOUR FAVORITE WINE REGION IN THE WORLD TODAY?
France. The way the French have adapted different grapes to different environments (given their diverse country) is brilliant.

WHAT LED YOU TO BECOME A SOMMELIER?
Taking a "Wines of the World" course twenty years ago.

WHAT ARE THE BEST ASPECTS OF YOUR JOB?
Helping customers new to wine with their selections and matching wines with our menu items.

IF YOU WERE NOT IN THE WINE PROFESSION, WHAT WOULD YOU BE DOING?
I'd be an anthropologist.

Atlas Bistro
2515 North Scottsdale Road
Scottsdale, Arizona 85257
phone 480-990-2433 fax 480-990-2435

David M. Johnson
SOMMELIER

WHAT ARE SOME OF YOUR ULTIMATE WINE AND FOOD PAIRINGS?
Scottish prime-aged Aberdeen Angus Chateaubriand slowly roasted over dead vines in a stone hearth rotisserie served with a properly decanted bottle of 1947 Chateau Cheval-Blanc.

DESCRIBE YOUR WINE PROGRAM AND WINE SELECTIONS.
Our wine offerings are extensive with 20,000 bottles in inventory from twelve wine producing countries. We have one of the most unique wine set-ups in the United States, offering a BYOB option as well.

WHAT IS YOUR FAVORITE REGION IN THE WORLD TODAY?
Bordeaux is the quintessential wine producing area on Earth. History, culture and pageantry add to the luster of each wine's finest expression. Without Bordeaux, the Napa Valley would be fruit orchards and mustard fields.

WHAT LED YOU TO BECOME A SOMMELIER?
It was a natural progression in my career in hospitality. I was always a specialist in Adult Beverages in all the houses I worked at around the country.

WHAT ARE THE BEST ASPECTS OF YOUR JOB?
Matching wine with the complex, yet subtle flavor profiles of Chef Carlos' exquisite cuisine.

IF YOU WERE NOT IN THE WINE PROFESSION, WHAT WOULD YOU BE DOING?
A cattle rancher or Hollywood screen writer.

Christopher's Fermier Brasserie and Paola's Wine Bar

2584 East Camelback Road
Phoenix, Arizona 85016
phone 602-522-2344 fax 602-468-0314
website www.fermier.com

Paola M. Embry-Gross
Owner and Sommelier

WHAT ARE SOME OF YOUR ULTIMATE FOOD AND WINE PAIRINGS?
Salad of goat cheese in a parmesan crust paired with Sancerre; Christopher's house-smoked salmon salad paired with a Rheingau Kabinett Riesling; seared tuna with red wine sauce paired with an Oregon Pinot Noir; wood oven–roasted foie gras with Tokaji Aszú 3-puttonyos from Hungary.

DESCRIBE YOUR WINE SELECTIONS.
We offer 100 wines by the glass and rotate about twenty wines per month to keep them fresh and exciting. Our focus is on "ABC" whites and reds from around the world.

WHAT CATEGORY OF WINE IS THE BEST VALUE IN YOUR RESTAURANT?
"ABC" whites and reds, especially from Portugal and Spain.

NAME RECENT WINE DISCOVERIES THAT HAVE EXCITED YOU.
Four favorites: 1999 Revello Dolcetto d'Alba, 2000 Villa del Borgo Pinot Grigio from Friuli, 1999 Pojer & Sandri Müller-Thurgau from Trentino and 2000 Vincent Delaporte Sancerre.

WHAT IS YOUR FAVORITE WINE REGION IN THE WORLD TODAY?
Southern Italy, with its exotic grape varieties like Negroamaro, Primitivo and Falaghina.

WHAT LED YOU TO BECOME A SOMMELIER?
Wine was a hobby when I began at Christopher's. Christopher Gross, my business partner, planted the seed.

WHAT ARE THE BEST ASPECTS OF YOUR JOB?
Turning guests on to new wines and encouraging them to branch out into something similar to yet slightly different from what they already know.

IF YOU WERE NOT IN THE WINE PROFESSION, WHAT WOULD YOU BE?
A disc jockey or a fashion designer!

Different Pointe of View at the Pointe-Hilton Tapatio Cliffs Resort

11111 North Seventh Street
Phoenix, Arizona 85020
phone 602-863-0912 fax 602-866-6358
website www.hilton.com

Eric A. Spragett
CELLAR MASTER

WHAT ARE SOME OF YOUR ULTIMATE FOOD AND WINE PAIRINGS?
Lobster bisque with Hirsch Grüner Veltliner; lychees and Gewürztraminer; foie gras and Tokaji Aszú.

DESCRIBE YOUR WINE SELECTIONS.
Global, with an emphasis on California Cabernet and Bordeaux.

WHAT CATEGORY OF WINE IS THE BEST VALUE ON YOUR WINE LIST?
Spanish, but not for long!

NAME A RECENT WINE DISCOVERY THAT EXCITED YOU.
Vivaldaia from Villa Pillo, a super-Tuscan at a great price.

WHAT IS YOUR FAVORITE WINE REGION IN THE WORLD TODAY?
Mendocino in California is the most unspoiled, but St.-Émilion in Bordeaux is classic!

WHAT LED YOU TO YOUR CURRENT POSITION?
No openings for a beer steward!

WHAT ARE THE BEST ASPECTS OF YOUR JOB?
Finding those wines that are so different that it is like starting all over tasting wine again.

IF YOU WERE NOT IN THIS PROFESSION, WHAT WOULD YOU BE DOING?
Brewing!

Mary Elaine's at the Phoenician Resort

6000 East Camelback Road
Scottsdale, Arizona 85251
phone 480-941-8200 fax 480-947-4311
website www.thephoenician.com

Greg A. Tresner
MASTER SOMMELIER

WHAT ARE SOME OF YOUR ULTIMATE FOOD AND WINE PAIRINGS?
Châteaubriand of buffalo with foie gras and béarnaise sauce paired with a ten-plus-year-old Cabernet Sauvignon; broadbill swordfish, cranberry beans, confit tomatoes, tomato jam and a fish-fennel broth paired with a medium-bodied Oregon Pinot Noir.

DESCRIBE YOUR WINE SELECTIONS.
An award-winning wine list, specializing in wines from the important wine regions.

WHAT CATEGORY OF WINE IS THE BEST VALUE IN YOUR RESTAURANT?
New Zealand white and red wines.

NAME RECENT WINE DISCOVERIES THAT HAVE EXCITED YOU.
Tokaji Aszú, the dessert wine of Hungary. Excellent quality and great value.

WHAT IS YOUR FAVORITE WINE REGION IN THE WORLD TODAY?
Burgundy, France. The variety of styles and flavors there never cease to amaze me.

WHAT LED YOU TO BECOME A SOMMELIER?
My love of wine.

WHAT ARE THE BEST ASPECTS OF YOUR JOB?
Guest satisfaction, a great chef and a large wine list.

IF YOU WERE NOT IN THIS PROFESSION, WHAT WOULD YOU BE DOING?
Playing guitar.

Mary Elaine's at the Phoenician Resort

6000 East Camelback Road
Scottsdale, Arizona 85251
phone 480-941-8200 fax 480-947-4311
website www.thephoenician.com

Paul T. Botamer
LEAD SOMMELIER

WHAT ARE SOME OF YOUR ULTIMATE FOOD AND WINE PAIRINGS?
Pan-seared foie gras with one-hundred-year-old balsamic and apricots with Tokaji Aszú; lobster with sliced apples and lobster butter sauce with a dry Alsace Muscat.

DESCRIBE YOUR WINE SELECTIONS.
Our list is designed to be user-friendly, starting with an excellent by-the-glass section. We also want to have the best half-bottle selection possible.

WHAT CATEGORIES OF WINE ARE THE BEST VALUES ON YOUR WINE LIST?
South Africa and Argentina.

NAME RECENT WINE DISCOVERIES THAT HAVE EXCITED YOU.
Malbec from Argentina. Tremendous price-to-quality ratio.

WHAT IS YOUR FAVORITE WINE REGION IN THE WORLD TODAY?
Alsace. The wines pair well with food and can be so diverse.

WHAT LED YOU TO BECOME A SOMMELIER?
Love of history and wine. Every wine has an interesting story.

WHAT ARE THE BEST ASPECTS OF YOUR JOB?
Sharing wine information with customers and recommending interesting and exciting new wines to our guests.

IF YOU WERE NOT IN THE WINE PROFESSION, WHAT WOULD YOU BE DOING?
Farming.

Mary Elaine's at the Phoenician Resort

6000 East Camelback Road
Scottsdale, Arizona 85251
phone 480-941-8200 fax 480-947-4311
website www.thephoenician.com

Thomas A. Ratcliff
SOMMELIER

WHAT ARE SOME OF YOUR ULTIMATE FOOD AND WINE PAIRINGS?
Riesling with lobster; Tokaji Aszú with foie gras; Sancerre with oysters; Hermitage rouge with lamb.

DESCRIBE YOUR WINE SELECTIONS.
We have 2,200 selections. Our list has won a major award for its breadth and depth.

WHAT CATEGORY OF WINE IS THE BEST VALUE ON YOUR WINE LIST?
Wines from South Africa.

NAME RECENT WINE DISCOVERIES THAT HAVE EXCITED YOU.
Sauvignon de St. Bris. I love Sauvignon Blanc and this is a new appellation contrôllée in France. Also, Sauvignon Blanc from Collio in Italy.

WHAT IS YOUR FAVORITE WINE REGION IN THE WORLD TODAY?
New Zealand. It is the one area that has all my favorites: sparkling wine, Riesling, Sauvignon Blanc and Pinot Noir.

WHAT LED YOU TO BECOME A SOMMELIER?
I have always had an interest in wine and turned it into a vocation.

WHAT IS THE BEST ASPECT OF YOUR JOB?
Having guests tell me the wine I chose made their experience extra special. It is very gratifying.

IF YOU WERE NOT IN THE WINE PROFESSION, WHAT WOULD YOU BE DOING?
Working in a bookstore or teaching history.

Mary Elaine's at the Phoenician Resort

6000 East Camelback Road
Scottsdale, Arizona 85251
phone 480-941-8200 fax 480-947-4311
website www.thephoenician.com

Troy J. Smith
SOMMELIER

WHAT ARE SOME OF YOUR ULTIMATE FOOD AND WINE PAIRINGS?
Alsace Sylvaner with white truffle risotto; seared beef tenderloin with porcini risotto paired with a mature Barolo.

DESCRIBE YOUR WINE SELECTIONS.
User-friendly, extensive selection from classic Old World and New World wines. We also have a tremendous selection of half-bottles.

WHAT COUNTRIES OFFER THE BEST VALUES ON YOUR WINE LIST?
South Africa and South America.

NAME RECENT WINE DISCOVERIES THAT HAVE EXCITED YOU.
Castellare's Chianti Classico and Vin Santo are exceptional; Malbec from Cahors, France, offers a great price-to-quality ratio.

WHAT IS YOUR FAVORITE WINE REGION IN THE WORLD TODAY?
Alsace. Its wines have a bright acidity and clean finish that allow them to pair well with a wide array of foods.

WHAT LED YOU TO BECOME A SOMMELIER?
To be able to learn new things about wine on a daily basis.

WHAT ARE THE BEST ASPECTS OF YOUR JOB?
Every day I get to taste wines from all over the world and share them with restaurant guests.

IF YOU WERE NOT IN THIS PROFESSION, WHAT WOULD YOU BE?
Maybe a real estate mogul.

Mastro's Steakhouse

8852 East Pinnacle Peak Road
Scottsdale, Arizona 85255
phone 480-585-9500 fax 480-585-2559
website www.mastrossteakhouse.com

Joi J. Graham
DIRECTOR OF WINE

WHAT ARE SOME OF YOUR ULTIMATE FOOD AND WINE PAIRINGS?
One of my personal favorites is shellfish with a beautiful white Burgundy or a great California Chardonnay. At the restaurant, the most popular food pairing is a California red wine and a juicy steak.

DESCRIBE YOUR WINE SELECTIONS.
The strength of our wine list definitely rests in California white and red wines.

WHAT CATEGORY OF WINE IS THE BEST VALUE ON YOUR WINE LIST?
Cabernet Sauvignon.

NAME RECENT WINE DISCOVERIES THAT HAVE EXCITED YOU.
My latest project has been creating an Italian red section on our list. I find the wines of Tuscany to be particularly fascinating.

WHAT IS YOUR FAVORITE WINE REGION IN THE WORLD TODAY?
The Pacific Northwest. I'm a huge fan of Washington and Oregon wines, especially Oregon Pinot Noirs.

WHAT LED YOU TO YOUR CURRENT POSITION?
I began selling wine in a fine wine shop in St. Thomas, U.S. Virgin Islands. It went from there.

WHAT ARE THE BEST ASPECTS OF YOUR JOB?
Introducing guests to great values. But finding those values is also my greatest challenge.

IF YOU WERE NOT IN THIS PROFESSION, WHAT WOULD YOU BE DOING?
Something to do with foreign language. My original college major was foreign language education.

Tarbell's

3213 East Camelback Road
Phoenix, Arizona 85018
phone 602-955-8100 fax 602-955-8181
website www.tarbells.com

Jim Gallen
OPERATIONS MANAGER AND WINE GUY

WHAT ARE SOME OF YOUR ULTIMATE FOOD AND WINE PAIRINGS?
Grilled double-cut pork chops with ancho vegetable and crispy potato hash with
a Shiraz from Australia; wood oven lamb tenderloin with roasted red pepper,
potato cakes, and balsamic vinaigrette with Pinot Noir from Oregon; white
Burgundy with shellfish; sweet Moscato with crème brûlée; Roquefort with vintage Port.

DESCRIBE YOUR WINE SELECTIONS.
We focus on exciting wines from regions all over the world that work with our
menu.

WHAT CATEGORIES OF WINE ARE THE BEST VALUES IN YOUR RESTAU-
RANT?
Wines from Bordeaux and Australia.

NAME A RECENT WINE DISCOVERY THAT EXCITED YOU.
Shiraz from the Barossa Valley. The wines both are drinkable and have aging
potential, so they are exciting for both cellaring and drinking!

WHAT IS YOUR FAVORITE WINE REGION IN THE WORLD TODAY?
Australia, a country that is innovative in how it makes wine accessible to everyone while keeping wine exciting.

WHAT LED YOU TO YOUR CURRENT POSITION?
I realized how much wine brings to the dining experience. I've wanted to be
involved ever since.

WHAT ARE THE BEST ASPECTS OF YOUR JOB?
Watching someone "get it."

IF YOU WERE NOT IN THE WINE PROFESSION, WHAT WOULD YOU BE
DOING?
I'd either be flying a B-52 or playing a professional sport. Seeing that I'm not
capable of doing either, I'll stay in the wine business.

The Terrace Dining Room at the Phoenician Resort

6000 East Camelback Road
Scottsdale, Arizona 85251-1949
phone 480-941-8200 fax 480-947-4311
website www.thephoenician.com

April Bloom
SOMMELIER

WHAT ARE SOME OF YOUR ULTIMATE FOOD AND WINE PAIRINGS?
Personal favorites include lobster bisque with rosé Champagne; foie gras with Tokaji Aszú; and chocolate flourless cake with Banyuls. In the restaurant, popular favorites are our caramelized diver scallops with a crisp, clean Sauvignon Blanc from France or New Zealand; pancetta-wrapped Atlantic salmon with a Carneros Pinot Noir.

DESCRIBE YOUR WINE SELECTIONS.
We focus on artisan wines of California and the Pacific Northwest, while not forgetting the classics.

WHAT CATEGORY OF WINE IS THE BEST VALUE ON YOUR WINE LIST?
"Aromatic Whites," including Viognier, Grüner Veltliner, Chenin Blanc, Pinot Grigio, Gewürztraminer and Riesling.

NAME RECENT WINE DISCOVERIES THAT HAVE EXCITED YOU.
Biodynamic wines which reflect a holistic approach to grape growing and winemaking.

WHAT IS YOUR FAVORITE WINE REGION IN THE WORLD TODAY?
Italy, because of its range of wine styles, from dry to sweet.

WHAT LED YOU TO BECOME A SOMMELIER?
When I was a dining room captain in charge of staff education, the more I read about wine, the more interested I became.

WHAT ARE THE BEST ASPECTS OF YOUR JOB?
Seeing the staff's growing interest in and enthusiasm for wine, and the reactions of guests who love the new wines I introduce them to.

IF YOU WERE NOT IN THE WINE PROFESSION, WHAT WOULD YOU BE?
A tour director, because I love to travel.

Wrigley Mansion Club

2501 East Telewa Trail
Phoenix, Arizona 85016
phone 602-955-4079 fax 602-956-8439
website www.wrigleymansionclub.com

David C. Torkko

RESTAURANT MANAGER AND SOMMELIER

WHAT ARE SOME OF YOUR ULTIMATE FOOD AND WINE PAIRINGS?
Duck breast with Russian River Pinot Noir; rack of lamb with Amador Zinfandel.

DESCRIBE YOUR WINE SELECTIONS.
We feature many of California's greatest wines, as well as quality wines from other regions. Bottom line: If it's not in the glass, it's not on the list.

WHAT CATEGORIES OF WINE ARE THE BEST VALUES ON YOUR WINE LIST?
New Zealand Sauvignon Blanc, Australian Shiraz, Washington Merlot and German Riesling.

NAME RECENT WINE DISCOVERIES THAT HAVE EXCITED YOU.
Australian Shiraz (d'Arenberg's Dead Arm) is unbelievable; South African Sauvignon Blanc (Neil Ellis) is amazingly complex and fairly priced.

WHAT IS YOUR FAVORITE WINE REGION IN THE WORLD TODAY?
Australia, without a doubt, is making the boldest and brightest flavored, most generous and compelling wines today.

WHAT LED YOU TO YOUR CURRENT POSITION?
My long-term appreciation of wine made becoming a sommelier a logical and easy choice.

WHAT ARE THE BEST ASPECTS OF YOUR JOB?
I love seeing "the light" go on in a staff member who has found the confidence to trust his own palate.

IF YOU WERE NOT IN THE WINE PROFESSION, WHAT WOULD YOU BE?
I would be a poet singing the praises of life's glories (or maybe in sales)!

Marquesa at the Fairmont Scottsdale Princess

REED GROBAN, FOOD AND
BEVERAGE DIRECTOR
7575 East Princess Drive, Scottsdale
480-585-4848

The Phoenician

KELLY KELLER, FOOD AND
BEVERAGE DIRECTOR
6000 East Camelback Road,
Scottsdale
480-941-8200

Rancho Pinot Grill

TOM KAUFMAN, SOMMELIER
6208 North Scottsdale Road,
Scottsdale
480-367-8030

Roxsand Restaurant

ROXSAND SCOCOS, PROPRIETOR
AND WINE BUYER
2594 East Camelback Road, Phoenix
602-381-0444

Vincent Guerithault on Camelback

VINCENT GUERITHAULT, OWNER,
CHEF AND WINE BUYER
3930 East Camelback Road, Phoenix
602-224-0225

Wright's at the Arizona Biltmore

PHILMAN CHAN, SOMMELIER
2400 East Missouri Avenue, Phoenix
602-954-2507

L'Auberge de Sedona

301 L'Auberge Lane
Sedona, Arizona 86339
phone 800-272-6777 fax 928-282-2885
website www.lauberge.com

Mark J. Buzan

SOMMELIER AND CELLAR MASTER
Team: Michael Steinhart, Cellar Master and Food and
Beverage Director

WHAT ARE SOME OF YOUR ULTIMATE FOOD AND WINE PAIRINGS?
Tokaji Eszencia with anything! The wine is so beautiful! Chocolate soufflé
dessert with an aged vintage Port or late-harvest red wine.

DESCRIBE YOUR WINE SELECTIONS.
We have a global list, with more than 800 selections, emphasizing French
wines, with a good representation in Bordeaux and Burgundy, as well as
California Cabernet Sauvignon.

WHAT CATEGORY OF WINE IS THE BEST VALUE ON YOUR WINE LIST?
The white wines of New Zealand.

NAME RECENT WINE DISCOVERIES THAT HAVE EXCITED YOU.
The dessert wines of Hungary. Tokaji Aszú is an incredible value when compared with Sauternes or other dessert wines.

WHAT IS YOUR FAVORITE WINE REGION IN THE WORLD TODAY?
Spain! The wines, both red and white, are of great quality at great prices. There
are so many new faces and wines every year.

WHAT LED YOU TO BECOME A SOMMELIER?
A love of wine! The culture, history, flavors and the ongoing challenge it provides to continue learning about it.

WHAT ARE THE BEST ASPECTS OF YOUR JOB?
Watching people enjoy a wine, whether it is new or an old favorite. Personal
satisfaction for me comes from the guests.

IF YOU WERE NOT IN THE WINE PROFESSION, WHAT WOULD YOU BE
DOING?
Something artistic with my hands, like carpentry.

Bistro Zin

1865 East River Road
Tucson, Arizona 85718
phone 520-299-7799 fax 520-615-4534
website www.tasteofbistrozin.com

Regan D. Jasper
CORPORATE SOMMELIER

WHAT ARE SOME OF YOUR ULTIMATE FOOD AND WINE PAIRINGS?
Pan-seared scallops over saffron Israeli couscous and lobster demi-glaze with
Viognier or Alsatian Pinot Gris; Mapleleaf duck with a drunken cherry sauce
with Russian River Valley Pinot Noir; foie gras with Sauternes; beef carpaccio
with Valpolicella.

DESCRIBE YOUR WINE SELECTIONS.
We offer seventy wines, all by the glass and all incorporated into flights. The
flights showcase wines from important growing regions for each varietal.

WHAT CATEGORY OF WINE IS THE BEST VALUE ON YOUR WINE LIST?
Pinot Gris in white, and Syrah and Shiraz in red.

NAME RECENT WINE DISCOVERIES THAT HAVE EXCITED YOU.
Soave from Italy. New Zealand Sauvignon Blanc, with its bright tropical fruit.
The wines of Alvaro Palacios from Spain are amazing.

WHAT IS YOUR FAVORITE WINE REGION IN THE WORLD TODAY?
Russian River, because of its Pinot Noir, which is my favorite varietal.

WHAT LED YOU TO BECOME A SOMMELIER?
I was a captain in a fine dining restaurant, where the sommelier was my
mentor. Wine became my favorite aspect of the dining experience.

WHAT IS THE BEST ASPECT OF YOUR JOB?
The thrill of the find. Discovering the next quality wine, varietal or region that
few yet recognize is both rewarding and thrilling.

**IF YOU WERE NOT IN THE WINE PROFESSION, WHAT WOULD YOU BE
DOING?**
Buying and selling real estate.

Janos
3770 East Sunrise Drive
Tucson, Arizona 85718
phone 520-615-6100 fax 520-615-3334
website www.janos.com

Ryan J. Schwartz
DIRECTOR OF WINE AND SOMMELIER

WHAT ARE SOME OF YOUR ULTIMATE FOOD AND WINE PAIRINGS?
Seared sea scallops, carrot nage, with lobster and potato galette paired with an Albariño from Rias Baixas, Spain. Mediterranean roast rack of lamb, pomegranate sauce and fingerling potatoes paired with a mature, traditional Barolo or Barbaresco.

DESCRIBE YOUR WINE SELECTIONS.
We have more than 800 selections, specializing in rare, artisan wines whose makers are dedicated to being the best while remaining unique.

WHAT CATEGORY OF WINE IS THE BEST VALUE ON YOUR WINE LIST?
Red Rhône.

NAME RECENT WINE DISCOVERIES THAT HAVE EXCITED YOU.
Schwarz wines from Austria. The winery is producing a wonderful Chardonnay, Zweigelt, and rosé of Zweigelt.

WHAT IS YOUR FAVORITE WINE REGION IN THE WORLD TODAY?
Rhône Valley. I can't think of any other region that consistently gives higher quality wine for the money.

WHAT LED YOU TO BECOME A SOMMELIER?
A passion and interest in the marriage of wine and food.

WHAT IS THE BEST ASPECT OF YOUR JOB?
Searching out small, artisan wines to give our guests unique experiences.

IF YOU WERE NOT IN THE WINE PROFESSION, WHAT WOULD YOU BE DOING?
Playing professional golf, which is what I did for a few years before I became a sommelier.

Stone Ashley

6400 East El Dorado Circle
Tucson, Arizona 85710
phone 520-886-9700 fax 520-886-9712
website www.stoneashley.com

Nina E. Rosas
WINE DIRECTOR AND LEAD SOMMELIER

WHAT ARE SOME OF YOUR ULTIMATE FOOD AND WINE PAIRINGS?
Our panko-crusted lamb with an au poivre sauce combined with classic wines from Ribera del Duero; a big Australian rosé of Grenache with our lobster soup or lobster tail; wild mushroom risotto with white truffle oil and aged Grand Cru Gewürztraminer from Alsace.

DESCRIBE YOUR WINE SELECTIONS.
We have a selection of wines that represent some of the best the wine world has to offer in quality and value while remaining true to regional styles and varietals.

WHAT CATEGORIES OF WINE ARE THE BEST VALUES ON YOUR WINE LIST?
Italian reds and wines from the Rhône, Loire Valley, and Germany.

NAME RECENT WINE DISCOVERIES THAT HAVE EXCITED YOU.
The fact that a mismatched wine can make a perfectly clean piece of fish taste horribly fishy, and that arsenic is a good way to precipitate heavy metals out of a wine. These both just seem like good things to know.

WHAT LED YOU TO BECOME A SOMMELIER?
The intense pleasure I derive from creating, sharing and perpetuating the "dining experience."

WHAT ARE THE BEST ASPECTS OF YOUR JOB?
Speaking to guests, trying to read them and providing them with that which will please their senses. It is all so intimate and legal!

IF YOU WERE NOT IN THE WINE PROFESSION, WHAT WOULD YOU BE DOING?
Researching bat iconography in Mesoamerica or writing comic books.

Ventana Room at Loews Ventana Canyon Resort

7000 North Resort Drive
Tucson, Arizona 85750
phone 520-299-2020
website www.loewshotels.com

Kevin P. Brady
MANAGER

WHAT ARE SOME OF YOUR ULTIMATE FOOD AND WINE PAIRINGS?
Lamb and Bordeaux; squab with Rioja Reserva; tripe with Pouilly-Fumé; Beaujolais with fondue; foie gras with Vouvray; and pizza with California Zinfandel.

DESCRIBE YOUR WINE SELECTIONS.
I try to represent important items that should appear on a good list such as Montrachet, Bordeaux, Chablis and Sancerre. We will have a petits châteaux list because of the interest in Bordeaux-style wines, and our barbecue has a Rhône list.

NAME RECENT WINE DISCOVERIES THAT HAVE EXCITED YOU.
Louis Martini Merlot. The wine has a spicy, smoky flavor.

WHAT IS YOUR FAVORITE WINE REGION IN THE WORLD TODAY?
I would be disappointed to have a favorite. I enjoy exploring new wines and new areas far too much to limit myself to a favorite.

WHAT LED YOU TO YOUR CURRENT POSITION?
My passion and thirst for knowledge, my love of wine, and the people involved in the wine industry.

WHAT ARE THE BEST ASPECTS OF YOUR JOB?
Finding great values and exchanging tasting notes.

IF YOU WERE NOT IN THE WINE PROFESSION, WHAT WOULD YOU BE DOING?
Acting. I was a theater major at Emerson College.

Anthony's in the Catalina

JOE MASCARI, PROPRIETOR AND
WINE BUYER
6440 North Campbell Avenue, Tucson
520-299-1771

The Grill at Hacienda Del Sol

DAN McCOOG, DIRECTOR OF
WINE AND SOMMELIER
5601 North Del Sol Road, Tucson
520-529-3500

The Tack Room

RICHARD TYLER, WINE BUYER
7300 East Vactor Ranch Trail, Tucson
520-722-2800

Wildflower

REGAN JASPER, CORPORATE
SOMMELIER
7037 North Oracle Road, Tucson
520-219-4230

A. P. Stumps

163 West Santa Clara Street
San Jose, California 95113
phone 408-292-9928 fax 408-292-9927

Randall W. Bertao
WINE DIRECTOR AND GENERAL MANAGER

WHAT ARE SOME OF YOUR ULTIMATE FOOD AND WINE PAIRINGS?
Grilled Muscovy duck breast with sautéed tatsoi, maitake mushrooms, potato galette and huckleberry sauce paired with Syrah or Shiraz; steamed Manila clams and Prince Edward Island mussels in a Thai curry broth with Riesling.

DESCRIBE YOUR WINE SELECTIONS.
I try to balance the New World, "hot" producers with the classic wine regions of the world.

WHAT CATEGORY OF WINE IS THE BEST VALUE ON YOUR WINE LIST?
Riesling and light white wines.

NAME RECENT WINE DISCOVERIES THAT HAVE EXCITED YOU.
Central Coast California Pinot Noir is offering good value right now.

WHAT IS YOUR FAVORITE WINE REGION IN THE WORLD TODAY?
Burgundy. I believe both the reds and whites are the most food-friendly wines in the world.

WHAT LED YOU TO YOUR CURRENT POSITION?
I have been passionate about wine since 1974.

WHAT ARE THE BEST ASPECTS OF YOUR JOB?
Working with great food and wine in a great restaurant. There is always something new to learn.

IF YOU WERE NOT IN THE WINE PROFESSION, WHAT WOULD YOU BE DOING?
Probably farming, vineyards in particular.

Ana Mandara

891 Beach Street
San Francisco, California 94109-1102
phone 415-771-6800 fax 415-771-5275
website www.anamandara.com

Joanna R. Breslin
SOMMELIER

WHAT ARE SOME OF YOUR ULTIMATE FOOD AND WINE PAIRINGS?
Turbinado sugar and chili–glazed freshwater prawns with a rich Pinot Gris
from Alsace or Austria; seared Mekong basa with lemon-chili sauce and off-dry
Riesling; lobster with Cognac and lobster roe sauce paired with Châteauneuf-
du-Pape blanc; oysters and Chablis; chocolate and young, fruity Banyuls.

DESCRIBE YOUR WINE SELECTIONS.
Our Vietnamese cuisine calls for wines with fruit and firm acidity, so we focus
on Riesling, Pinot Gris, and white Rhônes, as well as Pinot Noir and
Mediterranean red varietals and blends.

WHAT CATEGORIES OF WINE ARE THE BEST VALUES ON YOUR WINE LIST?
German whites and southern French reds offer particularly stellar quality for
the price.

NAME RECENT WINE DISCOVERIES THAT HAVE EXCITED YOU.
A modern-style Cahors that is 100-percent Malbec; Austrian Grauburgunder;
Pinot Noir from New Zealand; Sauvignon Blanc from South Africa.

WHAT LED YOU TO BECOME A SOMMELIER?
I started part-time at Ana Mandara to learn floor service, and loved it.

WHAT ARE THE BEST ASPECTS OF YOUR JOB?
The opportunity to taste the great range of wines available; the improvisational
element of working on the floor; the diversity of our clientele and co-workers;
being able to help people find wines they love that they would not have chosen
on their own.

IF YOU WERE NOT IN THIS PROFESSION, WHAT WOULD YOU BE DOING?
Coffee, or chocolate, or psychotherapy.

Aqua

252 California Street
San Francisco, California 94111
phone 415-956-9662 fax 415-956-5229
www.aqua-sf.com

Catherine Fallis
MASTER SOMMELIER, WINE DIRECTOR
Team: Matthew Turner, Sommelier

WHAT ARE SOME OF YOUR ULTIMATE FOOD AND WINE PAIRINGS?
Medallions of ahi tuna with foie gras and Pinot Noir; sautéed foie gras and 1993 Eszencia, Hungary; crab cakes and Domaine Matsa, Savatiano, Vieilles Vignes, Vin de Pays de Pallini, Greece.

DESCRIBE YOUR WINE SELECTIONS.
Aqua's wine list has 850 selections. Another fifty wines are used for the lunch and dinner tasting menus. We focus on Burgundy and California, and recently added a section for the wines of Greece.

WHAT CATEGORY OF WINE IS THE BEST VALUE ON YOUR WINE LIST?
I am proud to offer fifteen to twenty Burgundies under $100 and twenty to thirty under $50.

NAME RECENT WINE DISCOVERIES THAT HAVE EXCITED YOU.
Village-level Chablis from the 2000 vintage offer excellent value and quality.

WHAT IS YOUR FAVORITE REGION OR AREA IN THE WORLD TODAY?
Friuli. The level of quality and professionalism is impressive across the region.

WHAT LED YOU TO BECOME A SOMMELIER?
Backpacking around Europe in my college days introduced me to wine as an everyday beverage.

WHAT IS THE MOST CHALLENGING ASPECT OF YOUR JOB?
Creating custom, nine-course wine pairings on the fly is challenging and amazingly rewarding.

IF YOU WERE NOT IN THE WINE PROFESSION, WHAT WOULD YOU BE DOING?
Writing.

Bacar
448 Brannan Street
San Francisco, California 94107
phone 415-904-4100 fax 415-904-4113

Debbie F. Zachareas
WINE DIRECTOR

WHAT IS ONE OF YOUR ULTIMATE FOOD AND WINE PAIRINGS?
Gnocchi and Talenti Brunello di Montalcino 1995.

DESCRIBE YOUR WINE SELECTIONS.
All-encompassing, exciting, with something for everyone. We have sixty-five
wines by the glass, each served in four different portion sizes: by the 2-ounce
taste, 5-ounce glass, 250-milliliter decanter (1/3 bottle), and 500-milliliter
decanter (2/3 bottle). Our wine list has 1,200 to 1,400 selections from around
the world, including two pages of half-bottles.

WHAT IS YOUR FAVORITE WINE REGION IN THE WORLD TODAY?
The Loire Valley. It's a beautiful region and its white wines are food-friendly,
age-worthy and exciting.

WHAT LED YOU TO YOUR CURRENT POSITION?
I love wine!

WHAT ARE THE MOST CHALLENGING ASPECTS OF YOUR JOB?
Maintaining sixty-five wines by the glass and finding enough hours in the day.

IF YOU WERE NOT IN THE WINE PROFESSION, WHAT WOULD YOU BE
DOING?
Something good for the world, such as raising awareness and money for organi-
zations.

Boulevard Restaurant
1 Mission Street
San Francisco, California 94105
phone 415-543-6084 fax 415-495-2936

John M. Lancaster
WINE DIRECTOR AND SOMMELIER

WHAT IS ONE OF YOUR ULTIMATE FOOD AND WINE PAIRINGS?
Papardella pasta, pressed with truffles, with shaved truffles on top paired with a Paolo Scavino Barolo.

DESCRIBE YOUR WINE SELECTIONS.
California wines are the anchor of our list, but like the menu, we take a global view of food and wine.

WHAT IS YOUR FAVORITE WINE REGION IN THE WORLD TODAY?
Probably the south of France. I love the wines, and every trip I've taken has been magical.

WHAT LED YOU TO BECOME A SOMMELIER?
I was working in a restaurant and it became obvious I cared more than anyone about wine, so they made me the buyer. I've been doing it ever since.

WHAT ARE THE MOST CHALLENGING ASPECTS OF YOUR JOB?
Managing my time between meetings with purveyors, educating our staff, doing service and having a family life.

IF YOU WERE NOT IN THE WINE PROFESSION, WHAT WOULD YOU BE?
A sportswriter.

Campton Place Hotel and Restaurant

340 Stockton Street
San Francisco, California 94108
phone 415-781-5555 fax 415-955-5536
website www.camptonplace.com

Sean S. Crowley
WINE DIRECTOR AND SOMMELIER

WHAT ARE SOME OF YOUR ULTIMATE FOOD AND WINE PAIRINGS?
Spot prawns with Txakoli; sole and artichokes with Jurançon Blanc; triple crème cheese with Champagne.

DESCRIBE YOUR WINE SELECTIONS.
The wine program focuses on France and California. Champagne, Burgundy and domestic Pinot Noir take center stage.

WHAT CATEGORIES OF WINE OFFER THE BEST VALUE IN YOUR RESTAURANT?
Whites from Loire Valley, Alsace and southwestern France.

NAME A RECENT WINE DISCOVERY THAT EXCITED YOU.
A "spritz" (Prosecco and Campari over ice).

WHAT IS YOUR FAVORITE WINE REGION IN THE WORLD TODAY?
Champagne. The acidity in Champagne matches nicely with most foods.

WHAT LED YOU TO BECOME A SOMMELIER?
A passion for wine.

WHAT ARE THE BEST ASPECTS OF YOUR JOB?
Educating the staff and turning people on to wine.

IF YOU WERE NOT IN THE WINE PROFESSION, WHAT WOULD YOU BE DOING?
Designing roller coasters.

Cetrella Bistro and Café

845 Main Street
Half Moon Bay, California 94019
phone 650-726-4090 fax 650-726-4291
website www.cetrella.com

Saeed Amini
BEVERAGE DIRECTOR AND SOMMELIER

WHAT ARE SOME OF YOUR ULTIMATE FOOD AND WINE PAIRINGS?
Goat cheese, bacon, caramelized onion and thyme pizza with Pinot Gris; lamb kabob with Bordeaux; baked escargot with tarragon butter and Chablis; zarzuela and rosé; short ribs and Châteauneuf-du-Pape; grilled calamari and Chianti.

DESCRIBE YOUR WINE SELECTIONS.
Mediterranean; simple and affordable, with many unknown wines. I try to educate the customers without intimidation.

WHAT CATEGORY OF WINE IS THE BEST VALUE ON YOUR WINE LIST?
Italian whites.

NAME RECENT WINE DISCOVERIES THAT HAVE EXCITED YOU.
Refosco offers good value and diversity. Lagrein, it's elegant and complex.

WHAT IS YOUR FAVORITE REGION IN THE WORLD TODAY?
Tuscany. The wines are simple enough to drink every day, but age well and are food-friendly.

WHAT LED YOU TO BECOME A SOMMELIER?
Besides my love of wine, I feel that it brings people together in peace and harmony!

WHAT ARE THE BEST ASPECTS OF YOUR JOB?
Getting customers to experience new wines and watching them enjoy them.

IF YOU WERE NOT IN THE WINE PROFESSION, WHAT WOULD YOU BE DOING?
The Peace Corps. I love people and always want to help anyone in need.

Crustacean

1475 Polk Street
San Francisco, California 94109
phone 415-776-2722 fax 415-776-1069
website www.secretkitchen.com

David Glancy
SOMMELIER
Team: Ken Lew, Wine Buyer

IN YOUR RESTAURANT, WHAT FOOD AND WINE PAIRINGS HAVE GENERATED RAVE REVIEWS FROM CUSTOMERS?
Mussels with Asian pesto served with Marlborough Sauvignon Blanc; garlic-roasted crab with Alsace Gewürztraminer; Baked Alaska with Australian fortified Muscat.

DESCRIBE YOUR WINE SELECTIONS.
We feature an international selection with an extensive offering of wines by-the-glass and half-bottles. Our emphasis is on crisp, aromatic white wines that pair best with our Euro-Asian cuisine.

WHAT CATEGORIES OF WINE ARE THE BEST VALUES IN YOUR RESTAURANT?
Aromatic whites and dessert wines.

NAME RECENT WINE DISCOVERIES THAT HAVE EXCITED YOU.
Italy's Cannonau di Sardegna DOC has some super-ripe, Grenache-based wines that offer a great quality-to-price ratio.

WHAT IS YOUR FAVORITE WINE REGION IN THE WORLD TODAY?
Champagne, for what are undeniably the world's best sparkling wines.

WHAT LED YOU TO BECOME A SOMMELIER?
I started in the sommelier program to become a better manager, and discovered a new direction in my restaurant career.

WHAT IS THE BEST ASPECT OF YOUR JOB?
Turning a guest on to a new, favorite wine.

IF YOU WERE NOT IN THE WINE PROFESSION, WHAT WOULD YOU BE?
A park ranger, a professional soccer player, an astronaut, a computer programmer?

The Dining Room at the Ritz-Carlton

600 Stockton at California Street
San Francisco, California 94108
phone 415-296-7465 fax 415-951-8730

Stephane Lacroix
WINE DIRECTOR AND SOMMELIER

WHAT ARE SOME OF YOUR ULTIMATE FOOD AND WINE PAIRINGS?
Lobster salad paired with Sauvignon Blanc from New Zealand; squab breast paired with a Rhône such as Côte Rôtie; large asparagus, chicken with parmesan and olive oil paired with Chablis Premier Cru or Pouilly-Fumé from Dageneau; frog legs and snails meunière with white Rhônes.

DESCRIBE YOUR WINE SELECTIONS.
Our list offers 1,200 selections, mainly from California and France, with depth in old vintages and a good representation of top vineyards from around the world.

WHAT CATEGORY OF WINE IS THE BEST VALUE ON YOUR WINE LIST?
Red Rhône, especially selections from the smaller appellations of Crozes-Hermitage, Cairanne, Gigondas, and St. Joseph.

NAME A RECENT WINE DISCOVERY THAT EXCITED YOU.
The Rioja blanco from Remelluri is an incredible white from Spain with personality, complexity and balance.

WHAT IS YOUR FAVORITE WINE REGION IN THE WORLD TODAY?
Alsace. I love the tradition and the typicity of the wines. They are great, food-friendly wines.

WHAT LED YOU TO BECOME A SOMMELIER?
Passion for the restaurant business, good grades in wine class in catering school, interaction with the guests, and the staff's passion for wine.

WHAT ARE THE BEST ASPECTS OF YOUR JOB?
Discovering new people and new regions. Enjoying a passion as my job!

IF YOU WERE NOT IN THE WINE PROFESSION, WHAT WOULD YOU BE DOING?
I love the outdoors and exercise, so maybe I'd be a trainer.

Emile's

545 South Second Street
San Jose, California 95112
phone 408-289-1960 fax 408-998-1245
website www.emiles.com

Emile Mooser
CHEF AND OWNER

WHAT ARE SOME OF YOUR ULTIMATE FOOD AND WINE EXPERIENCES?
A dinner with Sauternes only; an all-sparkling wine dinner.

DESCRIBE YOUR WINE SELECTIONS.
Matching food and wine, in-house cooking school and a wine-tasting menu.

WHAT CATEGORY OF WINE IS THE BEST VALUE IN YOUR RESTAURANT?
All California wines.

NAME RECENT WINE DISCOVERIES THAT HAVE EXCITED YOU.
Some of the new blends, such as Sauvignon Blanc-Viognier and Zinfandel-Syrah.

WHAT IS YOUR FAVORITE WINE REGION IN THE WORLD TODAY?
Napa Valley.

HOW LONG HAVE YOU BEEN IN THE RESTAURANT BUSINESS?
For fifty-five years.

WHAT ARE THE BEST ASPECTS OF YOUR JOB?
Meeting people, sharing knowledge and constant change.

IF YOU WERE NOT IN THIS PROFESSION, WHAT WOULD YOU LIKE TO BE?
An architect.

Farallon
450 Post Street
San Francisco, California 94102
phone 415-956-6969 fax 415-834-1234
website www.farallonrestaurant.com

Peter J. Palmer
WINE DIRECTOR AND SOMMELIER

WHAT IS ONE OF YOUR ULTIMATE FOOD AND WINE PAIRINGS?
Prosciutto and summer melon with mint chiffonade paired with off-dry Gewürztraminer.

DESCRIBE YOUR WINE SELECTIONS.
I want our wine program to be fun, exciting and accessible. The list offers 475 international selections, with the majority from California and France. Our menu is mainly seafood, so lots of Burgundy and New World Pinot Noir is available for red wine drinkers.

WHAT CATEGORY OF WINE IS THE BEST VALUE IN YOUR RESTAURANT?
Italian whites. They are inexpensive and better than ever.

NAME RECENT WINE DISCOVERIES THAT HAVE EXCITED YOU.
Bonaccorsi Pinot Noir; the white wines from Francois Villard, Yves Gangloff and Yves Cuilleron in the northern Rhône; and the wines of Quintarelli in the Veneto—utterly unique and always memorable.

WHAT IS YOUR FAVORITE WINE REGION IN THE WORLD TODAY?
Burgundy, followed very closely by the northern Rhône Valley.

WHAT LED YOU TO BECOME A SOMMELIER?
I moved to San Francisco as a bartender and this, coupled with the proximity of the wine country and a couple of great bottles of Burgundy, got me hooked.

WHAT ARE THE BEST ASPECTS OF YOUR JOB?
The most rewarding by far is getting to know the people and personalities behind the wines.

IF YOU WERE NOT IN THIS PROFESSION, WHAT WOULD YOU BE DOING?
Something outdoors like nature and travel writing and photography.

La Folie Restaurant

2316 Polk Street
San Francisco, California 94109
phone 415-776-5577 fax 415-776-3431

George Passot

SOMMELIER, WINE BUYER AND MANAGER

WHAT IS ONE OF YOUR ULTIMATE FOOD AND WINE PAIRINGS?
Sautéed foie gras with wild huckleberries and a glass of Château d'Yquem 1989.

DESCRIBE YOUR WINE SELECTIONS.
A good balance between California and French wines. Not too large.
Customers are not intimidated by the wine list.

WHAT IS YOUR FAVORITE WINE REGION IN THE WORLD TODAY?
For the scenery I would say Beaujolais. For white wines, Bourgogne and
New Zealand. For red wines, the Rhône Valley and Bordeaux.

WHAT LED YOU TO BECOME A SOMMELIER?
The passion for wine and food pairing.

WHAT IS THE BEST ASPECT OF YOUR JOB?
Finding the right wine for my customer, whatever his budget.

IF YOU WERE NOT IN THE WINE PROFESSION, WHAT WOULD YOU BE?
A clown!

Gary Danko

800 North Point
San Francisco, California 94109
phone 415-749-2060 fax 415-775-1805
website www.garydanko.com

Christie R. Dufault
SOMMELIER

WHAT ARE SOME OF YOUR ULTIMATE FOOD AND WINE PAIRINGS?
French pumpkin soup with young Riesling Kabinett from the Mosel-Saar-Ruwer;
juniper-spiced venison medallions with classified left bank Bordeaux reds;
perfectly aged Citeaux cheese and white Burgundy; steak tartare and
Hermitage red.

DESCRIBE YOUR WINE SELECTIONS.
It is an award-winning wine list and thick in the classics: Champagne,
Burgundy, Bordeaux verticals. We also have a great selection of half-bottles.

WHAT CATEGORIES OF WINE ARE THE BEST VALUES IN YOUR RESTAURANT?
White wines from Austria and Germany. Red wines from Spain.

NAME RECENT WINE DISCOVERIES THAT HAVE EXCITED YOU.
Tasmania! The wines are pure, honest and delightful!

WHAT IS YOUR FAVORITE WINE?
Champagne! Acidity, complexity and that certain sparkle that it inspires in life.

WHAT LED YOU TO BECOME A SOMMELIER?
Being a sommelier is all I ever wanted to do.

WHAT IS THE MOST CHALLENGING ASPECT OF YOUR JOB?
The most challenging part of my job is trying to learn everything that I desire
to know about wine.

IF YOU WERE NOT IN THIS PROFESSION, WHAT WOULD YOU BE DOING?
Art restoration, truffle farming or spa testing.

Incanto

1550 Church Street
San Francisco, California 94131
phone 415-641-4500 fax 415-641-4546
website www.incanto.biz

Claudio Villani
SOMMELIER AND DINING ROOM MANAGER

WHAT IS ONE OF YOUR ULTIMATE FOOD AND WINE PAIRINGS?
Bread and extra virgin olive oil with Sassicaia 1985.

DESCRIBE YOUR WINE SELECTIONS.
Most of the list is Italian, with Californian and some French wines.

WHICH WINES ARE THE BEST VALUES IN YOUR RESTAURANT?
Southern Italian red and northern Italian white.

WHAT IS YOUR FAVORITE WINE REGION IN THE WORLD TODAY?
Southern Italy, which offers unusual grape varieties, unique terroir and great value.

WHAT LED YOU TO BECOME A SOMMELIER?
The love of wine.

WHAT IS THE BEST ASPECT OF YOUR JOB?
The opportunity to taste the best wines in the world.

IF YOU WERE NOT A SOMMELIER, WHAT WOULD YOU BE DOING?
Something in the restaurant business.

Mistral

370-6 Bridge Parkway
Redwood Shores, California 94065
phone 650-802-9222 fax 650-802-9221
website www.mistraldining.com

Morgan L. Plant
GENERAL MANAGER AND SOMMELIER

WHAT IS ONE OF YOUR ULTIMATE FOOD AND WINE PAIRINGS?
Our Thai crab and shrimp spring rolls with dry Alsatian wines.

DESCRIBE YOUR WINE SELECTIONS.
We have about 300 wines, primarily domestic, along with some Old World gems.

WHAT CATEGORY OF WINE IS THE BEST VALUE IN YOUR RESTAURANT?
Washington Cabernet Sauvignon. We sell it for less in order to get people to try it.

NAME RECENT WINE DISCOVERIES THAT HAVE EXCITED YOU.
Wines from South America. This region will be the next great wine spot.

WHAT IS YOUR FAVORITE WINE REGION IN THE WORLD TODAY?
The Northwest (Washington and Oregon). The wines are fresh, fun and still affordable. Their quality is just getting better and better.

WHAT LED YOU TO BECOME A SOMMELIER?
My father. He was always passionate about wine.

WHAT ARE THE BEST ASPECTS OF YOUR JOB?
I love turning a guest on to something new and having them order that same wine when they come back.

IF YOU WERE NOT IN THIS PROFESSION, WHAT WOULD YOU BE?
An accountant!

Navio at the Ritz-Carlton Half Moon Bay

1 Miramontes Point Road
Half Moon Bay, California 94109
phone 650-712-7000 fax 650-712-7070
website www.ritzcarlton.com

Michael H. Rasmussen
SOMMELIER

WHAT ARE SOME OF YOUR ULTIMATE FOOD AND WINE PAIRINGS?
Fresh Pacific oysters with great Pouilly-Fumé. Terrine of local goat cheese and golden beets paired with New Zealand Sauvignon Blanc.

DESCRIBE YOUR WINE SELECTIONS.
We feature mostly California wines, along with some of the best wines from the rest of the world.

WHAT CATEGORY OF WINE IS THE BEST VALUE IN YOUR RESTAURANT?
California Syrah is the most reasonably priced and pairs best with our menu.

NAME A RECENT WINE DISCOVERY THAT EXCITED YOU.
Tassinaia, a super-Tuscan, which was new to me.

WHAT IS YOUR FAVORITE WINES BY REGION?
Ribera del Duero, Spain. It is a great value, a great food wine, and has great power and finesse.

WHAT LED YOU TO BECOME A SOMMELIER?
A sommelier one evening paired the perfect wine with great food at dinner and it elevated both the food and wines to a height previously unknown to me.

WHAT IS THE BEST ASPECT OF YOUR JOB?
Meeting new people every day who want to learn about wine.

IF YOU WERE NOT IN THE WINE PROFESSION, WHAT WOULD YOU BE DOING?
Teaching high school world history.

The Plumed Horse

14555 Big Basin Way
Saratoga, California 95070
phone 408-867-4711 fax 408-867-6919
website www.plumedhorse.com

Paul S. Mekis
CELLAR MASTER

WHAT ARE SOME OF YOUR ULTIMATE FOOD AND WINE PAIRINGS?
Seared rare ahi tuna with Pinot Noir from the Russian River, Bien Nacido, Willamette Valley, Gevrey-Chambertin or Pommard; venison with Côte Rôtie; wood-roasted chicken with full-flavored, big-bodied Chardonnay; polenta with Viognier; chocolate with big, jammy Zinfandel.

DESCRIBE YOUR WINE SELECTIONS.
We have 800 selections, mostly from Californian and European wineries, including many wines from new wineries and older vintages.

WHAT CATEGORIES OF WINE OFFER THE BEST VALUE ON YOUR WINE LIST?
California's Rhône and Italian varietals; Australian, South African and German wines.

NAME RECENT WINE DISCOVERIES THAT HAVE EXCITED YOU.
Arietta Merlot from Napa Valley—dense, dark fruit with incredible balance. Also, Thunder Mountain Chardonnay, Santa Cruz Mountains—Meursault-like aromas and complexity.

WHAT IS YOUR FAVORITE WINE REGION IN THE WORLD TODAY?
Pauillac. In great vintages, there is nothing better than an aged one, with its complexity and length.

WHAT LED YOU TO BECOME A SOMMELIER?
I took a job as sommelier at Alioto's restaurant and was trained by Ronn Wiegand. Working with Nunzio Alioto inspired me to pursue a career in the wine field.

WHAT IS THE BEST ASPECT OF YOUR JOB?
Recommending a wine that pairs well with customers' food, that they have not tried before, and having it make their evening.

IF YOU WERE NOT IN THE WINE PROFESSION, WHAT WOULD YOU BE DOING?
Modern interior design.

Prima

1522 North Main Street
Walnut Creek, California 94596
phone 925-935-7780 fax 925-935-7780

J. D. (John) Massler
SOMMELIER
Team: Marcus Garcia, Assistant Sommelier

WHAT IS ONE OF YOUR ULTIMATE FOOD AND WINE PAIRINGS?
2000 Domaine Tempier Rosé with a bowl of steamed mussels—a little spicy.

DESCRIBE YOUR WINE SELECTIONS.
We have three wine lists: A 1,600-item, complete list from around the world; a 100-bottle "Selected List" (including a comparative tasting of five wines), with twenty to twenty-five wines by the glass; and a dessert wine list.

WHAT IS YOUR FAVORITE WINE REGION?
I love everything about Provence. The wines are improving, especially Bandol, and drink wonderfully with the Mediterranean cuisine of Provence.

WHAT LED YOU TO BECOME A SOMMELIER?
I've collected and loved wine for thirty years and have worked in all parts of the restaurant business.

WHAT ARE THE BEST ASPECTS OF YOUR JOB?
I love all aspects of my job. My major challenge is keeping the waiters pumped up about wine.

IF YOU WERE NOT A SOMMELIER, WHAT WOULD YOU BE DOING?
Another restaurant job: Owner, chef, waiter.

Redwood Park

600 Montgomery Street
San Francisco, California 94111
phone 415-283-1000 fax 415-283-3030
website www.redwoodpark-sf.com

Rajat Parr
WINE DIRECTOR

WHAT ARE SOME OF YOUR ULTIMATE FOOD AND WINE PAIRINGS?
Hudson foie gras with roasted pineapple paired with German Riesling Auslese;
farm-raised venison with young Châteauneuf-du-Pape; crab and avocado salad
with Austrian Muscat; salmon filet finished with an artichoke-and-sherry vinaigrette with Jurançon.

DESCRIBE YOUR WINE SELECTIONS.
We specialize in wines from Burgundy. We try to have a lot of old and mature
Burgundies.

WHICH WINES OFFER THE BEST VALUE ON YOUR WINE LIST?
Red Burgundy and red Rhône.

WHAT IS YOUR FAVORITE WINE REGION IN THE WORLD TODAY?
Burgundy.

WHAT LED YOU TO BECOME A SOMMELIER?
The magic of food and wine.

WHAT IS THE MOST CHALLENGING ASPECT OF YOUR JOB?
Trying to keep up with the customers' requests.

IF YOU WERE NOT IN THE WINE PROFESSION, WHAT WOULD YOU BE?
A chef.

Redwood Park

600 Montgomery Street
San Francisco, California 94111
phone 415-283-1000 fax 415-283-3030
website www.redwoodpark-sf.com

Mark E. Mendoza
SOMMELIER

WHAT ARE SOME OF YOUR ULTIMATE FOOD AND WINE PAIRINGS?
George's signature tuna foie gras with Pinot Noir; fallow deer with brandied cherry sauce and Côte Rôtie.

DESCRIBE YOUR WINE SELECTIONS.
We have an extensive commitment to Burgundy as well as wines from other great French appellations.

WHAT CATEGORIES OF WINE ARE THE BEST VALUES ON YOUR WINE LIST?
The white and red Burgundy selections.

NAME A RECENT WINE DISCOVERY THAT EXCITED YOU.
Clape Côtes-du-Rhône 2000. A juicy, young vine Syrah from the master of Cornas.

WHAT IS YOUR FAVORITE WINE REGION IN THE WORLD TODAY?
The Mosel wines of Germany. These wines are underestimated and are truly world-class food wines.

WHAT LED YOU TO BECOME A SOMMELIER?
I have always had restaurant jobs and it seemed a natural progression for me. Wine is a huge subject and constantly changing. You can never know it all.

WHAT IS THE MOST CHALLENGING ASPECT OF YOUR JOB?
To know when to ask people to "think outside the box."

IF YOU WERE NOT IN THE WINE PROFESSION, WHAT WOULD YOU BE?
A winemaker.

Rubicon

558 Sacramento Street
San Francisco, California 94111
phone 415-434-4100 fax 415-421-7648

Larry N. Stone
WINE DIRECTOR, MASTER SOMMELIER
AND PARTNER

WHAT ARE SOME OF YOUR ULTIMATE FOOD AND WINE PAIRINGS?
Père Pape Châteauneuf-du-Pape 1999 and pheasant saltimbocca with onion-sage tart and Serrano ham; Zinfandel and Stilton.

DESCRIBE YOUR WINE SELECTIONS.
We feature the best from all over the world and in every price range, but we also have a focus on Napa Valley Cabernet Sauvignon and red Burgundy.

WHAT CATEGORY OF WINE IS THE BEST VALUE IN YOUR RESTAURANT?
Rhône varietals, whether from California or France, tend to offer the most excitement for the dollar.

NAME RECENT WINE DISCOVERIES THAT HAVE EXCITED YOU.
Tomassi Valpolicella and Bussola Valpolicella, pretty amazing wines from a region on the rise.

WHAT IS YOUR FAVORITE WINE REGION IN THE WORLD TODAY?
Napa Valley is still full of surprises, and the wines are becoming more impressive with each successive vintage.

WHAT LED YOU TO BECOME A SOMMELIER?
Family meals where wine was enjoyed as a regular part of dining.

WHAT IS THE BEST ASPECT OF YOUR JOB?
Sharing the wines I love with friends and customers and watching their reactions.

IF YOU WERE NOT IN THIS PROFESSION, WHAT WOULD YOU BE DOING?
Teaching modern poetry—or a portrait photographer.

Valhalla Restaurant

201 Bridgeway
Sausalito, California 94965-2449
phone 415-332-2777

Nunzio S. Alioto
PRESIDENT, GENERAL MANAGER
AND MASTER SOMMELIER

WHAT ARE SOME OF YOUR ULTIMATE FOOD AND WINE PAIRINGS?
Ribs with Rhône, Zinfandel, or rosé; crab cakes with German Riesling.

DESCRIBE YOUR WINE SELECTIONS.
Well-priced, hard-to-find wines of all types, with a strong emphasis on Pinot Noir, white Burgundy and red Rhône.

WHAT CATEGORY OF WINE IS THE BEST VALUE IN YOUR RESTAURANT?
German Riesling and Italian whites.

NAME RECENT WINE DISCOVERIES THAT HAVE EXCITED YOU.
Müller-Thurgau. It is a food-friendly wine.

WHAT ARE YOUR FAVORITE WINE REGIONS IN THE WORLD TODAY?
Germany, southern France and Ribera del Duero, Spain.

WHAT LED YOU TO BECOME A SOMMELIER?
Love of the product and service of it.

WHAT IS THE BEST ASPECT OF YOUR JOB?
Being able to suggest wines that people have no clue about.

IF YOU WERE NOT IN THE WINE PROFESSION, WHERE WOULD YOU BE?
In the kitchen.

Wente Vineyards Restaurant

5050 Arroyo Road
Livermore, California 94550
phone 925-456-2450 fax 925-456-2401
website www.wentevineyards.com

Steve K. King

DINING ROOM MANAGER AND WINE PROGRAM
DIRECTOR

WHAT ARE SOME OF YOUR ULTIMATE FOOD AND WINE PAIRINGS?

Double thick, house-smoked pork loin chop with Pinot Noir; Pacific fish stew (prawns, mussels, clams, chilies, white wine broth) paired with Monterey County Chardonnay; caramel latte brûlée paired with Bual Madeira.

DESCRIBE YOUR WINE SELECTIONS.

Our list contains 500 items, with wines from virtually all California appellations. Glass wines are on the menu and change daily, as does the menu.

WHICH WINES OFFER THE BEST VALUE IN YOUR RESTAURANT?

Wines from Livermore Valley wineries. Also, California Rhône and Italian varietals, which are priced lower to encourage guests to try them.

NAME A RECENT WINE DISCOVERY THAT EXCITED YOU.

More California Chardonnay made with less malolactic and oak influences, allowing the grape's flavor to show and the wine to go with a wider variety of food.

WHAT IS YOUR FAVORITE WINE REGION IN THE WORLD TODAY?

Livermore Valley. It has great potential for making world-class wine.

WHAT LED YOU TO YOUR CURRENT POSITION?

Twenty years of restaurant experience coupled with an interest in food and a passion for wine.

WHAT IS THE BEST ASPECT OF YOUR JOB?

Seeing the results of our efforts. A guest's simple comment on how much he enjoyed our recommendations can make the tedious chores disappear.

IF YOU WERE NOT IN THE WINE PROFESSION, WHAT WOULD YOU BE DOING?

Something in sales or in a golf course–related business.

Asia de Cuba at the Clift Hotel

BENJAMIN GABRIEL, WINE BUYER
495 Geary Street, San Francisco
415-775-4700

Carnelian Room

MIKE AL-JABARI, SOMMELIER
555 California Street, San Francisco
415-433-7500

Charles Nob Hill

JANE RATE, SOMMELIER
1250 Jones Street, San Francisco
415-771-5400

Chez Panisse

JONATHAN WATERS, WINE BUYER
1517 Shattuck Avenue, Berkeley
510-548-5525

Club XIX at the Lodge at Pebble Beach

JOHN WINFIELD, BEVERAGE MANAGER
Seventeen Mile Drive, Pebble Beach
831-625-8519

Dal Baffo

VINCENZO LOGRASMO, CHEF, OWNER
AND WINE BUYER
878 Santa Cruz Avenue, Menlo Park
650-325-1588

Eastside West Restaurant and Bar

JOHN MARRS, SOMMELIER
3154 Fillmore Street, San Francisco
415-885-4000

El Paseo

GUNTHER KELLNER, WINE BUYER
7 El Paseo Lane, Mill Valley
415-388-0741

EOS Restaurant

DARIN SNOW, WINE DIRECTOR
901 Cole Street, San Francisco
415-566-3063

Fandango

PIERRE BAIN, WINE BUYER
223 17th Avenue, Pacific Grove
831-372-3456

Fleur De Lys

MICKEY CLEVINGER, WINE BUYER
777 Sutter Street, San Francisco
415-673-7779

Il Fornaio

SUE PEY, CORPORATE WINE BUYER
223 Town Center, Corte Madera
415-927-4400

Fournou's Ovens in the Renaissance Stanford Court Hotel

ABDULLAH VURAL, DIRECTOR OF
FOOD AND BEVERAGE
905 California Street, San Francisco
415-989-1910

Fresh Cream Restaurant

STEVE CHESNY, WINE BUYER
99 Pacific Street, Monterey
831-375-9798

Fusilli Ristorante

DAN GIACALONI, OWNER
AND WINE BUYER
620 Jackson Street, Fairmont
707-428-4211

Globe

JOSEPH AND MARY MANZARE,
CO-OWNERS
290 Pacific Avenue, San Francisco
415-391-4132

Hawthorne Lane
NABILE ABI'GHANEM, SOMMELIER
22 Hawthorne Street, San Francisco
415-777-9779

Jardinière
EUGENIO JARDIM, SOMMELIER
300 Grove Street, San Francisco
415-861-5555

Lafayette Park Hotel
JAY LIFSON, FOOD
AND BEVERAGE DIRECTOR
3287 Mount Diablo Boulevard, Lafayette
925-283-3700

Lark Creek Inn
JOHN HULIHAN, SOMMELIER
234 Magnolia Avenue, Larkspur
415-924-7766

Mandarin Oriental Hotel
JOSE GARCIA, EXECUTIVE CHEF
AND WINE BUYER
222 Sansome Street, San Francisco
415-276-9888

Marinus Restaurant at Bernardus Lodge
MARK JENSEN, WINE DIRECTOR
415 Carmel Valley Road, Carmel Valley
831-658-3500

Masa's
ALAN MURRAY, SOMMELIER
648 Bush Street, San Francisco
415-989-7154

Mecca
GENE TARTAGLIA, OWNER
AND WINE BUYER
2029 Market Street, San Francisco
415-621-7000

Moose's
BURTON BRADLEY, WINE DIRECTOR
1652 Stockton Street, San Francisco
415-989-7800

Oliveto
ADAM BRUCE, WINE STEWARD
5655 College Avenue, Oakland
510-547-5356

One Market Restaurant
LARRY DOWNEY, SOMMELIER
AND WINE BUYER
1 Market Street, San Francisco
415-777-5577

Pacific's Edge Restaurant at Highlands Inn
BERNABE DE LUNA, SOMMELIER
Highway One 4 Miles South of Carmel, Carmel
831-622-5445

Paolo's Restaurant
JALIL SAMAVAVARCHIAN, SOMMELIER
333 West San Carlos Street #150, San Jose
408-294-2558

Postrio
JOHN CASSANOS, WINE BUYER
545 Post Street, San Francisco
415-776-7825

Sardine Factory
MARC CUTINO, SOMMELIER
701 Wave Street, Monterey
831-373-3775

Sierra Mar at the Post Ranch Inn
DOMINIQUE DA CRUZ, WINE BUYER
Highway One, Big Sur
408-667-2800

XYZ Restaurant
at the W Hotel

JACK MOORE, GENERAL MANAGER
AND WINE BUYER
181 Third Street, San Francisco
415-817-7836

Equus Restaurant at the Fountain Grove Inn

101 Fountain Grove Parkway
Santa Rosa, California 95403
phone 707-578-6101 fax 707-544-9374

Larry A. Van Aalst
SOMMELIER

WHAT ARE SOME OF YOUR ULTIMATE FOOD AND WINE PAIRINGS?
Zinfandel and barbecued duck; Sauvignon Blanc and marinated crab.

DESCRIBE YOUR WINE SELECTIONS.
Mostly Sonoma and Napa wines.

WHAT IS YOUR FAVORITE WINE REGION IN THE WORLD TODAY?
California Russian River produces my favorite Pinots, Chardonnays, Sauvignon Blancs. The great fruit makes for bold wines.

WHAT ARE THE MOST CHALLENGING ASPECTS OF YOUR JOB?
Long hours and recordkeeping. Autograph hounds.

WHAT LED YOU TO BECOME A SOMMELIER?
A search for truth, because "In wine there's truth."

IF YOU WERE NOT IN THE WINE PROFESSION, WHAT WOULD YOU BE DOING?
Teaching, writing, traveling.

The French Laundry

6640 Washington Street
Yountville, California 94558
phone 707-944-2380 fax 707-944-1974

Bobby D. Stuckey
SOMMELIER
Team: Nate Ready, Sommelier

WHAT IS ONE OF YOUR ULTIMATE FOOD AND WINE PAIRINGS?
Bouget and white Rhône.

DESCRIBE YOUR WINE SELECTIONS.
We really champion half-bottles.

WHAT CATEGORY OF WINE IS THE BEST VALUE IN YOUR RESTAURANT?
German Riesling.

NAME A RECENT WINE DISCOVERY THAT EXCITED YOU.
The 2000 white, northern Rhônes. They have just enough acidity to balance
their exotic fruit.

WHAT IS YOUR FAVORITE WINE REGION IN THE WORLD TODAY?
I am more concerned with world-class wines than just one particular region.
As long as it's great, I enjoy it.

WHAT LED YOU TO BECOME A SOMMELIER?
I didn't really feel like selling professional liability insurance.

WHAT ARE THE BEST ASPECTS OF YOUR JOB?
I love everything about my job.

IF YOU WERE NOT IN THE WINE PROFESSION, WHAT WOULD YOU BE
DOING?
Pretending I was Haile Gebrselassie (possibly the best long-distance runner in
history).

The French Laundry
6640 Washington Street
Yountville, California 94558
phone 707-944-2380 fax 707-944-1974

Keith G. Fergel
ASSISTANT SOMMELIER

WHAT ARE SOME OF YOUR ULTIMATE FOOD AND WINE PAIRINGS?
Ruster Ausbruch with foie gras; Madeira with lobster consommé; pot au feu with young Cabernet (rich, fruity, forward style); Chasselas with celery and summer truffle salad; Monterey Bay sardines "cuit sous vide" with Fino Sherry; butter-poached lobster with yellow corn pudding and morel mushrooms with Meursault.

DESCRIBE YOUR WINE SELECTIONS.
Our wine list is designed to allow us to provide a perfect wine experience for every guest.

WHAT CATEGORIES OF WINE OFFER THE BEST VALUE IN YOUR RESTAURANT?
Austria and Germany wines. Both have a lot of great buys on a regular basis, and also work very well with food.

NAME A RECENT WINE DISCOVERY THAT EXCITED YOU.
Rudi Pichler's 1998 Weissburgunder Smaragd from Wosendorfer in the Wachau is a benchmark for quality, value and style.

WHAT IS YOUR FAVORITE WINE REGION IN THE WORLD TODAY?
If I could drink wine from only one region, it would be Burgundy.

WHAT LED YOU TO BECOME A SOMMELIER?
I read an article about a young sommelier and everything about his career appealed to me. Three months later, I began working as a food runner.

WHAT ARE THE BEST ASPECTS OF YOUR JOB?
New and exciting wine pairings; the perpetual discovery process involved with tasting wines blind.

IF YOU WERE NOT IN THE WINE PROFESSION, WHAT WOULD YOU BE?
A high-end furniture designer.

John Ash & Co.

4330 Barnes Road
Santa Rosa, California 95403
phone 707-527-7687 fax 707-527-1202
website www.vintnersinn.com

Walter R. Inman

BEVERAGE DIRECTOR AND SOMMELIER

WHAT ARE SOME OF YOUR ULTIMATE FOOD AND WINE PAIRINGS?
Buffalo ossobuco with Syrah; Dungeness crab cakes with Sancerre; venison loin with Zinfandel.

DESCRIBE YOUR WINE SELECTIONS.
We focus on California, but have many benchmarks from around the world.

WHAT CATEGORY OF WINE IS THE BEST VALUE ON YOUR WINE LIST?
Southern Rhône.

NAME RECENT WINE DISCOVERIES THAT HAVE EXCITED YOU.
Wines of the southern Rhône. We vacationed there in 2001 and it is a remarkable area with very diverse wines.

WHAT IS YOUR FAVORITE WINE REGION IN THE WORLD TODAY?
Rhône Valley wines. The wines range widely in style and price, and are very food-friendly.

WHAT LED YOU TO BECOME A SOMMELIER?
An evolving love of wine and sharing wines with people. It seemed like such a perfect career: food, wine and conversation.

WHAT IS THE BEST ASPECT OF YOUR JOB?
Guiding customers to wines that they probably wouldn't have tried otherwise.

IF YOU WERE NOT IN THE WINE PROFESSION, WHAT WOULD YOU BE?
A game warden.

Martini House

1245 Spring Street
St. Helena, California 94574
phone 707-963-2233 fax 707-967-9237
website www.martinihouse.com

Lisa E. Minucci

SOMMELIER

WHAT ARE SOME OF YOUR ULTIMATE FOOD AND WINE PAIRINGS?

Napa Valley Cabernet Sauvignon with venison and game sauce; Tokaji Aszú with foie gras; white Burgundy with lobster; Willamette Valley Pinot Noir with veal cheeks; crisp, northern Italy white wines with cheese; tawny Ports with chocolate desserts.

DESCRIBE YOUR WINE SELECTIONS.

We feature more than forty-five wines by the glass and an international selection of 700 wines on our wine list. Most wines are from smaller producers.

WHAT CATEGORY OF WINE IS THE BEST VALUE IN YOUR RESTAURANT?

Wines over $100 per bottle, which have the lowest markup (two times cost).

NAME RECENT WINE DISCOVERIES THAT HAVE EXCITED YOU.

Napa Valley Merlot from high-quality producers, German Riesling and Burgundy from small producers.

WHAT IS YOUR FAVORITE WINE REGION IN THE WORLD TODAY?

Napa Valley, whose best wines are produced by creative, fastidious winemakers interested in achieving the absolute best.

WHAT LED YOU TO BECOME A SOMMELIER?

I worked in retail in New York City and learned a great deal, especially about French and German wines, so I decided to study wine seriously.

WHAT ARE THE BEST ASPECTS OF YOUR JOB?

Working with the chef to create sublime matches. Introducing guests to new wines and new regions, and pairing wines to specific dishes.

IF YOU WERE NOT IN THE WINE PROFESSION, WHAT WOULD YOU BE?

A diplomat based in the Middle East, an Italian art restorer, or an antique dealer.

La Toque at the Rancho Caymus Inn

1140 Rutherford Road
Rutherford, California 94573
phone 707-963-9770 fax 707-963-9072
website www.latoque.com

Scott Tracy
SOMMELIER

WHAT ARE SOME OF YOUR ULTIMATE FOOD AND WINE PAIRINGS?
Foie gras with Sauternes; Banyuls with chocolate; sashimi with Tocai Friulano; ginger desserts with Malvasia delle Lipari; and properly chilled French Champagne with the reading of a fine dining menu.

DESCRIBE YOUR WINE SELECTIONS.
We have an extensive wine list, but most guests order wines that I have paired with the eleven dishes on our menu, which changes weekly.

WHAT CATEGORY OF WINE IS THE BEST VALUE IN YOUR RESTAURANT?
The concept of "value" for our guests is in the value of the experience. Most of our diners are not concerned with the best buys of the wine world because they are on vacation, often with their spouses. The pleasure of sharing ten dishes and ten wines with the one you love is a very valuable memory.

NAME RECENT WINE DISCOVERIES THAT HAVE EXCITED YOU.
Loire Valley Chenin Blanc. Dry versions with cheese and sweet versions with strawberries.

WHAT IS YOUR FAVORITE WINE REGION IN THE WORLD TODAY?
Napa Valley.

WHAT LED YOU TO BECOME A SOMMELIER?
I found that wine returned the passion that I had for it exponentially.

WHAT IS THE BEST ASPECT OF YOUR JOB?
The ever-changing, nightly wine pairing allows for a wonderful opportunity to learn and teach and share the love of wine.

IF YOU WERE NOT IN THE WINE PROFESSION, WHAT WOULD YOU BE DOING?
Teaching.

Auberge du Soleil Restaurant

KRIS MARGERUM, SOMMELIER
180 Rutherford Hill Road, Rutherford
707-963-1211

Domaine Chandon

DAVID BRIDGES, WINE BUYER
1 California Drive, Yountville
707-944-2892

Dry Creek Kitchen

JIM FERGUSON, SOMMELIER
317 Healdsburg Avenue, Healdsburg
707-431-0330

The Girl and the Gaucho

SONDRA BERNSTEIN, PROPRIETOR AND
WINE BUYER
13690 Arnold Drive, Glen Ellen
707-938-2130

Greystone at the Culinary Institute of America

MICHAEL PRYOR, FOOD AND
BEVERAGE DIRECTOR
2555 Main Street, St. Helena
707-967-1010

Madrona Manor

KEN STIRITZ, SOMMELIER
1001 Westside Road, Healdsburg
707-433-4231

Mustard's Grill

NATALIE SCHLEIP, WINE BUYER
7399 St. Helena Highway, Yountville
707-944-2424

The Restaurant at Meadowood

JOHN THOREEN, DIRECTOR OF WINE
900 Meadowood Lane, St. Helena
707-963-3646

Restaurant 301

MARK CARTER, OWNER
AND WINE BUYER
301 L Street, Eureka
707-444-8062

Citronelle

901 East Cabrillo Boulevard
Santa Barbara, California 93103
phone 805-963-0111 fax 805-966-6584
website www.citronelle.com

Adam R. Mahler

ASSISTANT RESTAURANT MANAGER
AND SOMMELIER

WHAT ARE SOME OF YOUR ULTIMATE FOOD AND WINE PAIRINGS?
California Cabernet Franc with salmon baked with spinach crust and a carrot curry sauce; Vouvray demi-sec with mushroom-based cauliflower soup and sautéed foie gras; red Zinfandel with lamb and garlic demi-glaze.

DESCRIBE YOUR WINE SELECTIONS.
We specialize in Central Coast wines, but we do have an extensive selection from Napa, Sonoma, Washington, Oregon and France.

WHAT CATEGORY OF WINE IS THE BEST VALUE IN YOUR RESTAURANT?
California Syrahs and Rhône wines.

NAME A RECENT WINE DISCOVERY THAT EXCITED YOU.
High-profile Cabernet Franc, for its richness and ability to enhance flavors in food pairings.

WHAT IS YOUR FAVORITE WINE REGION IN THE WORLD TODAY?
Santa Barbara. It's exciting to see such a young region get its feet under it so quickly.

WHAT LED YOU TO BECOME A SOMMELIER?
Five years ago I fell in love with the mystique, beauty and tradition of wine. I've always felt that wine needs to be fun and that there are not enough sommeliers who feel that way.

WHAT ARE THE BEST ASPECTS OF YOUR JOB?
Education and learning. In the wine industry we all help to educate each other.

IF YOU WERE NOT IN THE WINE PROFESSION, WHAT WOULD YOU BE DOING?
Teaching cultural studies or film.

Miro at Bacara Resort and Spa

8301 Hollister Avenue
Santa Barbara, California 93103
phone 805-968-0100 fax 805-571-3271
website www.bacararesort.com

Gillian M. Ballance
WINE DIRECTOR

WHAT ARE SOME OF YOUR ULTIMATE FOOD AND WINE PAIRINGS?
Vidal sparkling ice wine with our Peach Mille-Feuille; Brunello di Montalcino Riserva with glazed veal shank.

DESCRIBE YOUR WINE SELECTIONS.
Bacara has three restaurants: Spa Café's wine list features organic and biodynamic wines; Bistro's casual dining list focuses on local Santa Barbara wines; Miro, our flagship restaurant, has an international list of more than 600 wines.

WHAT CATEGORY OF WINE IS THE BEST VALUE ON YOUR WINE LIST?
Probably Spanish. Anyone savvy enough to know the Miro list of world-class Spanish producers deserves a little break on price.

WHAT IS YOUR FAVORITE WINE REGION IN THE WORLD TODAY?
Italy, for its unique wines and diverse styles.

WHAT LED YOU TO BECOME A SOMMELIER?
I was in the restaurant business and selling wine was the best part of being on the floor.

WHAT ARE THE BEST ASPECTS OF YOUR JOB?
Enhancing and being the best part of someone's dining experience.

IF YOU WERE NOT IN THE WINE PROFESSION, WHAT WOULD YOU BE DOING?
Teaching ballet to young students.

Ranch House Restaurant

MICHAEL DENNEY, WINE BUYER

500 South Lomita Avenue, Ojai

805-646-2360

San Ysidro Ranch

SCOTT ABATE, WINE BUYER

900 San Ysidro Lane, Montecito

805-969-5046

Wine Cask Restaurant

CHRIS ROBLES, SOMMELIER

813 Anacapa Street, Santa Barbara

805-966-9463

Aqua at St. Regis Monarch Beach Hotel

1 Monarch Beach Resort
Dana Point, California 92677
phone 949-234-3200 fax 949-234-3201
website www.stregismonarchbeach.com

Olivier Zardoni
SOMMELIER

WHAT ARE SOME OF YOUR ULTIMATE FOOD AND WINE PAIRINGS?
Our lobster pot pie and Viognier; Japanese yellowtail or hamachi and Austrian Grüner Veltliner; truffle popcorn and Brut rosé Champagne.

DESCRIBE YOUR WINE SELECTIONS.
We offer a broad selection of wines from different areas of the world, including a generous selection of light red wines such as Pinot Noir.

WHAT CATEGORY OF WINE IS THE BEST VALUE IN YOUR RESTAURANT?
California Pinot Noir.

NAME RECENT WINE DISCOVERIES THAT HAVE EXCITED YOU.
Sauvignon Blanc and Gewürztraminer from the Alto Adige in Italy are outstanding values.

WHAT IS YOUR FAVORITE WINE REGION IN THE WORLD TODAY?
Burgundy, because of the complexity of the soil and the dimension and evolution of flavors that are derived from just two grape varieties, Chardonnay and Pinot Noir.

WHAT LED YOU TO BECOME A SOMMELIER?
I grew up in a wine area (Languedoc-Roussillon) that had a good restaurant school and fine restaurants where I was able to learn more about the fascinating world of wine.

WHAT ARE THE BEST ASPECTS OF YOUR JOB?
It is very satisfying to be able to turn customers on to a new varietal or winery and share in their delight and discovery. I particularly enjoy hearing guest feedback, which is very helpful in fine-tuning our list.

IF YOU WERE NOT IN THE WINE PROFESSION, WHAT WOULD YOU BE?
A professional scuba diver.

Barney Greengrass Restaurant at Barneys New York

9570 Wilshire Boulevard, Fifth Floor
Beverly Hills, California 90212
phone 310-777-5877 fax 310-777-5760

Sharyn L. Kervyn de Volkaersbeke

GENERAL MANAGER AND SOMMELIER

WHAT ARE SOME OF YOUR ULTIMATE FOOD AND WINE PAIRINGS?
Our Nova Scotia salmon with Sauvignon Blanc; peppered ahi salad with Pinot Noir; breast of chicken and crispy artichokes with full-bodied Chardonnay; southwestern corn and chicken salad with Viognier; chilled soups with Champagne; chocolate raspberry cake with Cabernet Sauvignon; steamed shellfish with white Burgundy; rosemary grilled lamb with Meritage blends.

DESCRIBE YOUR WINE SELECTIONS.
Our current wine list is small and to the point, with a focus on California wines and Champagne.

WHAT CATEGORY OF WINE IS THE BEST VALUE IN YOUR RESTAURANT?
Rhône varietals. They are affordable and featured by the glass to encourage our patrons to try them.

NAME RECENT WINE DISCOVERIES THAT HAVE EXCITED YOU.
For style and quality, the 1988 Mongeard-Mugneret Vosne-Romanée and 1989 Château Grand Barrail Lamarzelle Figeac, St.-Émilion Grand Cru.

WHAT IS YOUR FAVORITE WINE REGION IN THE WORLD TODAY?
California's Central Coast, for its growing diversity, the wonderful people involved in the industry and the superb wines.

WHAT LED YOU TO BECOME A SOMMELIER?
My parents are restaurant owners and I have worked in food and beverage for years. I started cellaring wines in 1988.

WHAT ARE THE BEST ASPECTS OF YOUR JOB?
Having an active role in increasing the bottom line, and chatting with our regular customers, many of whom are celebrities.

IF YOU WERE NOT IN THE WINE PROFESSION, WHAT WOULD YOU DO?
Either paint or own a winery.

The Cellar

305 North Harbor Boulevard
Fullerton, California 92832
phone 714-525-5682 fax 714-525-3853
website www.imenu.com/thecellar

Ernest Zingg
OWNER AND MANAGER

WHAT ARE SOME OF YOUR ULTIMATE FOOD AND WINE PAIRINGS?
Roasted breast of Muscovy duck and sour cherries with a fruity Australian or
Central Coast Syrah; Châteaubriand bouquetière with a Côte de Beaune
(Burgundy).

DESCRIBE YOUR WINE SELECTIONS.
We are next to a major convention center and our wine selection caters to
international customers. We carry wines from more than fifteen countries.

WHAT CATEGORY OF WINE IS THE BEST VALUE IN YOUR RESTAURANT?
The older wines, especially red Burgundies and California Cabernets, where a
ten- to twenty-year-old bottle is priced only a little less than the latest release
from the same producer.

NAME A RECENT WINE DISCOVERY THAT EXCITED YOU.
A Marsanne from Chateau Tahbilk in Victoria, Australia.

WHAT IS YOUR FAVORITE WINE REGION IN THE WORLD TODAY?
Burgundy is my favorite region and Pinot Noir my favorite wine.

WHAT LED YOU TO BECOME A SOMMELIER?
Wine service has always been close to my heart and when I became a proprietor, I continued to serve and recommend wine.

WHAT IS THE BEST ASPECT OF YOUR JOB?
Tasting all the new wines. I have personally tasted 98 percent of the wine I buy.

IF YOU WERE NOT IN THE WINE PROFESSION, WHAT WOULD YOU DO?
Return to the hotel business.

Chez Melange

1716 South Pacific Coast Highway
Redondo Beach, California 90277
phone 310-540-1222 fax 310-316-9283
website www.chezmelange.com

Michael I. Franks
CO-OWNER

WHAT ARE SOME OF YOUR ULTIMATE FOOD AND WINE PAIRINGS?
Sausage and Zinfandel; Cajun meatloaf and southern Rhône; oysters and
California Pinot Gris; lamb ossobuco and Pinot Noir; chicken curry and
California Gewürztraminer.

DESCRIBE YOUR WINE SELECTIONS.
We specialize in California wines, new releases, hard-to-find wines and great
values.

WHAT CATEGORY OF WINE IS THE BEST VALUE ON YOUR WINE LIST?
Interesting reds.

NAME RECENT WINE DISCOVERIES THAT HAVE EXCITED YOU.
Joe Gott Cabernet Sauvignon 2000—a great value; Waterbrook Melange 1999-
—a Cabernet Merlot-Sangiovese blend. It is a great value and has a great name.

WHAT IS YOUR FAVORITE WINE REGION IN THE WORLD TODAY?
Napa Valley, for its quality, people and innovation.

WHAT LED YOU TO YOUR CURRENT POSITION?
Passion for wine.

WHAT ARE THE BEST ASPECTS OF YOUR JOB?
The constant motivation to get things right.

IF YOU WERE NOT IN THE WINE PROFESSION, WHAT WOULD YOU BE
DOING?
I would be in marketing.

The Hobbit Restaurant

2932 East Chapman Avenue
Orange, California 92869-3798
phone 714-997-1972 fax 714-997-3181
website www.hobbitrestaurant.com

Brian W. Harley
MANAGER AND SOMMELIER

WHAT ARE SOME OF YOUR ULTIMATE FOOD AND WINE PAIRINGS?
Australian Shiraz and Cabernet blends with our beef Wellington; New Zealand
Pinot Noir and herb-crusted lamb loin.

DESCRIBE YOUR WINE SELECTIONS.
We have nearly 1,100 selections and offer two different tasting selections,
which are paired with our fixed-price menu.

WHAT CATEGORIES OF WINE ARE THE BEST VALUES IN YOUR RESTAURANT?
German Rieslings and Loire Valley wines.

NAME RECENT WINE DISCOVERIES THAT HAVE EXCITED YOU.
Wines from Argentina. They offer value and quality.

WHAT IS YOUR FAVORITE WINE REGION IN THE WORLD TODAY?
Burgundy. It's magical.

WHAT LED YOU TO BECOME A SOMMELIER?
I needed the money.

WHAT IS THE BEST ASPECT OF YOUR JOB?
Trying many of the world's finest wines.

IF YOU WERE NOT IN THE WINE PROFESSION, WHAT WOULD YOU BE?
A musician.

James' Beach Café

60 North Venice Boulevard
Venice, California 90291
phone 310-823-5396 fax 310-827-8560

Daniel C. Samakow
PROPRIETOR

WHAT ARE SOME OF YOUR ULTIMATE FOOD AND WINE PAIRINGS?
Steak and Cabernet Sauvignon; foie gras and Château d'Yquem 1989; salmon and Pouilly-Fumé.

DESCRIBE YOUR WINE SELECTIONS.
We specialize in comfort food. Our list is a comfort list of great names and exciting newcomers, all sold at excellent prices.

WHAT CATEGORY OF WINE IS THE BEST VALUE IN YOUR RESTAURANT?
California wines.

NAME RECENT WINE DISCOVERIES THAT HAVE EXCITED YOU.
1999 Justin Isosceles, for its great complexity and value; 1997 Peter Michael "Bellecote" Chardonnay and 1999 Kistler Chardonnay for their wonderful balance.

WHAT ARE YOUR FAVORITE WINE REGIONS IN THE WORLD TODAY?
Rhône for its quality and versatility with food; Bordeaux for complexity.

WHAT LED YOU TO YOUR CURRENT POSITION?
I create perfume for my cosmetic company and for other companies. There are many similarities regarding notes and understanding complexity that made me appreciate wine when I started my restaurants.

WHAT ARE THE BEST ASPECTS OF YOUR JOB?
Buying wine at auction, explaining rare vintages to customers and trying new, exciting producers.

IF YOU WERE NOT IN THE WINE PROFESSION, WHAT WOULD YOU BE DOING?
Making art. I am a painter.

Jer-ne Restaurant at the Ritz-Carlton Marina Del Rey

4375 Admiralty Way
Marina Del Rey, California 90292
phone 310-823-1700 fax 310-821-3830

Alison Junker
SOMMELIER

WHAT ARE SOME OF YOUR ULTIMATE FOOD AND WINE PAIRINGS?
Sauternes with several types of crème brûlée; Champagne and potato chips.

DESCRIBE YOUR WINE SELECTIONS.
Our wine list is not extremely extensive, but wines from almost every fine wine–producing region are represented.

WHAT CATEGORY OF WINE IS THE BEST VALUE ON YOUR WINE LIST?
California blends of red Rhône and Italian varietals.

NAME RECENT WINE DISCOVERIES THAT HAVE EXCITED YOU.
White Bordeaux more than ten years old. They evolve and show nuances that are well worth the wait.

WHAT IS YOUR FAVORITE WINE REGION IN THE WORLD TODAY?
France. A pretty broad region but, within its borders, there is the perfect manifestation of many varietals.

WHAT LED YOU TO BECOME A SOMMELIER?
I took a sommelier course in New York taught by Andrea Immer because I personally wanted to learn more about wine. After the first class, I was hooked.

WHAT ARE THE BEST ASPECTS OF YOUR JOB?
You can study wine your whole life and never learn everything you need to know.

IF YOU WERE NOT IN THE WINE PROFESSION, WHAT WOULD YOU BE DOING?
Armed with my degree in geography and cartography, I would make maps of wine regions.

Lucques

8474 Melrose Avenue
Los Angeles, California 90069
phone 323-655-6277 fax 323-655-3925
website www.lucques.com

Caroline P. Styne
CO-OWNER AND WINE DIRECTOR

WHAT ARE SOME OF YOUR ULTIMATE FOOD AND WINE PAIRINGS?
Our suckling pig paired with an earthy Côte Rôtie is a perfect marriage. I love pairing wines and cheeses, such as a beautiful chèvre with a flinty Sancerre.

DESCRIBE YOUR WINE SELECTIONS.
We specialize in small-production, boutique wineries. Our list is known for showcasing wines that are off the beaten path.

WHAT CATEGORY OF WINE IS THE BEST VALUE ON YOUR WINE LIST?
The wines of Provence and southern France, an area of great, rich wines at reasonable prices.

NAME RECENT WINE DISCOVERIES THAT HAVE EXCITED YOU.
Australian wines. I have found some that are hearty and structured.

WHAT IS YOUR FAVORITE WINE REGION IN THE WORLD TODAY?
For the moment I am obsessed with Russian River Pinot Noirs. It's so rich and earthy.

WHAT LED YOU TO BECOME A SOMMELIER?
A combination of restaurant management and an adoration of wine.

WHAT ARE THE BEST ASPECTS OF YOUR JOB?
The daily expansion of my wine knowledge and the sharing of it with my staff.

IF YOU WERE NOT IN THE WINE PROFESSION, WHAT WOULD YOU DO?
I'd hate to even contemplate that question!

Melisse
1104 Wilshire Boulevard
Santa Monica, California 90401
phone 310-395-0881 fax 310-395-3810

Paul S. Einbund
SOMMELIER

WHAT ARE SOME OF YOUR ULTIMATE FOOD AND WINE PAIRINGS?
Lobster and mature Savennières. The textures mirror each other exactly. (Add some cream or butter to the equation and look out!) I can also be brought to tears by foie gras and Sauternes any day of the week.

WHAT IS YOUR FAVORITE WINE REGION IN THE WORLD TODAY?
The Russian River has elegant Chardonnay and Pinot and jammy Zins, not to mention the charm of a small remote area. So between the diversity of wines available and the attitudes of the people, that would be my number one region.

WHAT LED YOU TO BECOME A SOMMELIER?
A visit to Napa Valley. As soon as I saw the first vineyard, I became obsessed.

WHAT IS THE MOST CHALLENGING ASPECT OF YOUR JOB?
Convincing people (servers, assistants, managers) not to make things up, that it is okay to say "I don't know."

IF YOU WERE NOT IN THE WINE PROFESSION, WHAT WOULD YOU BE DOING?
Chef, restaurant general manager or winemaker.

Michael's Restaurant

1147 Third Street
Santa Monica, California 90403
phone 310-451-0843 fax 310-394-1830

Jennifer L. Benzie

SOMMELIER

WHAT ARE SOME OF YOUR ULTIMATE FOOD AND WINE PAIRINGS?
Oysters and Sancerre; duck and Syrah.

DESCRIBE YOUR WINE SELECTIONS.
We have about 500 selections from different regions, grape varieties and price points.

WHAT CATEGORY OF WINE IS THE BEST VALUE ON YOUR WINE LIST?
Nontraditional regions and grape varieties.

NAME RECENT WINE DISCOVERIES THAT HAVE EXCITED YOU.
The wines from Lewis Cellars. There's not a bad one in the bunch!

WHAT IS YOUR FAVORITE WINE REGION IN THE WORLD TODAY?
Italy, a country which is examining its Old World concepts and now evolving with New World ideas.

WHAT LED YOU TO BECOME A SOMMELIER?
I worked in many restaurants around the country waiting tables. Eventually, I took a job as a wine steward in the Virgin Islands.

WHAT ARE THE BEST ASPECTS OF YOUR JOB?
Learning about where the wine really comes from (cultures and the land) and the people that produce such fine products. There is always something more to learn.

IF YOU WERE NOT IN THE WINE PROFESSION, WHAT WOULD YOU BE?
A pastry chef.

Morton's of Chicago at the Beverly Hills Nikko

435 South La Cienega Boulevard
Los Angeles, California 90048
phone 310-246-1501 fax 310-246-1203
website www.mortons.com

Jonathan L. Mitchell
WINE CAPTAIN

WHAT ARE SOME OF YOUR ULTIMATE FOOD AND WINE PAIRINGS?
Napa Valley Cabernet and Morton's Porterhouse steak; Australian Shiraz with
our double-cut filet mignon; ML-style Chardonnay with baked Maine lobster!

DESCRIBE YOUR WINE SELECTIONS.
We have wines from most areas, but really emphasize American red wines.

WHAT CATEGORIES OF WINE ARE THE BEST VALUES ON YOUR WINE LIST?
California Zinfandels, Syrahs, Petite Syrahs and Sangioveses.

NAME RECENT WINE DISCOVERIES THAT HAVE EXCITED YOU.
Santa Barbara Sangioveses are wonderful. They are incredibly fruit-packed with
lots of structure and are great values, as are Amador County and El Dorado
wines.

WHAT IS YOUR FAVORITE WINE REGION IN THE WORLD TODAY?
I'd have to say I love Northern California for its consistency of climate and
diversity of soils. Every winegrape variety seems to thrive somewhere in
Northern California.

WHAT LED YOU TO BECOME A SOMMELIER?
After frequent visits to Napa Valley and ten years as a waiter in fine dining
restaurants, I couldn't help but get excited and inspired about wines and winemaking.

WHAT ARE THE BEST ASPECTS OF YOUR JOB?
Exceeding people's expectations. We have a great wine list, too, which makes it
enjoyable to recommend wines!

IF YOU WERE NOT IN THE WINE PROFESSION, WHAT WOULD YOU BE?
A full-time drummer, which is what I do part-time on a freelance basis.

Napa Rose at the Disneyland Grand Californian Resort

1600 South Disneyland Drive
Anaheim, California 92802
phone 714-300-7170 fax 714-300-7122

Michael A. Jordan
SOMMELIER, GENERAL MANAGER
AND WINE EDUCATOR

WHAT ARE SOME OF YOUR ULTIMATE FOOD AND WINE PAIRINGS?
Seared scallops with coastal-style Chardonnay; pork rack with Zinfandel; Scharffen Berger chocolate velvet pâté with Pinot Noir Port; Sauternes with seared foie gras; venison with California Zinfandel; oysters and Sancerre; braised rabbit ragoût with Chianti Classico Riserva.

DESCRIBE YOUR WINE SELECTIONS.
There are 330 wines on the list and fifty by the glass. Ninety percent are California wines, from cult wines to affordable "discovery" wines.

WHAT CATEGORIES OF WINE ARE THE BEST VALUES ON YOUR WINE LIST?
Rhône varietals, Cal-Italian varietals, Pinot Noir and Zinfandel.

NAME RECENT WINE DISCOVERIES THAT HAVE EXCITED YOU.
Fanucchi Trousseau Gris is a crisp, fruity, limited-production wine at a great price; Tantara Pinot Noir is a fine version of the varietal.

WHAT IS YOUR FAVORITE WINE REGION IN THE WORLD TODAY?
California. With seventy-one AVAs and so many varieties being grown well, there is both diversity and great quality among them.

WHAT LED YOU TO BECOME A SOMMELIER?
I am passionate about the experience of great dining, and of enhancing meals with selected wines. And I enjoy sharing that.

WHAT ARE THE BEST ASPECTS OF YOUR JOB?
Teaching wine classes that have resulted in the certification of thirty sommeliers on staff at the resort and managing the wine program at the restaurant.

IF YOU WERE NOT IN THE WINE PROFESSION, WHAT WOULD YOU BE DOING?
Helping children with special needs.

The Pacific Club
4110 MacArthur Boulevard
Newport Beach, California 92660
phone 949-955-1123 fax 949-252-7680

René E. Chazottes
DIRECTOR OF WINE AND MAÎTRE SOMMELIER
Team: Erick Strong, Assistant Sommelier

WHAT ARE SOME OF YOUR ULTIMATE FOOD AND WINE PAIRINGS?
Roasted partridge with fresh raisin with Château Gazin 1995 Pomerol; yellow-tail with oyster mushrooms, fresh ginger and roasted peppers with King Estate 1998 Pinot Gris from Oregon.

DESCRIBE YOUR WINE SELECTIONS.
Open-minded, balanced and affordable.

WHAT IS YOUR FAVORITE WINE REGION IN THE WORLD TODAY?
Burgundy. Great people, fantastic food, amazing wines.

WHAT LED YOU TO BECOME A SOMMELIER?
Passion.

WHAT IS THE BEST ASPECT OF YOUR JOB?
Objectivity.

IF YOU WERE NOT IN THE WINE PROFESSION, WHAT WOULD YOU BE?
A clown.

Pinot Provence

686 Anton Boulevard
Costa Mesa, California 92626
phone 714-444-5900 fax 714-444-5906

Scott S. Teruya
GENERAL MANAGER AND SOMMELIER

WHAT ARE SOME OF YOUR ULTIMATE FOOD AND WINE PAIRINGS?
Braised rabbit with grilled portobella mushroom, foie gras raviolis and braised red chard with red Burgundy or Gigondas; our Belgian endive and wild cress salad with candied pecans Roquefort and walnut vinaigrette pairs well with an Alsatian Gewürztraminer with some residual sugar.

DESCRIBE YOUR WINE SELECTIONS.
A 500-selection list of older and current vintages from all major wine regions and in all price categories, including many great finds at reasonable prices. We also feature fifty to seventy-five half-bottles.

WHAT CATEGORY OF WINE IS THE BEST VALUE ON YOUR WINE LIST?
The "Old World Interesting Alternatives" section of our list, featuring the wines of Spain and Portugal.

NAME RECENT WINE DISCOVERIES THAT HAVE EXCITED YOU.
Spanish red and white wines. Many are extremely good values, high quality and consistent from vintage to vintage.

WHAT IS YOUR FAVORITE WINE REGION IN THE WORLD TODAY?
Burgundy. It is amazing that a wine produced from Pinot Noir can develop flavors, concentration, complexity and be defined by terroir.

WHAT IS THE BEST ASPECT OF YOUR JOB?
Wine education is the most rewarding.

IF YOU WERE NOT IN THE WINE PROFESSION, WHAT WOULD YOU BE DOING?
Something in the medical field. I was ready to run off to medical school before I decided to attend the Culinary Institute of America.

Rembrandt's Beautiful Food
909 East Yorba Linda Boulevard
Placentia, California 92870
phone 714-528-6222 fax 714-528-6202

Bernie Gordon
WINE BUYER AND SOMMELIER

WHAT IS ONE OF YOUR ULTIMATE FOOD AND WINE PAIRINGS?
Salmon with Pinot Noir or Burgundy.

DESCRIBE YOUR WINE PROGRAM.
Above average in selection and below average in price.

WHAT LED YOU TO BECOME A SOMMELIER?
I own a restaurant and love wine.

WHAT ARE THE BEST ASPECTS OF YOUR JOB?
Teaching and educating in a nice way.

IF YOU WERE NOT IN THE WINE PROFESSION, WHAT WOULD YOU BE?
A wine sales rep.

La Rive Gauche

320 Tejon Place
Palos Verdes Estate, California 90274-1204
phone 310-378-0267 fax 310-373-5837

Jacques J. Grenier
WINE BUYER

WHAT IS ONE OF YOUR ULTIMATE FOOD AND WINE PAIRINGS?
Veal Oscar with crab meat and red Bordeaux from St. Julien.

DESCRIBE YOUR WINE SELECTIONS.
We're known for having an excellent wine list and good prices.

WHAT CATEGORY OF WINE IS THE BEST VALUE ON YOUR WINE LIST?
Red Bordeaux.

NAME RECENT WINE DISCOVERIES THAT HAVE EXCITED YOU.
Kalin Cellars wines for their taste and finish.

WHAT IS YOUR FAVORITE WINE REGION IN THE WORLD TODAY?
Spain, for good Rioja.

WHAT IS THE BEST ASPECT OF YOUR JOB?
Knowing I have the best collection of wines.

IF YOU WERE NOT IN THE WINE PROFESSION, WHAT WOULD YOU BE?
A winemaker.

Röckenwagner Restaurant

2435 Main Street
Santa Monica, California 90405
phone 310-399-6504 fax 310-399-7984
website www.rockenwagner.com

David Osenbach

GENERAL MANAGER AND WINE DIRECTOR

WHAT ARE SOME OF YOUR ULTIMATE FOOD AND WINE PAIRINGS?
White asparagus with Black Forest ham and Austrian Grüner Veltliner; sautéed foie gras with raisin brioche, tangerine gastrique and Tokaji Aszú from Hungary; Roquefort and Sauternes.

DESCRIBE YOUR WINE SELECTIONS.
Our menu is based on French technique with a strong California influence. Wines from Germany, Austria and Alsace go incredibly well with our food. There is a very large presence of these on our list, as well as fine wines from California and several other regions.

WHAT CATEGORY OF WINE IS THE BEST VALUE ON YOUR WINE LIST?
German Riesling.

NAME RECENT WINE DISCOVERIES THAT HAVE EXCITED YOU.
Menetou-Salon from the Loire, and a great Chablis-style Chardonnay from Schneider on Long Island.

WHAT IS YOUR FAVORITE WINE REGION IN THE WORLD TODAY?
Campania. Right now I am on a big Taurasi and Greco di Tufo binge.

WHAT LED YOU TO YOUR CURRENT POSITION?
Fate.

WHAT ARE THE BEST ASPECTS OF YOUR JOB?
Having guests initially turn their nose up at one of my favorite, obscure recommendations and then having them fall in love with it by the end of the evening.

IF YOU WERE NOT IN THE WINE PROFESSION, WHAT WOULD YOU BE DOING?
Conducting a symphony orchestra.

Valentino Ristorante

3115 Pico Boulevard
Santa Monica, California 90405
phone 310-829-4313 fax 310-315-2791
website www.welovewine.com

Alessandro Sbrendola
SOMMELIER

WHAT ARE SOME OF YOUR ULTIMATE FOOD AND WINE PAIRINGS?
Maine scallops and Italian white; Piemontese beef and Sicilian red; tagliatelle with white truffles and Piedmont red.

DESCRIBE YOUR WINE PROGRAM.
Our goal is to accumulate the most well-rounded cellar of Italian wines in the United States.

WHAT CATEGORY OF WINE IS THE BEST VALUE IN YOUR RESTAURANT?
Red wine from southern Italy.

NAME RECENT WINE DISCOVERIES THAT HAVE EXCITED YOU.
Lebanese wine, particularly Chateau Musar, for its exotic character, and southern Italian wine for its prices.

WHAT IS YOUR FAVORITE WINE REGIONS IN THE WORLD TODAY?
Tuscany and Umbria for superior quality wines and attractive prices.

WHAT LED YOU TO BECOME A SOMMELIER?
After completing hotel and restaurant management school, I realized there was even more to learn about wine and pursued further education.

WHAT ARE THE BEST ASPECTS OF YOUR JOB?
The opportunity to taste rare wines and to share my knowledge.

IF YOU WERE NOT IN THE WINE PROFESSION, WHAT WOULD YOU BE DOING?
Training horses for dressage, jumping and cutting.

Villa Nova Restaurant

3131 West Pacific Coast Highway
Newport Beach, California 92663
phone 949-642-7880 fax 949-642-0674
website www.villanovarestaurant.com

John W. Caneer
WINE BUYER

DESCRIBE YOUR WINE SELECTIONS.
We have many Californian and Italian wines.

WHAT CATEGORY OF WINE IS THE BEST VALUE ON YOUR WINE LIST?
We have bargains scattered throughout the wine list, especially on the captain's list.

WHAT IS YOUR FAVORITE WINE REGION IN THE WORLD TODAY?
Oregon, for its development of Pinot Noir.

WHAT LED YOU TO YOUR CURRENT POSITION?
I grew into the job.

WHAT IS THE BEST ASPECT OF YOUR JOB?
Talking to people with similar experience in wine.

IF YOU WERE NOT IN THE WINE PROFESSION, WHAT WOULD YOU BE DOING?
Fishing.

Alto Palato Trattoria
DANILLO TERRIBILI, OWNER
AND WINE BUYER
755 North La Cienega Boulevard,
Los Angeles
310-657-9271

Antonello Ristorante
STEVE NEBOL, SOMMELIER
1611 Sunflower Avenue, Santa Ana
714-751-7153

Aubergine
TIM GOODELL, OWNER,
CHEF AND WINE BUYER
508 29th Street, Newport Beach
714-723-4150

Café Del Rey
BILL PRIESTLEY, MANAGER
AND WINE STEWARD
4451 Admiralty Way, Marina Del Rey
310-823-6395

Café La Bohème
RAY CACCIOLI, WINE BUYER
8400 Santa Monica Boulevard,
West Hollywood
323-848-2360

Campanile Restaurant
GEORGE COSSETTE, WINE BUYER
624 South La Brea Avenue, Los Angeles
323-938-1447

Capo Restaurant
BRUCE MARDER, SOMMELIER
1810 Ocean Avenue, Santa Monica
310-394-5550

Chanteclair
BILL BLANK, SOMMELIER
18921 MacArthur Boulevard, Irvine
949-752-8001

Le Dome
EDDY KERKHOFS, WINE BUYER
8720 Sunset Boulevard, Los Angeles
310-659-6919

Doug Arango's
ROBERT EVANS, WINE BUYER
73520 El Paseo, Palm Desert
760-341-4120

Duane's Prime Steaks at the Mission Inn
TOM SZALLAY, WINE BUYER
3649 Mission Inn Avenue, Riverside
909-784-0300

Five Crowns Restaurant
CHRIS SZCHENYI, WINE BUYER
3801 East Coast Highway,
Corona Del Mar
949-760-0331

Gardens Restaurant at the Four Seasons Hotel
EKREN TERANOGLU, FOOD
AND BEVERAGE DIRECTOR
Four Seasons, Los Angeles
300 South Doheny Drive, Los Angeles
310-273-2222

Granita
PHOITOS KYRIAKOUZIS, WINE BUYER
23725 West Malibu Road, Malibu
310-456-0488

JiRaffe
STEPHEN PARRA, WINE BUYER
502 Santa Monica Boulevard,
Santa Monica
310-917-6671

CALIFORNIA, LOS ANGELES AREA

Linq
STEVEN THOMPSON, SOMMELIER
8338 West Third Street, Los Angeles
323-655-4555

Los Angeles Country Club
BRUCE PRUITT, GENERAL MANAGER
AND WINE BUYER
10101 Wilshire Boulevard, Los Angeles
323-272-2134

Morton's of Chicago
WILLIAM LEWIS, WINE BUYER
1641 West Sunflower, Santa Ana
714-444-4834

Mr. Stoxx
RON MARSHALL, SOMMELIER
1105 East Katella Avenue, Anaheim
714-634-2994

Napa Valley Grille
RAFAEL DUMAS, SOMMELIER
Westwood Center, 1100 Glendon Avenue,
Los Angeles
310-824-3322

Oceanfront
MARC NEUBERT, WINE BUYER
1910 Ocean Front Walk, Santa Monica
310-581-7714

L'Orangerie
ELIZABETH SCHWEITZER, SOMMELIER
Stephane Clasquin, Manager
and Sommelier
903 North La Cienega Boulevard,
Los Angeles
310-652-9770

Patina Restaurant
CHRISTOPHER MEESKE, SOMMELIER
5955 Melrose Avenue, Los Angeles
323-467-1108

The Polo Lounge at the Beverly Hills Hotel
CLAUDE BOUDOUX, FOOD
AND BEVERAGE DIRECTOR
9641 Sunset Boulevard, Beverly Hills
310-276-2251

The Regency Club
MATHIAS ORELLANA, FOOD
AND BEVERAGE DIRECTOR
10900 Wilshire Boulevard, Los Angeles
310-208-1443

Renato Restaurant at Portofino Beach Hotel
KEN RICAMORE, OWNER
AND WINE BUYER
2306 West Ocean Front Boulevard,
Newport Beach
949-673-7030

Ritz-Carlton Laguna Niguel
CRAIG LARSON, SOMMELIER
1 Ritz-Carlton Drive, Dana Point
949-240-2000

Saddle Peak Lodge
GERHARD TRATTER, GENERAL
MANAGER AND WINE BUYER
419 Cold Canyon Road, Calabasas
818-222-3888

Spago Beverly Hills
KEVIN O'CONNOR, SOMMELIER
David Organizak, Manager and Sommelier
176 North Canon Drive, Beverly Hills
310-385-0880

Le St. Germain

MICHEL DESPARS, OWNER
AND WINE BUYER
74-985 Highway 111, Indian Wells
760-773-6511

Troquet

SYLVIE CAHUZAC, SOMMELIER
333 Bristol Street, Costa Mesa
714-708-6865

La Vie en Rose

JOEL RICHARD, WINE BUYER
240 South State College Boulevard,
Brea
714-529-8333

Vincenti Ristorante

GARY FREEDMAN, WINE BUYER
11930 San Vincente Boulevard,
Los Angeles
310-207-0127

Azzura Point Restaurant at Loews Coronado Bay Resort

4000 Coronado Bay Road
Coronado, California 92118
phone 619-424-4000 fax 619-628-5468
website www.loews.com

Kurt A. Kirschenman
SOMMELIER

WHAT ARE SOME OF YOUR ULTIMATE FOOD AND WINE PAIRINGS?
Lobster risotto paired with Italian white (Gavi, Greco di Tufo); seared ahi tuna with dry Riesling from Alsace or Austria; roasted venison loin wrapped in bacon with massive Australian Shiraz blend.

DESCRIBE YOUR WINE SELECTIONS.
We are strong on California white and red wines, but also feature wines from many regions around the world.

WHAT CATEGORIES OF WINE ARE THE BEST VALUES ON YOUR WINE LIST?
California Sauvignon Blancs, Bordeaux and Australian wines.

NAME RECENT WINE DISCOVERIES THAT HAVE EXCITED YOU.
Australia whites are outstanding; its reds great value.

WHAT IS YOUR FAVORITE WINES REGION IN THE WORLD TODAY?
Whites and reds from the Rhône Valley. They are tremendous. Also, Australian wines are outstanding and are usually great values.

WHAT LED YOU TO BECOME A SOMMELIER?
I became highly motivated to learn about wine both during my time as a bartender here at the restaurant and during my travels to the major wine regions in Europe.

WHAT ARE THE BEST ASPECTS OF YOUR JOB?
It is very rewarding to have guests say "Wow!" when they try a wine I've recommended for the first time.

IF YOU WERE NOT IN THIS PROFESSION, WHAT WOULD YOU BE DOING?
Making wine, growing grapes or being a travel guide.

El Bizcocho at the Rancho Bernardo Inn

17550 Bernardo Oaks Drive
San Diego, California 92128
phone 858-675-8500 fax 858-675-8501
website www.jcresorts.com

Michael D. Dalton
HEAD SOMMELIER

WHAT ARE SOME OF YOUR ULTIMATE FOOD AND WINE PAIRINGS?
Spanish red pepper–lacquered scallops with orange and corn ravioli, white asparagus and vanilla bean butter with rich Australian Sauvignon Blanc; our roasted duck with caramelized root vegetables and Pinot Noir; sautéed sea bass with braised short ribs and Port wine reduction with jammy Australian Shiraz; grilled veal chop with morel mushroom sauce and red Bordeaux.

DESCRIBE YOUR WINE SELECTIONS.
Our list features 1,600 selections with breadth and depth in many areas. We encourage our guests to allow us to guide and assist them with their selections, and this is indicated on our cover page.

WHAT CATEGORIES OF WINE ARE THE BEST VALUES ON YOUR WINE LIST?
California Zinfandel and wines from the southern Rhône.

NAME RECENT WINE DISCOVERIES THAT HAVE EXCITED YOU.
New Zealand Sauvignon Blancs—tremendous character and great value; Australian Shirazs and blends, which offer a lot of character and early accessibility.

WHAT IS YOUR FAVORITE WINE REGION IN THE WORLD TODAY?
The Rhône. I love the terroir of the wines and their compatibility with our chef's cuisine.

WHAT LED YOU TO BECOME A SOMMELIER?
A love of wine and an exposure to a great wine program.

WHAT IS THE BEST ASPECT OF YOUR JOB?
The opportunity to sell, serve and taste the best wines in the world nightly.

IF YOU WERE NOT IN THE WINE PROFESSION, WHAT WOULD YOU BE DOING?
Professional golf.

George's at the Cove

1250 Prospect Place
La Jolla, California 92037
phone 858-454-4244 fax 858-454-5458
website www.georgesatthecove.com

Steve J. Josefski

RESTAURANT MANAGER AND WINE BUYER

WHAT ARE SOME OF YOUR ULTIMATE FOOD AND WINE PAIRINGS?
A carrot–coconut milk soup with lemongrass and ginger with lobster cannelloni and mint paired with Mendocino Gewürztraminer; roasted grouper with a ragoût of corn, cranberry beans, zucchini blossom, calamari and Spanish chorizo with lightly oaked Tempranillo.

DESCRIBE YOUR WINE SELECTIONS.
We have 500 selections on the list and hundreds more in the cellar. Our focus is on California, but we incorporate all styles from most wine-growing regions in the world at reasonable prices.

WHAT CATEGORY OF WINE IS THE BEST VALUE ON YOUR WINE LIST?
Rhône-style wines, which offer great value. We feature selections from many regions of the world, such as France, Australia and California.

NAME RECENT WINE DISCOVERIES THAT HAVE EXCITED YOU.
Spanish wines. Better viticulture, marketing and shipping have brought these wines to a higher level in the United States.

WHAT IS YOUR FAVORITE WINE REGION IN THE WORLD TODAY?
I love them all. After thirty years in the business, I couldn't pick just one.

WHAT LED YOU TO YOUR CURRENT POSITION?
The support of George Hauer (owner of the restaurant), who recognized my passion for wine and provided the means for pursuing it.

WHAT IS THE MOST CHALLENGING PART OF YOUR JOB?
The minute-to-minute challenge of providing a high level of service and satisfaction (and succeeding most of the time).

IF YOU WERE NOT IN THE WINE PROFESSION, WHAT WOULD YOU BE DOING?
Gardening.

Mille Fleurs

6009 Paseo Delisias
Rancho Santa Fe, California 92067
phone 858-756-3085 fax 858-756-9945
website www.millefleurs.com

Bertrand R. Hug
OWNER AND WINE BUYER

DESCRIBE YOUR WINE SELECTIONS.

Our selections reflect my personal taste, although I do try to please more people by having an eclectic selection. Our wine cellar offers more than 700 choices, a selection of wines spanning the globe which includes all price ranges.

WHAT IS YOUR FAVORITE WINE REGION IN THE WORLD TODAY?

I love all the regions.

WHAT LED YOU TO BECOME A SOMMELIER?

I am the owner, but I handle all the wine purchases and training for both restaurants.

WHAT IS THE MOST CHALLENGING ASPECT OF YOUR JOB?

Wine list management is a constant, evolving job. I taste twenty to fifty wines every day, Monday through Thursday, and write a wine column for the Rancho Santa Fe Review.

IF YOU WERE NOT IN THE WINE PROFESSION, WHAT WOULD YOU BE?

An actor.

Bertrand at Mister A's

BERTRAND HUG, OWNER
AND WINE BUYER
2550 Fifth Avenue, San Diego
619-239-1377

Brigantine

JOHN AZEVEDO, GENERAL MANAGER
AND WINE BUYER
3263 Camino del Mar, Del Mar
858-481-1166

Thee Bungalow

EDMUND MOORE, OWNER AND WINE BUYER
4996 West Point Loma Boulevard, San Diego
619-224-2884

Croce's

CHRIS MILLER, RESTAURANT MANAGER
AND BEVERAGE DIRECTOR
802 Fifth Avenue, San Diego
619-233-4355

Delicias

KEVIN MABBUTT, OWNER
AND WINE BUYER
6106 Paseo Delicias B, Rancho Santa Fe
858-756-8000

Donovan's Steak and Chop House

CARL ESSERT, SOMMELIER
4340 La Jolla Village Drive, La Jolla
858-450-9466

Harbor House Restaurant

JEB CARTER, BEVERAGE MANAGER
831 West Harbor Drive, San Diego
619-232-1141

Hornblower Yacht

HILARY ROSSI, FOOD
AND BEVERAGE MANAGER
2825 Fifth Avenue, San Diego
619-686-8700

Jake's Del Mar

CHRIS HOWE, WINE SPECIALIST
1660 Coast Boulevard, Del Mar
858-755-2002

Pacifica Del Mar

ROBERT CARTER, WINE BUYER
1555 Camino Del Mar, Suite 321, Del Mar
858-792-0476

Pamplemousse Grille

CARLOS SERAFIM, SOMMELIER
514 Via De La Valle, Solana Beach
858-792-9090

Rainwater's

LAUREL RAINWATER, OWNER
AND WINE BUYER
1202 Kettner Boulevard, San Diego
619-233-5757

Rancho Valencia Restaurant

DON BRIGHT, SOMMELIER
5921 Valencia Circle, Rancho Santa Fe
858-756-1123

Star of the Sea

BRIAN JOHNSTON, EXECUTIVE CHEF
AND WINE BUYER
1360 North Harbor Drive, San Diego
619-232-7408

Top of the Cove

JOSEF HELPHINSTINE, SOMMELIER
1216 Prospect Street, La Jolla
858-454-7779

The Winesellar & Brasserie

DAVID DERBY, WINE BUYER
9550 Waples Street, San Diego
858-450-9557

Enotria Café and Wine Bar

1431 Del Paso Boulevard
Sacramento, California 95621
phone 916-922-6792 fax 916-922-6794
website www.enotria.com

Michael L. Jones
ASSISTANT MANAGER AND WINE BUYER

WHAT ARE SOME OF YOUR ULTIMATE FOOD AND WINE PAIRINGS?
Pinot Noir with our salmon Niçoise; Syrah with our pepper-crusted pork ten-derloin with Cabernet sauce or grilled medallions of lamb with spiced cider Port wine demi-glace.

DESCRIBE YOUR WINE SELECTIONS.
An expansive international collection of wines that is reasonably priced.

WHAT CATEGORIES OF WINE ARE THE BEST VALUES ON YOUR WINE LIST?
California Cabernet Sauvignon and red Burgundy.

NAME RECENT WINE DISCOVERIES THAT HAVE EXCITED YOU.
We just started using a decanting pour spout that actually is the equivalent of decanting wine for 90 minutes. It really enhances the wine, provided you know which wines it works well with.

WHAT IS YOUR FAVORITE WINE REGION IN THE WORLD TODAY?
Rhône wines. I have always liked Viogniers and I love the soft finish of Rhône reds.

WHAT LED YOU TO YOUR CURRENT POSITION?
It was a combination of being a server for so long, wanting to go to the next level and working with Dave Bagley.

WHAT ARE THE BEST ASPECTS OF YOUR JOB?
Meeting all of the people involved in what we do, from the guests to those who bring us the wine.

IF YOU WERE NOT IN THE WINE PROFESSION, WHAT WOULD YOU BE DOING?
Skiing 100 days per year, instead of the 35 I do now.

Nepheles

1169 Ski Run Boulevard
South Lake Tahoe, California 96150
phone 530-544-8130 fax 530-544-8131
website www.nepheles.com

Timothy R. Halloran
PRESIDENT AND CELLAR MASTER

WHAT ARE SOME OF YOUR ULTIMATE FOOD AND WINE PAIRINGS?
Rack of New Zealand lamb roasted with a grain mustard crust, then finished
with a tequila, garlic, feta cheese demi-glaze with a Shiraz or Zinfandel;
Château d'Yquem with foie gras.

DESCRIBE YOUR WINE SELECTIONS.
Current and aged California wines at reasonable prices with more than 100
items on the list and 3,500 bottles in the cellar.

WHAT CATEGORY OF WINE IS THE BEST VALUE IN YOUR RESTAURANT?
California Cabs that are ten years old or more.

NAME A RECENT WINE DISCOVERY THAT EXCITED YOU.
A 1985 Mondavi Reserve Napa Valley Cabernet Sauvignon.

WHAT IS YOUR FAVORITE WINE REGION IN THE WORLD TODAY?
California, with its cutting-edge technology.

WHAT LED YOU TO YOUR CURRENT POSITION?
My love of food and wine and a B.S. in hotel and restaurant administration
from Oklahoma State University, 1974.

WHAT IS THE BEST ASPECT OF YOUR JOB?
Having a well-trained, experienced staff to work with.

IF YOU WERE NOT IN THE WINE PROFESSION, WHAT WOULD YOU BE
DOING?
I'd be retired.

Elbow Room

MICHAEL SHIRNIAN, SOMMELIER

731 West San Jose, Fresno

559-227-1234

Erna's Elderberry House

CHRIS SHACKELFORD, WINE BUYER

48688 Victoria Lane, Oakhurst

209-683-6800

Lahontan Country Club Lake Tahoe

JAY JAY MORGAN, SOMMELIER

AND WINE BUYER

12700 Lodge Trail Drive, Truckee

530-550-2400

Ajax Tavern
685 East Durant Avenue
Aspen, Colorado 81611
phone 970-920-9333 fax 970-920-2004
website www.ajaxtavern.com

Sabine Fowler
MANAGER AND SOMMELIER

DESCRIBE YOUR WINE SELECTIONS.
We feature mostly California wines, but part of the wine list includes Italian and French wines. Most of our California wines are from small producers.

WHAT CATEGORY OF WINE IS THE BEST VALUE ON YOUR WINE LIST?
"Interesting Whites," which includes Sauvignon Blancs, Chenin Blancs and so on.

WHAT LED YOU TO BECOME A SOMMELIER?
I love wine and food.

WHAT ARE THE BEST ASPECTS OF YOUR JOB?
The constant tasting of wines, discovering new wines and then selling them to the customer.

IF YOU WERE NOT IN THE WINE PROFESSION, WHAT WOULD YOU BE DOING?
I'd be a veterinarian.

Antares Restaurant
57-1/2 Eighth Street
Steamboat Springs, Colorado 80477
phone 970-879-9939 fax 970-879-0718

Douglas W. Enochs
OWNER AND SOMMELIER

WHAT ARE SOME OF YOUR ULTIMATE FOOD AND WINE PAIRINGS?
Pistachio-crusted rack of lamb with Napa Valley Cabernet Sauvignon; Thai curry prawns over jasmine rice with New Zealand Riesling.

DESCRIBE YOUR WINE SELECTIONS.
We offer twenty wines by the glass and have an international list of 175 selections, with an emphasis on American wines.

WHAT CATEGORY OF WINE IS THE BEST VALUE IN YOUR RESTAURANT?
California Chardonnay.

NAME RECENT WINE DISCOVERIES THAT HAVE EXCITED YOU.
Rancho Zabaco Dancing Bull Zinfandel. Well priced with big flavors.

WHAT IS YOUR FAVORITE WINE REGION IN THE WORLD TODAY?
Piedmont. Barolos are my current favorites. I visited the region last year and fell in love.

WHAT LED YOU TO BECOME A SOMMELIER?
Love of wine and the restaurant business.

WHAT ARE THE BEST ASPECTS OF YOUR JOB?
Drinking wine and socializing with the guests.

IF YOU WERE NOT IN THE WINE PROFESSION, WHAT WOULD YOU BE DOING?
Catering.

Barolo Grill
3030 East Sixth Avenue
Denver, Colorado 80206
phone 303-393-1040 fax 303-333-9240

Mark S. Sandusky
SOMMELIER

WHAT ARE SOME OF YOUR ULTIMATE FOOD AND WINE PAIRINGS?
Our signature dish of duckling braised in red wine paired with aged Barolo (sublime!); Stilton with vintage Port; New Mexican cuisine with Châteauneuf-du-Pape.

DESCRIBE YOUR WINE SELECTIONS.
We specialize in the wines of Italy with a strong selection of wines from Barolo and Barbaresco, Tuscany and the Veneto.

WHAT CATEGORY OF WINE IS THE BEST VALUE IN YOUR RESTAURANT?
Barbera.

NAME RECENT WINE DISCOVERIES THAT HAVE EXCITED YOU.
The wines of Sicily. They are good values and have an entirely different flavor profile from wines from other Italian regions.

WHAT IS YOUR FAVORITE WINE REGION IN THE WORLD TODAY?
The Piedmont region of northern Italy for its Barolo and Barbaresco wines. They're powerful, yet polished and elegant.

WHAT LED YOU TO BECOME A SOMMELIER?
Fourteen years in the restaurant business, a love of wine and the excitement in introducing people to the joys of great food and wine.

WHAT ARE THE BEST ASPECTS OF YOUR JOB?
When a customer leaves happy and satisfied, satiated by food and wine, that's rewarding.

IF YOU WERE NOT IN THE WINE PROFESSION, WHAT WOULD YOU BE DOING?
Playing trombone in a jazz combo.

Bravo! Ristorante at the Adams Mark Hotel

1550 Court Place
Denver, Colorado 80202
phone 303-893-3333 fax 303-626-2542

Maxence Ariza
SOMMELIER

WHAT IS ONE OF YOUR ULTIMATE FOOD AND WINE PAIRINGS?
Dessilani Spanna Riserva 1997 served with roasted rack of lamb and rosemary polenta.

DESCRIBE YOUR WINE SELECTIONS.
The wine list covers Italy extensively, as well as California and France. We also have a good selection of wines by the glass and half-bottle.

WHAT IS YOUR FAVORITE WINE REGION IN THE WORLD TODAY?
Southern Rhône, more specifically Châteauneuf-du-Pape. As a kid, I had my first professional wine tasting there.

WHAT LED YOU TO BECOME A SOMMELIER?
As a restaurant manager, I assumed both management and sommelier duties, and naturally moved to sommelier when the opportunity was presented.

WHAT IS THE MOST CHALLENGING ASPECT OF YOUR JOB?
Trying to keep up with the ever-expanding wine world.

IF YOU WERE NOT IN THE WINE PROFESSION, WHAT WOULD YOU BE DOING?
I'd be a stunt man.

Brook's Steak House
6538 South Yosemite Circle
Greenwood Village, Colorado 80111
phone 303-770-1177 fax 303-770-0193

Marcus J. Brown
SOMMELIER

WHAT IS ONE OF YOUR ULTIMATE FOOD AND WINE PAIRINGS?
Château d'Yquem 1990 with a Stilton blue cheese tartine.

DESCRIBE YOUR WINE SELECTIONS.
Our wine list is strong in California Cabernets and red Bordeaux. It is now at
850 items and is constantly evolving.

WHAT IS YOUR FAVORITE WINE REGION IN THE WORLD TODAY?
Burgundy, because of the sheer elegance and purity in the wines and the natural
surroundings.

WHAT LED YOU TO BECOME A SOMMELIER?
My love of wine since childhood when I had my own engraved wine glass and
champagne flute.

WHAT IS THE MOST CHALLENGING ASPECT OF YOUR JOB?
Ensuring the best possible experience for my guests on a daily basis.

IF YOU WERE NOT IN THIS PROFESSION, WHAT WOULD YOU BE?
An enologist.

The Century Room at the Hotel Jerome

330 East Main Street
Aspen, Colorado 81611
phone 970-920-1000 fax 970-925-2784
website www.hoteljerome.com

Jamie Jamison

HOTEL SOMMELIER AND DIRECTOR
OF RESTAURANT OPERATIONS

DESCRIBE YOUR WINE SELECTIONS.
We specialize in the wines from California and France.

WHAT CATEGORY OF WINE IS THE BEST VALUE ON YOUR WINE LIST?
Older Bordeaux.

WHAT ARE YOUR FAVORITE WINE REGIONS IN THE WORLD TODAY?
Rhône Valley, Burgundy and Napa Valley.

WHAT LED YOU TO BECOME A SOMMELIER?
Love of fine wine, food and service.

WHAT ARE THE BEST ASPECTS OF YOUR JOB?
Visiting with people from all over the world and introducing them to great food and wine.

IF YOU WERE NOT IN THE WINE PROFESSION, WHAT WOULD YOU BE?
A chef.

Larkspur Restaurant

458 Vail Valley Drive
Vail, Colorado 81657
phone 970-479-8050 fax 970-479-8052
website www.larkspurvail.com

Kevin M. Furtado

BEVERAGE DIRECTOR AND SOMMELIER

DESCRIBE YOUR WINE SELECTIONS.
Very diverse, with an emphasis on wines that are food-friendly and good values.

WHAT CATEGORY OF WINE IS THE BEST VALUE IN YOUR RESTAURANT?
Italian wines. With the run of great vintages, there have been many great, affordable wines available.

WHAT IS YOUR FAVORITE REGION OR AREA IN THE WORLD TODAY?
Alsace. This exceptional region produces wine of elegance and intensity. It is also a thrill to see the look of enjoyment and amazement when a person tastes an Alsatian Pinot Gris for the first time.

WHAT LED YOU TO BECOME A SOMMELIER?
My passion for food led me to restaurants, which led me to wine.

WHAT ARE THE BEST AND MOST CHALLENGING ASPECTS OF YOUR JOB?
Educating myself, my staff and our guests.

IF YOU WERE NOT IN THE WINE PROFESSION, WHAT WOULD YOU BE DOING?
I could not imagine not being in the restaurant business.

Larkspur Restaurant

458 Vail Valley Drive
Vail, Colorado 81657
phone 970-479-8050 fax 970-479-8052
website www.larkspurvail.com

John (Mick) TerHaar
BEVERAGE DIRECTOR AND SOMMELIER

WHAT IS ONE OF YOUR ULTIMATE FOOD AND WINE PAIRINGS?
Our seared foie gras with tangerine-infused French toast and ruby grapefruit
with a 1989 Château d'Yquem. A classic match.

DESCRIBE YOUR WINE SELECTIONS.
We have an emphasis on California and French wines with a focus on boutique
wineries and highly allocated wines from around the world.

WHAT IS YOUR FAVORITE WINE REGION IN THE WORLD TODAY?
The Rhône region. It has great food wines which are very versatile, still affordable, with a wide range of flavors.

WHAT LED YOU TO BECOME A SOMMELIER?
My passion for wine and desire to learn more about the wine industry.

WHAT IS THE MOST CHALLENGING ASPECT OF YOUR JOB?
The constant turnover in our staff. In a resort town such as Vail, our staff
changes with the season.

IF YOU WERE NOT IN THE WINE PROFESSION, WHAT WOULD YOU BE
DOING?
Designing websites or developing software.

The Lodge at Vail

174 East Gore Creek Road
Vail, Colorado 81657
phone 970-476-5011 fax 970-476-7425
website www.lodgeatvail.com

Willem A. Johnson
SOMMELIER AND CELLAR MASTER

WHAT ARE SOME OF YOUR ULTIMATE FOOD AND WINE PAIRINGS?
Lamb T-bone with big, red Côte de Nuits and big, domestic Syrah; arborio-crusted sea scallops with a potato, atop parsnip purée with an older-style Soave Classico Superiore.

DESCRIBE YOUR WINE PROGRAM.
We have one of the largest wine programs in the state. Our selections have an emphasis on the wines of California, Burgundy and Italy.

WHAT CATEGORIES OF WINE ARE THE BEST VALUES ON YOUR WINE LIST?
Red Italian and white Californian wines.

NAME RECENT WINE DISCOVERIES THAT HAVE EXCITED YOU.
White Spanish wine has intrigued me of late for its varied complexity, drink-ablility with or without food and its unquestionable value.

WHAT IS YOUR FAVORITE WINE REGION IN THE WORLD TODAY?
I would have to toss a coin. It would be between Alsace and Italy.

WHAT LED YOU TO BECOME A SOMMELIER?
A love of wine that began about fifteen years ago.

WHAT IS THE BEST ASPECT OF YOUR JOB?
The look on someone's face when I describe or introduce them to a new wine.

IF YOU WERE NOT IN THE WINE PROFESSION, WHAT WOULD YOU BE DOING?
Flying helicopters.

Montagna at
The Little Nell

675 East Durant Avenue
Aspen, Colorado 81611
phone 970-920-6330 fax 970-920-6328

W. Richard Betts

WINE DIRECTOR AND SOMMELIER
Team: Alyson Heller, Food and Beverage Director

COLORADO

WHAT IS ONE OF YOUR ULTIMATE FOOD AND WINE PAIRINGS?
Riesling with curry, many different curries.

DESCRIBE YOUR WINE SELECTIONS.
Both classic and cutting-edge. We are really excited about new wines from old places like Spain, the south of France and Austria.

WHAT IS YOUR FAVORITE WINE REGION IN THE WORLD TODAY?
The Rhône Valley, because the wines are diverse, unique and offer power while remaining seductive.

WHAT LED YOU TO BECOME A SOMMELIER?
I fell in love with food and wine in Italy and just had to learn more about it!

WHAT IS THE MOST CHALLENGING ASPECT OF YOUR JOB?
The biggest challenge also brings the greatest reward: always working to personalize our guests' experience and making it special for them.

IF YOU WERE NOT IN THE WINE PROFESSION, WHAT WOULD YOU BE DOING?
Cooking. No question about it!

Renaissance Restaurant & Bistro

304 East Hopkins Avenue
Aspen, Colorado 81611-1906
phone 970-925-2402 fax 970-925-6634

Gerald B. Theron
SOMMELIER

WHAT ARE SOME OF YOUR ULTIMATE FOOD AND WINE PAIRINGS?
Hudson Valley foie gras with Sauternes; Tasmanian salmon with red Burgundy (Pommard).

DESCRIBE YOUR WINE SELECTIONS.
We feature more than 550 selections with particular strength in California, Burgundy, Bordeaux, the Rhône Valley and Australia. We are known for our six- and nine-course nightly food and wine pairings.

WHAT CATEGORIES OF WINE ARE THE BEST VALUES IN YOUR RESTAURANT?
Australian reds and Rhône wines.

NAME RECENT WINE DISCOVERIES THAT HAVE EXCITED YOU.
Languedoc-Roussillon, for its vast array of microclimates and terroirs, and the great wine values coming from them.

WHAT IS YOUR FAVORITE WINE REGION IN THE WORLD TODAY?
Stellenbosch and Paarl in South Africa, for the beauty, the history and the people.

WHAT LED YOU TO BECOME A SOMMELIER?
A passion for wine and an opportunity to travel to wine regions around the world.

WHAT ARE THE BEST ASPECTS OF YOUR JOB?
Traveling to wine regions and the friendships made.

IF YOU WERE NOT IN THE WINE PROFESSION, WHAT WOULD YOU BE DOING?
Playing golf.

Sweet Basil

193 Gore Creek Drive
Vail, Colorado 81657-4549
phone 970-476-0125 fax 970-476-0137
website www.sweetbasil-vail.com

Patrick T. Welch

BEVERAGE DIRECTOR

WHAT ARE SOME OF YOUR ULTIMATE FOOD AND WINE PAIRINGS?
Beef tenderloin and béarnaise sauce with a big California Cabernet Sauvignon; Colorado rack of lamb with a red Hermitage or Châteauneuf-du-Pape.

DESCRIBE YOUR WINE SELECTIONS.
Our list consists of 425 selections and we offer twenty wines by the glass. We focus on California and France, but we also have a broad selection of wines from all over the world.

WHAT CATEGORY OF WINE IS THE BEST VALUE IN YOUR RESTAURANT?
Rhône varietals.

NAME RECENT WINE DISCOVERIES THAT HAVE EXCITED YOU.
The wines from Priorat, Ribero del Duero and other lesser-known wines of Spain and Portugal have excited me recently.

WHAT IS YOUR FAVORITE WINE REGION IN THE WORLD TODAY?
Burgundy. I love its rich history and the extensive microclimates that create such diverse wines in this small region.

WHAT LED YOU TO YOUR CURRENT POSITION?
I became involved in fine dining after high school and fell in love with how wine is made, its history and, of course, the taste.

WHAT ARE THE BEST ASPECTS OF YOUR JOB?
Training the staff and inspiring younger servers to learn about wine.

IF YOU WERE NOT IN THE WINE PROFESSION, WHAT WOULD YOU BE DOING?
Something related to art or art history.

Tante Louise

4900 East Colfax Avenue
Denver, Colorado 80220-1208
phone 303-355-4488 fax 303-321-6312
website www.tantelouise.com

Emma M. Healion
SOMMELIER

WHAT ARE SOME OF YOUR ULTIMATE FOOD AND WINE PAIRINGS?
Ribera del Duero reds with deer rack; white Châteauneuf-du-Pape with scallops; pan-seared foie gras with Monbazillac; lamb and truffles with Échezeaux; wild mushroom charlotte with Rioja.

DESCRIBE YOUR WINE SELECTIONS.
Our 500-item wine list is predominantly French, with an emphasis on Burgundy.

WHAT CATEGORY OF WINE IS THE BEST VALUE ON YOUR WINE LIST ?
Spanish whites.

NAME A RECENT WINE DISCOVERY THAT EXCITED YOU.
Carmelo Rodero Ribera del Duero Riserva 1996 is a beautiful wine with unique character.

WHAT IS YOUR FAVORITE WINE REGION IN THE WORLD TODAY?
The Rhône Valley. It has a huge variety of wines, many great values and some dynamic new winemakers. There also have been some phenomenal vintages here in the late 1990s.

WHAT LED YOU TO BECOME A SOMMELIER?
I have a passion for food and wine pairing and was approached to take this position.

WHAT ARE THE BEST ASPECTS OF YOUR JOB?
Seeing customers try something different and get really excited about it. It is extremely rewarding to see customers return again and again to the restaurant, asking for recommendations and totally trusting my judgment.

IF YOU WERE NOT IN THE WINE PROFESSION, WHAT WOULD YOU BE DOING?
Sculpting, or something in the perfume business or art world.

Trios Enoteca

1730 Wynkoop Street
Denver, Colorado 80202
phone 303-293-2887 fax 303-293-8475
website www.triosenoteca.com

Gabriele (Gibbie) G. Whelehan

MANAGER AND SOMMELIER

WHAT ARE SOME OF YOUR ULTIMATE FOOD AND WINE PAIRINGS?
Sauvignon Blanc with fresh ripe tomatoes (wonderfully refreshing in the summer); rich Australian Shiraz with Stilton cheese.

DESCRIBE YOUR WINE SELECTIONS.
Our wine list is strong in California and French selections, but has other wines from around the world. We also have an extensive by-the-glass program.

WHAT CATEGORY OF WINE IS THE BEST VALUE ON YOUR WINE LIST?
The "French Red" section, which includes France's lesser-known areas, with fun and interesting wines.

NAME RECENT WINE DISCOVERIES THAT HAVE EXCITED YOU.
Enjoying a rich Zinfandel with a cigar, rather than the traditional Cognac or Scotch.

WHAT IS YOUR FAVORITE WINE REGION IN THE WORLD TODAY?
Sicily. The wines are really spectacular, especially the reds. The whites are refreshing, yet have some depth.

WHAT LED YOU TO BECOME A SOMMELIER?
I began working here as a waitress after college. We change our list quarterly and I found myself becoming more and more passionate about what I was selling.

WHAT ARE THE BEST ASPECTS OF YOUR JOB?
The opportunity of tasting wines from all over the world. The look on the faces of guests when you turn them onto their new favorite wine. It is personally rewarding.

IF YOU WERE NOT IN THE WINE PROFESSION, WHAT WOULD YOU BE DOING?
I couldn't imagine doing anything else. I'm having too much fun!

Trios Wine Bar & Grille
1155 Canyon Boulevard
Boulder, Colorado 80302
phone 303-442-8400

David R. Miller
WINE MANAGER

WHAT ARE SOME OF YOUR ULTIMATE FOOD AND WINE PAIRINGS?
Farmstead cheese with late-harvest wines; halibut and seared greens with
Vouvray.

DESCRIBE YOUR WINE SELECTIONS.
It is ever-changing and includes wines from new and exciting viticultural areas.

WHAT CATEGORY OF WINE IS THE BEST VALUE IN YOUR RESTAURANT?
Rhône styles.

NAME RECENT WINE DISCOVERIES THAT HAVE EXCITED YOU.
Northwestern American Syrah and Riesling: great value and an awesome
expression of terroir.

WHAT ARE YOUR FAVORITE WINE REGIONS IN THE WORLD TODAY?
Barossa, Australia, and Columbia Valley, Washington.

WHAT LED YOU TO YOUR CURRENT POSITION?
An odd twist of fate.

WHAT ARE THE BEST ASPECTS OF YOUR JOB?
Taking the fear out of wine and service.

IF YOU WERE NOT IN THE WINE PROFESSION, WHAT WOULD YOU BE?
National park ranger.

Beano's Cabin
ROBERT BATTLE, WINE BUYER
Beaver Creek Service Center, Avon
970-949-9090

The Broker Restaurant
JERRY FRITZLER, WINE BUYER
821 17th Street, Denver
303-292-5065

The Caribou Club
OLIVER JADERKO, WINE BUYER
411 East Hopkins, Aspen
970-925-2929

Charles Court at the Broadmoor
C. W. CRAIG REED, FOOD
AND BEVERAGE DIRECTOR
Tim Weustneck, Sommelier
1 Lake Avenue, Colorado Springs
719-634-7711

Flagstaff House Restaurant
SCOTT MONETTE, MANAGING
PARTNER AND WINE BUYER
1138 Flagstaff Road, Boulder
303-442-4640

Giovanni's Ristorante and Trattoria
MIMI WITZER, WINE BUYER
127 11th Street, Steamboat Springs
970-879-4141

Krabloonik
DAN MACEACHEN, OWNER
AND WINE BUYER
4250 Divide Road, Snowmass Village
970-923-3953

Ludwigs Restaurant
THOMAS GUTMANN, MANAGER
AND WINE BUYER
20 Vail Road, Vail
970-476-5656

Mirabelle Restaurant at Beaver Creek
DANIEL JOLY, OWNER AND CHEF
55 Village Road, Avon
970-949-7728

Olives at the St. Regis Aspen
STEPHEN PARZIALE, WINE DIRECTOR
315 East Dean Street, Aspen
970-920-3300

Palace Arms
MEHRAN ASMAILI, WINE BUYER
321 17th Street, Denver
303-297-3111

Piñons
JEFF WALKER, WINE BUYER
105 South Mill Street, Aspen
970-920-2021

Primitivo
ANASTACIA LAMMEY, SOMMELIER
28 South Tejon Street, Colorado Springs
719-473-4900

Syzygy Restaurant
WALT HARRIS, SOMMELIER
520 East Hyman Avenue, Second Floor, Aspen
970-925-3700

The Tyrolean Inn
SETH MATASAR, GENERAL MANAGER
AND WINE BUYER
400 East Meadow Drive, Vail
970-476-2204

Jean-Louis

61 Lewis Street
Greenwich, Connecticut 08630
phone 203-622-8450 fax 203-622-5845
website www.restaurantjeanlouis.com

Jean-Claude Vassalle

SOMMELIER

WHAT ARE SOME OF YOUR ULTIMATE FOOD AND WINE PAIRINGS?
Wood pigeon with Hermitage; filet of beef with St.-Émilion (château); cod
with Meursault; Sauternes with foie gras or Roquefort; spicy or fusion food
with Gewürztraminer or Riesling; lamb with herbs and Châteauneuf-du-Pape;
grilled fish with Chassagne-Montrachet.

DESCRIBE YOUR WINE SELECTIONS.
We specialize in French wines overall, but are known also for our wide selection
of Californian and other wines.

WHAT CATEGORIES OF WINE ARE THE BEST VALUES ON YOUR WINE LIST?
Burgundy, Port and some Bordeaux.

NAME RECENT WINE DISCOVERIES THAT HAVE EXCITED YOU.
Rioja and Ribera del Duero for value; New Zealand Sauvignon Blanc for style;
and wines from the northern Rhône for quality.

WHAT IS YOUR FAVORITE WINE REGION IN THE WORLD TODAY?
Northern Rhône, home to Côte Rôtie and Hermitage. I love Syrah, especially
from this area, and the last few vintages have been great.

WHAT LED YOU TO BECOME A SOMMELIER?
Working in restaurants as a waiter, captain and maître d'.

WHAT ARE THE BEST ASPECTS OF YOUR JOB?
I love to match dishes with wine and introduce guests to new styles of wine.

IF YOU WERE NOT IN THE WINE PROFESSION, WHAT WOULD YOU BE
DOING?
Medicine, the sciences or languages.

Rebecca's

265 Glenville Road
Greenwich, Connecticut 06831
phone 203-532-9270 fax 203-532-9271

Rebecca Kirhoffer

CO-OWNER

WHAT ARE SOME OF YOUR ULTIMATE FOOD AND WINE PAIRINGS?
Foie gras dumpling in a truffle broth and red Burgundy; tartare of salmon and oysters with chives and a white Burgundy; pear tarte Tatin and toasted almond ice cream with Tokaji Aszú; sashimi of kampachi with an Asian salad and wasabi vinaigrette and Pouilly-Fumé.

DESCRIBE YOUR WINE SELECTIONS.
I have chosen wines that are well-suited to our cuisine. The list changes often, sometimes as frequently as four times in one week.

WHAT CATEGORY OF WINE IS THE BEST VALUE ON YOUR WINE LIST?
French red, Burgundy and Bordeaux.

NAME RECENT WINE DISCOVERIES THAT HAVE EXCITED YOU.
Ramey Chardonnay, Quarts de Chaume, Sauzet white Burgundies and Dujac red Burgundies.

WHAT IS YOUR FAVORITE WINE REGION IN THE WORLD TODAY?
Burgundy. So incredibly complex and yet so simple.

WHAT LED YOU TO YOUR CURRENT POSITION?
A love of wine, and of wine and food together.

WHAT ARE THE BEST ASPECTS OF YOUR JOB?
People actually care about my opinion and I think that since I've tasted everything on the list, I have a lot to share with them.

IF YOU WERE NOT IN THE WINE PROFESSION, WHAT WOULD YOU BE?
A designer for homes, clothing or jewelry.

Cavey's Restaurant

NANCY HAMMARSTROM, SOMMELIER

Steven Cavagnaro, Wine Buyer

45 East Center Street, Manchester

860-649-0344

Elms Restaurant
and Tavern

GUY LOZOCH, SOMMELIER

500 Main Street, Ridgefield

203-438-9206

Columbus Inn

CLAIRE MAUK, WINE STEWARD

2216 Pennsylvania Avenue, Wilmington

302-571-1492

Café Milano

3251 Prospect Street Northwest
Washington, District of Columbia 20007
phone 202-965-8990 fax 202-965-7119
website www.cafemilano.net

Franco Nuschese
PRESIDENT
Team: Laurent Menoud, Sommelier

WHAT ARE SOME OF YOUR ULTIMATE FOOD AND WINE PAIRINGS?
Pastas go very well with California wines; Italian wines with salads and cheeses.

DESCRIBE YOUR WINE SELECTIONS.
We have a great Italian and American wine list.

WHAT CATEGORY OF WINE IS THE BEST VALUE ON YOUR WINE LIST?
Super-Tuscans.

NAME A RECENT WINE DISCOVERY THAT EXCITED YOU.
Almaviva from Chile.

WHAT IS YOUR FAVORITE WINE REGION IN THE WORLD TODAY?
Number one is Tuscany, Italy. And I also like Napa Valley.

WHAT LED YOU TO YOUR CURRENT POSITION?
My background in Italy.

WHAT ARE THE BEST ASPECTS OF YOUR JOB?
Meeting new people every day and the ability to share the knowledge of wine with customers.

IF YOU WERE NOT IN THIS PROFESSION, WHAT WOULD YOU BE DOING?
Show business.

The Caucus Room

401 Ninth Street Northwest
Washington, District of Columbia 20004
phone 202-393-1300
website www.thecaucusroom.com

Steven Goldstein
CORPORATE WINE DIRECTOR
AND SOMMELIER

WHAT ARE SOME OF YOUR ULTIMATE FOOD AND WINE PAIRINGS?
Risotto cakes with Pinot Blanc; rack of venison with Pomerol; oysters with Champagne; and sweet potatoes with Pinot Noir.

DESCRIBE YOUR WINE SELECTIONS.
At The Caucus Room, we have worldwide selections, of which 60 percent are American. With such diversity in our dishes, the list contains wines from many regions and many styles.

WHAT CATEGORY OF WINE IS THE BEST VALUE ON YOUR WINE LIST?
Spanish reds.

NAME RECENT WINE DISCOVERIES THAT HAVE EXCITED YOU.
Spanish wines imported by Jorge Ordoñez offer absolutely incredible value. Montes wines from Chile are also great.

WHAT IS YOUR FAVORITE WINE REGION IN THE WORLD TODAY?
Puligny-Montrachet. I love the incredible balance and complexity of the wines.

WHAT LED YOU TO YOUR CURRENT POSITION?
A passion for wine and great people to share it with.

WHAT ARE THE BEST ASPECTS OF YOUR JOB?
Meeting people with similar passions about wine. There is no greater pleasure than turning your clients on to amazing wines that they fall in love with over dinner. There is also a great sense of achievement when I overhear a server communicating to a guest the ideas that I have expressed during our educational training.

IF YOU WERE NOT IN THE WINE PROFESSION, WHAT WOULD YOU BE DOING?
Finance. Raising capital and funding for projects.

The Historic George Town Club

1580 Wisconsin Avenue Northwest
Washington, District of Columbia 20007
phone 202-333-9330 fax 202-333-3183

Gino Ballarin
WINE DIRECTOR AND SOMMELIER

WHAT IS ONE OF YOUR ULTIMATE FOOD AND WINE PAIRINGS?
Caymus Conundrum with Oriental or curried food preparations.

DESCRIBE YOUR WINE SELECTIONS.
Designed and tailored to increase awareness and sales to a limited audience.

WHAT ARE YOUR FAVORITE WINE REGIONS IN THE WORLD TODAY?
New Zealand for Sauvignon Blanc; Oregon for Pinot Noir. Both are very versatile wines.

WHAT LED YOU TO BECOME A SOMMELIER?
I was raised in a wine culture.

WHAT ARE THE BEST ASPECTS OF YOUR JOB?
Educating staff and members about food, and educating the wine committee about wine selection and service.

IF YOU WERE NOT IN THIS PROFESSION, WHAT WOULD YOU BE DOING?
Growing Chardonnay grapes at Wolf Crag, Virginia.

Kinkeads, an American Brasserie

2000 Pennsylvania Avenue Northwest
Washington, District of Columbia 20006
phone 202-296-7700 fax 202-296-7688
website www.kinkead.com

Michael Flynn
WINE DIRECTOR AND SOMMELIER

WHAT ARE SOME OF YOUR ULTIMATE FOOD AND WINE PAIRINGS?
Red Burgundy with a walnut and horseradish–crusted flounder served with cauliflower and Sherry beet sauce; New Zealand Sauvignon Blanc and raw oysters; Barolo and truffles; Quarts de Chaume and foie gras.

DESCRIBE YOUR WINE SELECTIONS.
Comprehensive, idiosyncratic and global with an emphasis on quality, food-friendliness, price and rarity.

WHAT CATEGORY OF WINE IS THE BEST VALUE ON YOUR WINE LIST?
Sherry.

NAME RECENT WINE DISCOVERIES THAT HAVE EXCITED YOU.
A Jurançon sweet wine, which shows great value and style. South African Pinotage, which is better than ever and suggests South Africa's potential.

WHAT IS YOUR FAVORITE WINE REGION IN THE WORLD TODAY?
Alsace for its marvelous variety of superb wines, hearty food, hospitality and charm, and excellent weather.

WHAT LED YOU TO BECOME A SOMMELIER?
My passion for food, my love of the limelight and an educational background in French and linguistics.

WHAT ARE THE BEST ASPECTS OF YOUR JOB?
The opportunity to see the results of my work almost instantaneously, to consult with the best and the brightest, and to travel the world.

IF YOU WERE NOT IN THE WINE PROFESSION, WHAT WOULD YOU BE DOING?
Teaching French literature at the graduate level.

The Occidental

1475 Pennsylvania Avenue Northwest
Washington, District of Columbia 20004
phone 202-783-1475 fax 202-783-1478
website www.occidentaldc.com

Kathryn Morgan
WINE DIRECTOR

WHAT ARE SOME OF YOUR ULTIMATE FOOD AND WINE PAIRINGS?
Roasted lobster with foie gras sauce and chestnut spaetzle with Meursault;
roasted quail with country ham gravy with Rioja; crab spring roll with Chenin
Blanc/Viognier blend; goat cheese, carrot and dill terrine with South African
Sauvignon Blanc; lamb shank with California Syrah; filet mignon with white
truffle sauce with Barolo.

DESCRIBE YOUR WINE SELECTIONS.
Our wines reflect a broad range of styles and regions from quality, smaller producers.

WHAT CATEGORIES OF WINE ARE THE BEST VALUES ON YOUR WINE LIST?
Riesling and Alsace varietals and Italian reds.

NAME RECENT WINE DISCOVERIES THAT HAVE EXCITED YOU.
The value and flavors of Spanish wines and Loire Valley Chenin Blancs.

WHAT IS YOUR FAVORITE WINE REGION IN THE WORLD TODAY?
I am fascinated by the strength and longevity of seemingly delicate German
Rieslings.

WHAT LED YOU TO YOUR CURRENT POSITION?
My father has a great collection of Bordeaux and vintage Port. It seemed a natural progression from my years in the restaurant business.

WHAT ARE THE BEST ASPECTS OF YOUR JOB?
There is nothing more rewarding than helping a guest choose a wine that he
loves, especially if it is a good value.

IF YOU WERE NOT IN THE WINE PROFESSION, WHAT WOULD YOU BE?
A travel writer.

1789 Restaurant

WILLIAM WATTS, WINE BUYER
1224 36th Street Northwest,
Washington
202-965-1789

Café Atlantico

FRANCISCO ASTUDILLO, RESTAURANT
MANAGER AND SOMMELIER
405 Eighth Street Northwest,
Washington
202-393-0812

The Capital Grille

BILL BUTLER, WINE BUYER
601 Pennsylvania Avenue, Washington
202-737-6200

Citronelle at the Latham Hotel

MARK SLATER, SOMMELIER
3000 M Street Northwest, Washington
202-625-2150

Galileo Restaurant

MICHAEL NAYERI, GENERAL
MANAGER AND WINE BUYER
11021st Street Northwest, Washington
202-293-7191

Jaleo at the Lansburgh

SANDY LEWIS, WINE BUYER
480 Seventh Street Northwest,
Washington
202-628-7949

Jeffrey's at the Watergate Hotel

SEBASTIAN ARNAUD,
BEVERAGE DIRECTOR
2650 Virginia Avenue Northwest,
Washington
202-298-4455

Morrison-Clark Restaurant

VERONICA COOL, MANAGER
AND WINE BUYER
Massachusetts Avenue & Eleventh
Street, Northwest, Washington
800-332-7898

Olives

BEN FEVILLA
1600 K Street Northwest, Washington
202-452-1866

The Prime Rib

JIM ROSS, WINE BUYER
2020 K Street Northwest, Washington
202-466-8811

Red Sage

RALPH ROSENBURG, MANAGER
AND WINE BUYER
605 14th Street Northwest, Washington
202-638-4444

Sam & Harry's

STEVEN GOLDSTEIN, CORPORATE
WINE DIRECTOR AND SOMMELIER
1201 19th Street Northwest,
Washington
202-296-4333

Smith & Wollensky

RICHARD FITZGERALD, SOMMELIER
1112 19th Street Northwest,
Washington
202-466-1100

Taberna del Alabardero

JAVIER REGATTO, WINE BUYER
1776 Eye Street Northwest, Washington
202-429-2200

Vidalia

MICHAEL NEVAREZ, GENERAL
MANAGER AND WINE BUYER
1990 M Street Northwest, Washington
202-659-1990

Willard International Continental

GERARD MADANI, EXECUTIVE CHEF
AND WINE BUYER
1401 Pennsylvania Avenue Northwest,
Washington
202-637-7440

Bern's Steak House

1208 South Howard Avenue
Tampa, Florida 33606
phone 813-251-2421 fax 813-251-5001
website www.bernssteakhouse.com

Eric A. Renaud
SOMMELIER

WHAT ARE SOME OF YOUR ULTIMATE FOOD AND WINE PAIRINGS?
Steak and Rhône wines; foie gras and Sauternes; shellfish with Austrian white wines; barbecue with Zinfandel or Ribera del Duero.

DESCRIBE YOUR WINE SELECTIONS.
We have 6,500 table wines, 1,000 dessert wines and about 185 wines by the glass from vintages dating back to 1971. We want to offer all styles of wine.

WHAT CATEGORY OF WINE IS THE BEST VALUE IN YOUR RESTAURANT?
Older red wines from virtually any region. Our pricing is inexpensive because Bern Laxer, the founder, began buying wines in quantity in the 1960s.

NAME RECENT WINE DISCOVERIES THAT HAVE EXCITED YOU.
The crisp, refreshing white wines of Austria and South African wines, which are rapidly improving in quality and are very reasonably priced.

WHAT IS YOUR FAVORITE WINE REGION IN THE WORLD TODAY?
Burgundy, for white and red wines. For everyday reds, Spain.

WHAT LED YOU TO BECOME A SOMMELIER?
It happened by accident. I began working part-time at the restaurant as a wine steward. I began studying and asking questions.

WHAT IS THE MOST REWARDING ASPECT OF YOUR JOB?
Finding the wine my guests say they love, a wine they might not have ever thought of asking for, from a region they may not ever have known existed.

IF YOU WERE NOT IN THE WINE PROFESSION, WHAT WOULD YOU BE?
A jet mechanic.

Café de France

526 Park Avenue South
Winter Park, Florida 32789
phone 407-647-1869 fax 407-679-9930
website www.lecafedefrance.com

Dominique M. Gutierrez
PRESIDENT, OWNER AND WINE PURCHASER

WHAT ARE SOME OF YOUR ULTIMATE FOOD AND WINE PAIRINGS?
Our rack of lamb with hearty Spanish red and our ossobuco with Carneros Pinot Noir; venison with Teofilo Reyes or Vega Sicilia; sea bass or fresh Scottish sea scallops with Caymus Conundrum.

DESCRIBE YOUR WINE SELECTIONS.
We are a nineteen-table restaurant and carry eighty-five different wines, mostly American and French, but also Spanish, Italian and South African wines.

WHAT CATEGORIES OF WINE ARE THE BEST VALUES IN YOUR RESTAURANT?
Red Bordeaux and Riojas.

NAME RECENT WINE DISCOVERIES THAT HAVE EXCITED YOU.
Conundrum from Caymus. It is so easy to sell and pleases every palate.

WHAT IS YOUR FAVORITE WINE REGION IN THE WORLD TODAY?
Ribera del Duero, Spain. Full-bodied reds with hearty flavor. They mature quickly so you can drink them early.

WHAT LED YOU TO YOUR CURRENT POSITION?
I was raised in France, where one grows up with an acquired taste for good wine.

WHAT IS THE BEST ASPECT OF YOUR JOB?
Teaching wine to such an array of customers, especially the liquor-drinking patrons.

IF YOU WERE NOT IN THIS PROFESSION, WHAT WOULD YOU BE DOING?
Traveling for a travel guide and continuing to sample wine and food.

The Colony Beach and Tennis Resort

1620 Gulf of Mexico Drive
Longboat Key, Florida 34228
phone 941-383-6464 fax 941-383-7549
website www.colonyfl.com

David D. Crandell
FOOD AND BEVERAGE DIRECTOR

WHAT ARE SOME OF YOUR ULTIMATE FOOD AND WINE PAIRINGS?
Local fish with Sauvignon Blanc; big Cabernet with bittersweet chocolate;
mango sorbet and tropical fruit with Muscat-based wines.

DESCRIBE YOUR WINE SELECTIONS.
We specialize in age-worthy, older Cabernet Sauvignon.

WHAT CATEGORIES OF WINE ARE THE BEST VALUES IN YOUR RESTAURANT?
Estate-bottled red and white Burgundies and Rhône wines.

NAME RECENT WINE DISCOVERIES THAT HAVE EXCITED YOU.
New World Sauvignon Blanc. It's so diverse and pairs well with a lot of very
unique menu items.

WHAT IS YOUR FAVORITE WINE REGION IN THE WORLD TODAY?
Rutherford, for astounding Cabernet Sauvignon.

WHAT LED YOU TO YOUR CURRENT POSITION?
I made my first wine at age fifteen, took a job as a waiter at a winery, then
became a sommelier in a five-star resort.

WHAT ARE THE BEST ASPECTS OF YOUR JOB?
Juggling an entire resort staff with different needs.

IF YOU WERE NOT IN THIS PROFESSION, WHAT WOULD YOU BE?
A fisherman or a farmer.

Flying Fish Café at Walt Disney World's Boardwalk Resort

2101 North Epcot Resort Boulevard
Lake Buena Vista, Florida 32830
phone 407-939-3463 fax 407-939-5158

Robert T. Dunham
RESTAURANT MANAGER AND SOMMELIER

WHAT ARE SOME OF YOUR ULTIMATE FOOD AND WINE PAIRINGS?
Whole yellowtail snapper with Gewürztraminer; salmon with Pinot Noir; chocolate lava cake with Brachetto.

DESCRIBE YOUR WINE SELECTIONS.
Our wines have been chosen because they are of good quality and match the food we serve.

WHAT CATEGORY OF WINE IS THE BEST VALUE ON YOUR WINE LIST?
Alternative whites, such as Riesling, Pinot Gris and Albariño.

NAME RECENT WINE DISCOVERIES THAT HAVE EXCITED YOU.
White Châteauneuf-du-Pape pairs well with almost any dish on our menu. Sauvignon de St. Bris is also a great value.

WHAT IS YOUR FAVORITE WINE REGION IN THE WORLD TODAY?
Last year it was Burgundy. Today it is Australia. I love the Shiraz and Chardonnay being produced there.

WHAT LED YOU TO BECOME A SOMMELIER?
A trip through Burgundy inspired me to learn more.

WHAT ARE THE BEST ASPECTS OF YOUR JOB?
I love sharing what I have learned with the many guests I come into contact with.

IF YOU WERE NOT IN THE WINE PROFESSION, WHAT WOULD YOU BE?
A chef. I like to cook.

The Grill Room at the Ritz-Carlton

4750 Amelia Island Parkway
Fernandina Beach, Florida 32034
phone 904-277-1100 fax 904-277-1144
website www.ritzcarlton.com

John L. Pugliese
WINE STEWARD

WHAT IS ONE OF YOUR ULTIMATE FOOD AND WINE PAIRINGS?
Foie gras with Austrian dessert wines such as Eiswein and Beerenauslese.

DESCRIBE YOUR WINE SELECTIONS.
Our wine list is diverse and complex.

WHAT CATEGORY OF WINE IS THE BEST VALUE ON YOUR WINE LIST?
California Zinfandel.

NAME RECENT WINE DISCOVERIES THAT HAVE EXCITED YOU.
Austrian wines. They are good values and taste wonderful!

WHAT IS YOUR FAVORITE WINE REGION IN THE WORLD TODAY?
Alsace. The wines are so food-friendly.

WHAT LED YOU TO BECOME A SOMMELIER?
A passion for food and wine.

WHAT ARE THE BEST ASPECTS OF YOUR JOB?
Meeting guests who love to try new wines. The rewards are the smiles I receive for choosing a great wine.

IF YOU WERE NOT IN THE WINE PROFESSION, WHAT WOULD YOU BE?
A chef, because I love to cook.

Maison & Jardin Restaurant

430 South Wymore Road
Altamonte Springs, Florida 32714
phone 407-862-4410 fax 407-862-5507

William R. Beuret
OWNER AND SOMMELIER

WHAT IS ONE OF YOUR ULTIMATE FOOD AND WINE PAIRINGS?
1970 Vega Sicilia Unico with fresh-roasted, whole suckling lamb.

DESCRIBE YOUR WINE SELECTIONS.
We have 1,300 selections from all the major wine areas of the world, with special emphasis on California, Bordeaux, Burgundy, Germany and Italy. Food and wine pairings are on the wine list.

WHAT ARE YOUR FAVORITE WINE REGIONS IN THE WORLD TODAY?
The Mosel, for the beauty; Burgundy, for the wine; and Italy, for food and wine compatibility.

WHAT LED YOU TO YOUR CURRENT POSITION?
Love of wine and dining, and it's a part of the job owning a fine restaurant.

WHAT IS THE MOST CHALLENGING ASPECT OF YOUR JOB?
Never-ending staff training. Finding motivated and enthusiastic staff in a tight labor market.

IF YOU WERE NOT IN THE WINE PROFESSION, WHAT WOULD YOU BE DOING?
Teaching.

Mia's

1633 Snow Avenue in Old Hyde Park Village
Tampa, Florida 33606
phone 813-258-9400 fax 813-258-6838

Christopher D. Enos

GENERAL MANAGER AND WINE PURCHASER

WHAT ARE SOME OF YOUR ULTIMATE FOOD AND WINE PAIRINGS?
Syrah with our prime aged filet mignon topped with Gorgonzola and walnut pesto, wrapped in applewood-smoked bacon; Sauvignon Blanc with hazelnut-crusted grouper with broken brown butter sauce; Marsanne and Viognier with truffled Russian fingerling potatoes, sizzled greens and seared foie gras medallion, finished with pear and brandy demi-glaze.

DESCRIBE YOUR WINE SELECTIONS.
We offer a small, fun selection of wines that change frequently.

WHAT CATEGORY OF WINE IS THE BEST VALUE IN YOUR RESTAURANT?
Rhône-style blends from both France and the United States, particularly California.

NAME RECENT WINE DISCOVERIES THAT HAVE EXCITED YOU.
For value, quality and style I look to wines like Petite Sirah, Mourvèdre, Roussanne, Marsanne, Grenache and Viognier.

WHAT IS YOUR FAVORITE WINE REGION IN THE WORLD TODAY?
It is not so much where, but what is being done with wines. The distinct flavors of regional wines are broadening. I like the playfulness.

WHAT LED YOU TO YOUR CURRENT POSITION?
Becoming involved in restaurants at an early age. It sparked my fascination with and respect for wine.

WHAT IS THE BEST ASPECT OF YOUR JOB?
The synergy between food and wine.

IF YOU WERE NOT IN THIS PROFESSION, WHAT WOULD YOU BE?
I would be …

Michael's on East Restaurant
1212 East Avenue South
Sarasota, Florida 34239
phone 941-366-0007 fax 941-955-1945

Michael Klauber
PROPRIETOR, SOMMELIER AND WINE BUYER

WHAT IS ONE OF YOUR ULTIMATE FOOD AND WINE PAIRINGS?
Roasted quail with rich, red Burgundy.

DESCRIBE YOUR WINE SELECTIONS.
We focus primarily on estate and domain-bottled wines, with 200 to 250 wines
and twelve to fifteen wine flights.

WHAT IS YOUR FAVORITE WINE REGION IN THE WORLD TODAY?
Burgundy! I love the wines. It is a place where the style of food is so beautifully
complemented by the amazing wines.

WHAT LED YOU TO BECOME A SOMMELIER?
Actually, I was thrown into it while working at Arnaud's Restaurant in
New Orleans.

WHAT ARE THE MOST CHALLENGING ASPECTS OF YOUR JOB?
To constantly create opportunities for our guests to experience new wines. To
continue to find emerging wineries and wine regions.

IF YOU WERE NOT IN THIS PROFESSION, WHAT WOULD YOU BE DOING?
Living in the wine country, growing grapes and making wine.

Sawgrass Marriott Resort and Beach Club

1000 PGA Tour Boulevard
Ponte Vedra Beach, Florida 32082
phone 904-285-7777 fax 904-285-0906
website www.sawgrassmarriott.com

Vincenzo E. D'Agostino
FOOD AND BEVERAGE MANAGER
AND WINE BUYER

WHAT ARE SOME OF YOUR ULTIMATE FOOD AND WINE PAIRINGS?
Kumamoto oysters and osetra caviar with Sauvignon Blanc or Champagne; seared diver scallops and Hudson Valley foie gras with Alsace Gewürztraminer; Riesling with various types of soft cheeses like Brie, Fontina, Morbier, and Teleme.

DESCRIBE YOUR WINE SELECTIONS.
We offer quality wines from all over the world, with an emphasis on California and France, followed by Germany and Australia.

NAME RECENT WINE DISCOVERIES THAT HAVE EXCITED YOU.
Wines from Portugal. They are a great value and there are many interesting grape varieties used in making table wines.

WHAT IS YOUR FAVORITE WINE REGION IN THE WORLD TODAY?
Italy. It has a very long wine history and produces great wines like Amarone and Barolo, which are my favorites.

WHAT LED YOU TO YOUR CURRENT POSITION?
The restaurant world inspired in me a desire for more wine knowledge. I wanted to learn more.

WHAT ARE THE BEST ASPECTS OF YOUR JOB?
When guests try new wines that they are not familiar with.

IF YOU WERE NOT IN THIS PROFESSION, WHAT WOULD YOU BE?
I would travel and be a food and wine writer.

The Summerhouse

6101 Midnight Pass Road
Sarasota, Florida 34242
phone 941-349-1100 fax 941-346-1755
website www.sarasotarestaurants.com

Anthony J. Sherman
WINE DIRECTOR

WHAT IS ONE OF YOUR ULTIMATE FOOD AND WINE PAIRINGS?
Baked salmon en croûte with Merlot.

DESCRIBE YOUR WINE SELECTIONS.
We specialize in American whites and reds.

WHAT CATEGORY OF WINE IS THE BEST VALUE IN YOUR RESTAURANT?
Medium to high-end Cabernets.

WHAT IS YOUR FAVORITE WINE REGION IN THE WORLD TODAY?
Napa Valley, because of the care that is put into the wine.

WHAT LED YOU TO YOUR CURRENT POSITION?
A love of food and wine.

WHAT IS THE MOST REWARDING ASPECT OF YOUR JOB?
Getting the staff to stand behind a product I believe in.

IF YOU WERE NOT IN THIS PROFESSION, WHAT WOULD YOU BE DOING?
There is no other profession for me. I have been in the restaurant business all
my life.

Al & Linda's La Cantina

KAREN HART, SOMMELIER
4721 East Colonial Drive, Orlando
407-894-4491

Antonio's La Fiamma

JOSE JANER, WINE BUYER
611 South Orlando Avenue, Maitland
407-645-1043

Armani's

CHERYL WHITE, WINE BUYER
6200 West Courtney Campbell
Causeway, Tampa
813-281-9165

Arthur's 27 at the Wyndham Palace Resort

KEVIN STURGEON, MANAGER
AND WINE BUYER
1900 Lake Buena Vista Drive,
Lake Buena Vista
407-827-2727

Bacco Italian Restaurant

LILIANA BADAMO, SOMMELIER
10065 University Boulevard, Orlando
407-678-8833

Bay Hill Country Club

RAY EASLER, BEVERAGE DIRECTOR
6200 Bay Hill Boulevard, Orlando
407-876-2429

Beech Street Grill

ELIZABETH SMIDDY, PROPRIETOR
AND SOMMELIER
801 Beech Street, Fernandina Beach
904-277-3662

Café L'Europe

MICHAEL GAREY, GENERAL MANAGER
AND WINE BUYER
431 Saint Armands Circle, Sarasota
941-388-4415

Charlie's Lobster House

JEFF EICHER, WINE BUYER
8445 International Drive, Suite 122,
Orlando
407-352-6929

Chatham's Place

MAURICE COLINDRES, MANAGING
PARTNER AND WINE BUYER
7575 Dr. Phillips Boulevard, Orlando
407-345-2992

Christinis Restaurant

CHRIS CHRISTINI, OWNER
AND WINE BUYER
7600 Dr. Phillips Boulevard, Orlando
407-345-8770

Citricos at the Disney Grand Floridian Resort

JOHN BLAZON, CORPORATE
WINE DIRECTOR
4401 Grand Floridian Way,
Lake Buena Vista
407-566-5808

Criolla's

MICHEL THIBAULT, SOMMELIER
170 East Scenic Highway, 30-A,
Santa Rosa Beach
850-267-1267

Del Frisco's Double Eagle Steak House

DAN COLGAN, SOMMELIER
729 Lee Road, Orlando
407-645-4443

Destin Chops

JIM ALTAMURA, OWNER
AND WINE BUYER
320 Highway 98 East, Destin
850-654-4944

The Dining Room at the Ritz-Carlton

BILL HARRIS, HOTEL SOMMELIER
280 Vanderbilt Beach, Naples
941-598-6644

Donatello

TED LEWIS, SOMMELIER
232 North Dale Mabry, Tampa
813-875-6660

Elephant Walk Restaurant at Sandestin Resort

STEWART SMITH, SOMMELIER
9300 Highway 98 West, Destin
850-267-4800

Emeril's Restaurant

DAVID PENISI, SOMMELIER
6000 Universal Boulevard, Orlando
407-224-2424

Enzo's Restaurant

ENZO PERLINI, CO-OWNER
AND WINE BUYER
1130 South Highway 17-92, Longwood
407-834-9872

Epping Forest Yacht Club

CHRIS MILLER, BEVERAGE MANAGER
1830 Epping Forest Drive, Jacksonville
904-739-7200

Fulton's Crab House

GED ZIEGLER, WINE BUYER
1670 North Buena Vista Drive,
Lake Buena Vista
407-934-2628

Governor's Club

BARRY HERMAN, SOMMELIER
202 South Adams Street, Tallahassee
850-222-4065

Grosvenor Resort

MICHAEL GRAY, FOOD
AND BEVERAGE DIRECTOR
1850 Hotel Plaza Boulevard,
Lake Buena Vista
407-828-4444

Hilton in the Walt Disney World Resort

ADRIAN GONZALEZ, FOOD
AND BEVERAGE DIRECTOR
1751 Hotel Plaza Boulevard,
Lake Buena Vista
407-827-4000

Hilton Melbourne Airport Hotel

MICHAEL KHATIB, DIRECTOR OF
OPERATIONS AND WINE BUYER
200 Rialto Place, Melbourne
321-768-0200

Hyatt Grand Cypress Resort

FRED HOFFMAN, FOOD
AND BEVERAGE DIRECTOR
1 Grand Cypress Boulevard, Orlando
407-239-1234

Interlachen Country Club

RYAN KLING, SOMMELIER
2245 Interlachen Center, Winter Park
407-657-0850

Island Way Grill

BRAD DIXON, WINE
AND SPIRITS MANAGER
20 Island Way, Clearwater Beach
727-461-6617

Isleworth Country Club

RANDY LUEDDERS, CHEF
AND WINE BUYER
6100 Deacon Drive, Windermere
407-876-6034

Jack's Place at the Rosen Plaza Hotel

SCOTT E. GALLOWAY,
RESTAURANT MANAGER
9700 International Drive
Orlando, Florida 32819
407-996-9700

Jiko's at Disney's Animal Kingdom Lodge

KEITH LANDRY, SOMMELIER
2901 Osceola Parkway, Bay Lake
407-938-3000

Karlings Inn

KARL CAENERS, WINE BUYER
4640 North US Highway 17,
Deleon Springs
386-985-5535

Lafite at the Registry Resort

IAN HAWTHORNE, FOOD
AND BEVERAGE DIRECTOR
475 Seagate Drive, Naples
239-597-3232

Manuel's on the 28th

DARREL HORMEL, FOOD
AND BEVERAGE DIRECTOR
390 North Orange Avenue, Orlando
407-246-6580

Marina Café

JIM ALTAMURA, WINE BUYER
404 Highway 98 East, Destin
850-837-7960

Marker 32

BEN GROSHELL, OWNER
AND WINE BUYER
14549 Beach Boulevard, Jacksonville
904-223-1534

Mise en Place

JAY KILLMARTIN, GENERAL MANAGER
AND WINE BUYER
442 West Kennedy Boulevard, Tampa
813-254-5373

Orlando Airport Marriott

KIM ARNOLD, FOOD
AND BEVERAGE DIRECTOR
7499 Augusta National Drive, Orlando
407-851-9000

Peter Scott's

DAVID MILES, GENERAL MANAGER
AND WINE BUYER
1811 West State Road 434, Longwood
407-834-4477

Radisson Plaza Hotel Orlando

RICHARD BITNER, FOOD
AND BEVERAGE DIRECTOR
60 South Ivanhoe Boulevard, Orlando
407-425-4455

Ramada Resort Parkway

DANIEL MEYS, FOOD
AND BEVERAGE DIRECTOR
2900 Parkway Boulevard, Kissimmee
407-396-7000

Renaissance Orlando Resort at Sea World

BERNARD SUN, FOOD
AND BEVERAGE DIRECTOR
6677 Sea Harbour Drive, Orlando
407-351-5555

Roy's

AARON RADMAN, WINE DIRECTOR
4342 West Boy Scout Boulevard, Tampa
813-873-7697

Sergio's

SCOTT COOK, GENERAL MANAGER
AND SOMMELIER
355 North Orange Avenue, Orlando
407-428-6162

Silver Lake Golf and Country Club

KATHLEEN KING, WINE BUYER
9435 Silver Lake Drive, Leesburg
352-787-4035

Vivaldi's Restaurant

SAM FILLEPI, SOMMELIER
107 West Pine Street, Orlando
407-423-2335

Walt Disney World Swan and Dolphin

MENZE HEROIAN, WINE BUYER
1200 Epcot Resort, Lake Buena Vista
407-934-3000

Wyndham Palace Resort

LUC ANDRES, FOOD
AND BEVERAGE DIRECTOR
1900 Lake Buena Vista Drive,
Lake Buena Vista
407-827-2727

The Addison

2 East Camino Real
Boca Raton, Florida 33432
phone 561-395-9335 fax 561-393-6255
website www.theaddison.com

Zachary N. Smith
SOMMELIER

WHAT ARE SOME OF YOUR ULTIMATE FOOD AND WINE PAIRINGS?
Lobster potstickers with a chile-ponzu broth and a daikon sprout salad paired with Alsace white wine; mustard and herb crumb–crusted rack of Colorado lamb with California Syrah; wild mushroom risotto and duck breast with Pinot Noir; cold water oysters on the half shell with a Champagne mignonette paired with Sancerre.

DESCRIBE YOUR WINE SELECTIONS.
We offer 280 wines on our list and twenty wines by the glass, focused on Californian, French and Italian wines, but also including wines from most of the other wine-producing regions of the world.

WHAT CATEGORIES OF WINE ARE THE BEST VALUES ON YOUR WINE LIST?
Red wines from the Rhône, Provence and Australia.

NAME RECENT WINE DISCOVERIES THAT HAVE EXCITED YOU.
California Meritages and Cabernets, 1999 Oregon Pinot Noirs, and super-Tuscan and IGT reds from Italy.

WHAT IS YOUR FAVORITE WINE REGION IN THE WORLD TODAY?
California. There is so much going on: the restaurants, the wonderful people, the diversity and styles of wines.

WHAT LED YOU TO BECOME A SOMMELIER?
A love of wine and great food and a desire to expand my horizons beyond waiting tables.

WHAT ARE THE BEST ASPECTS OF YOUR JOB?
Talking about wine with wine-loving customers and inspiring the restaurant staff to understand, appreciate and sell wine.

IF YOU WERE NOT IN THIS PROFESSION, WHAT WOULD YOU BE?
A fishing guide or a commercial pilot.

Café des Artistes

1007 Simonton Street
Key West, Florida 33040
phone 305-294-7100

Charles A. Seitz

MANAGER

WHAT ARE SOME OF YOUR ULTIMATE FOOD AND WINE PAIRINGS?
Lobster Tango Mango with Loire Valley white wine; foie gras with Sauternes or
late-harvest Riesling; rack of lamb with Pinot Noir; seafood with white
Burgundy or Loire Valley white; desserts with late-harvest Riesling.

DESCRIBE YOUR WINE SELECTIONS.
While our specialty is red Bordeaux, we offer our clientele a broad selection of
wines that offer quality, consistency and good value, and complement our
menu.

WHAT CATEGORY OF WINE IS THE BEST VALUE ON YOUR WINE LIST?
Loire Valley. Superior wines that are very affordable.

NAME RECENT WINE DISCOVERIES THAT HAVE EXCITED YOU.
Onyx, a Spanish red that is well-balanced and inexpensive; Miner Pinot Noir,
an incredible wine.

WHAT IS YOUR FAVORITE WINE REGION IN THE WORLD TODAY?
Rhône Valley, because of its history, terroir and styles of wines.

WHAT LED YOU TO BECOME A SOMMELIER?
Love of wine. I am also intrigued by the history of wine regions and wine
estates.

WHAT ARE THE BEST ASPECTS OF YOUR JOB?
I enjoy searching for new products and reading about and tasting wines. It is
rewarding when customers enjoy a wine I introduced them to.

IF YOU WERE NOT IN THIS PROFESSION, WHAT WOULD YOU BE DOING?
I cannot imagine doing anything else.

Jackson's Steakhouse

450 East Las Olas Boulevard
Fort Lauderdale, Florida 33301
phone 954-522-4450 fax 954-522-1911
website www.jacksonssteakhouse.com

Patrick E. Morey

MANAGER AND DIRECTOR OF WINE

WHAT ARE SOME OF YOUR ULTIMATE FOOD AND WINE PAIRINGS?
Filet mignon with Côte Rôtie or Crozes-Hermitage; bone-in ribeye with
American Syrah; New York strip with estate Shiraz from Australia; crab-stuffed
yellowtail snapper filet with unwooded American Pinot Blanc; goat cheese or
foie gras with Tokaji Aszú (5 or 6 puttonyos); grilled sea scallops with rich
Monterey Chardonnay; stone crabs with Alsatian Gewürztraminer; roast pork
with Russian River Pinot Noir; herb-crusted rack of lamb with Barbera d'Alba.

DESCRIBE YOUR WINE SELECTIONS.
We offer between 280 and 310 selections on our list with an emphasis on
American wines, especially Cabernet Sauvignon.

WHAT CATEGORIES OF WINE ARE THE BEST VALUES ON YOUR WINE LIST?
Australian and New Zealand wines.

NAME RECENT WINE DISCOVERIES THAT HAVE EXCITED YOU.
A late-harvest Chardonnay from Lolonis Vineyards; 1999 red Burgundies;
Syrahs from small producers in the Languedoc.

WHAT IS YOUR FAVORITE WINE REGION IN THE WORLD TODAY?
Australia. Its wines offer great quality and drinkability in all price ranges.

WHAT LED YOU TO YOUR CURRENT POSITION?
My father had an exceptional wine collection. I grew more curious about wine
as I worked for restaurants in high school.

WHAT IS THE BEST ASPECT OF YOUR JOB?
Nothing brings more elation than the applause of departing guests.

IF YOU WERE NOT IN THIS PROFESSION, WHAT WOULD YOU BE DOING?
Restoring old homes and buildings.

Joe's Stone Crab Restaurant

11 Washington Avenue
Miami Beach, Florida 33139
phone 305-673-0365 fax 305-673-0295

Paul R. Kozolis
BEVERAGE DIRECTOR

WHAT IS YOUR ULTIMATE FOOD AND WINE PAIRING?
Kim Crawford Sauvignon Blanc with ice-cold Florida stone crab and Joe's mustard sauce, garlic spinach and french-fried sweet potatoes.

DESCRIBE YOUR WINE SELECTIONS.
We have a good selection of wines from around the world.

WHAT IS YOUR FAVORITE WINE REGION IN THE WORLD TODAY?
Burgundy. I am so passionate about Pinot Noir.

WHAT LED YOU TO YOUR CURRENT POSITION?
An insatiable desire for knowledge of wine.

WHAT ARE THE MOST CHALLENGING ASPECTS OF YOUR JOB?
Keeping my list fresh, and training my staff to understand fine wine and how to sell it.

IF YOU WERE NOT IN THIS PROFESSION, WHAT WOULD YOU BE DOING?
Living on a boat in Key West and fishing for a living.

Mar-a-Lago Club

1100 South Ocean Boulevard
Palm Beach, Florida 33480
phone 561-832-2600

Bernd-Michael Schweizer

ASSISTANT SOMMELIER AND WINE
CONSULTANT

DESCRIBE YOUR WINE PROGRAM AND WINE SELECTIONS.

My specialty is recommending wines and wine programs depending on the company's needs. I attempt to continually teach through tasting, selling and talking about wine with anyone who asks questions.

NAME RECENT WINE DISCOVERIES THAT HAVE EXCITED YOU AND TELL WHY.

Petit Verdot is full-bodied with spicy pepper tannins and Petite Sirah is robust and peppery. Both are used for blending.

WHAT IS YOUR FAVORITE REGION IN THE WORLD TODAY?

California. In just a few years it is producing the finest wines and challenging the rest of the world.

WHAT LED YOU TO BECOME A SOMMELIER?

Growing up in Germany with wine, learning about and understanding wine from all over the world.

WHAT ARE THE BEST ASPECTS OF YOUR JOB?

People ask me for help in selecting wines, pairing food and wine, and finding new wines.

IF YOU WERE NOT IN THE WINE PROFESSION, WHAT WOULD YOU BE DOING?

There is no other business. Wine is my life!

La Palme d'Or at the Biltmore Hotel

1200 Anastasia Street
Miami, Florida 33136
phone 605-445-1926 fax 305-913-3156

Sebastien Verrier
SOMMELIER

WHAT IS ONE OF YOUR ULTIMATE FOOD AND WINE PAIRINGS?
Lobster fricassee with a bisque rosé sauce reduction, infused with morels and paired with a Morey St. Denis Les Ruchots.

DESCRIBE YOUR WINE SELECTIONS.
We have wines from around the world, but our strength is in French and California wines.

WHAT IS YOUR FAVORITE WINE REGION IN THE WORLD TODAY?
I don't have a preference, but we can talk about La Provence, with its different varietals and great values.

WHAT LED YOU TO BECOME A SOMMELIER?
The passion for the taste of wine and the process of winemaking.

WHAT ARE THE BEST ASPECTS OF YOUR JOB?
Pairing the chef's dishes with wine and, of course, satisfying my customers.

IF YOU WERE NOT IN THE WINE PROFESSION, WHAT WOULD YOU BE DOING?
I would be a chef.

La Petite Maison

366 East Palmetto Park Road
Boca Raton, Florida 33432
phone 561-750-7483 fax 561-362-8434

Olivier Adams

SOMMELIER

WHAT IS ONE OF YOUR ULTIMATE FOOD AND WINE PAIRINGS?
Duck breast in a red wine sauce with leg confit and St. Estèphe.

DESCRIBE YOUR WINE SELECTIONS.
A small wine list with special, weekly selections, geared toward the adventurer.

WHAT CATEGORY OF WINE IS THE BEST VALUE ON YOUR WINE LIST?
Bordeaux.

NAME RECENT WINE DISCOVERIES THAT HAVE EXCITED YOU.
The quality of American wines in recent years has gone to the top.

WHAT IS YOUR FAVORITE WINE REGION IN THE WORLD TODAY?
Burgundy. Every flavor is just a few miles from each other.

WHAT LED YOU TO BECOME A SOMMELIER?
Career change and the challenge.

WHAT IS THE BEST ASPECT OF YOUR JOB?
Seeing a woman smile.

IF YOU WERE NOT IN THIS PROFESSION, WHAT WOULD YOU BE DOING?
I would be interested in wines, stable returns and long-term profit.

Pierre's Restaurant at Morada Bay

81600 Overseas Highway
Islamorada, Florida 33036
phone 305-664-3225 fax 305-664-3227

Yoann A. Bagat
SOMMELIER

WHAT ARE SOME OF YOUR ULTIMATE FOOD AND WINE PAIRINGS?
Seared breast of duck with mushroom risotto cake and reduction of crème de cassis de Dijon with Pinot Noir Reserve (Los Carneros/Napa); ribeye with sautéed onions marinated in red wine sauce, with potato gratin and grilled mushroom, with a Pauillac.

DESCRIBE YOUR WINE SELECTIONS.
We encourage our guests to try wines from new regions represented on our wine list. We also specialize in selections of old Bordeaux and rare American Cabernet.

WHAT CATEGORY OF WINE IS THE BEST VALUE ON YOUR WINE LIST?
California Meritage.

NAME RECENT WINE DISCOVERIES THAT HAVE EXCITED YOU.
Red wines from Washington because of great quality and value.

WHAT IS YOUR FAVORITE WINE REGION IN THE WORLD TODAY?
Bordeaux, where I have my roots.

WHAT LED YOU TO BECOME A SOMMELIER?
I was raised in the middle of a vineyard in St. Estèphe in a wine-loving family.

WHAT IS THE BEST ASPECT OF YOUR JOB?
Discovering new wines and new vintages every day from around the world.

IF YOU WERE NOT A SOMMELIER, WHAT WOULD YOU BE?
A bartender.

La Tavernetta

926 Northeast 20th Avenue
Fort Lauderdale, Florida 33338
phone 954-463-2566 fax 954-524-0777
website www.latavernetta.net

Ute E. M. Stork
CHEF AND RESTAURANT MANAGER

WHAT ARE SOME OF YOUR ULTIMATE FOOD AND WINE PAIRINGS?
Chilean sea bass with Pinot Grigio and veal entrées with Chianti.

DESCRIBE YOUR WINE SELECTIONS.
We are an Italian bistro. Nearly 60 percent of our selection is Italian, 30 percent is American and 10 percent is French Champagne.

WHAT CATEGORY OF WINE IS THE BEST VALUE ON YOUR WINE LIST?
Amarone della Valpolicella.

NAME A RECENT WINE DISCOVERY THAT EXCITED YOU.
Col di Sasso from Banfi. Everybody has been surprised by the taste of this Sangiovese and Cabernet blend. It is easy to recommend great, expensive wines, but people also are looking for value.

WHAT IS YOUR FAVORITE WINE REGION IN THE WORLD TODAY?
Burgundy. The first great wines I tasted were Burgundies.

WHAT LED YOU TO YOUR CURRENT POSITION?
My career has always been in the restaurant and hotel business, and wine knowledge has always been a part of it.

WHAT IS THE BEST ASPECT OF YOUR JOB?
Tasting great wines at no cost.

IF YOU WERE NOT IN THIS PROFESSION, WHAT WOULD YOU BE?
Retired.

Arturo's Restaurant

VINCENT GISMALDE, WINE BUYER

6750 North Federal Highway, Boca Raton

561-997-7373

Bambu

MILOVAN TELLEZ, WINE BUYER

1661 Meridian Avenue, Miami Beach

305-531-4800

Bistro Jean Pierre

DAVID LEVERRIER, WINE BUYER

132 North County Road, Palm Beach

561-833-1171

Brazilian Court Hotel

ROLAND GIRAUDY, FOOD

AND BEVERAGE DIRECTOR

301 Australian Avenue, Palm Beach

561-655-7740

Burt & Jack's

STEVE BROWN, SOMMELIER

Berth 23 — Port Everglades,

Fort Lauderdale

954-522-5225

Café Chardonnay

BRIAN CHAMIS, SOMMELIER

4533 PGA Boulevard, Palm Beach

561-627-2662

Café L'Europe

RAINER SCHONHERR, SOMMELIER

331 South County Road, Palm Beach

561-655-4020

Café Maxx

RON LABADIE, BEVERAGE MANAGER

2601 East Atlantic Boulevard,

Pompano Beach

954-782-0606

Chef Allen

ALLEN SUSSER, CHEF AND OWNER

19088 North East 29th Avenue, Miami

305-935-2900

Eden Roc at the Renaissance Resort and Spa

MARK BUTCHER, WINE BUYER

4525 Collins Avenue, Miami Beach

305-531-0000

L'Escalier at the Breakers Hotel

VIRGINIA PHILIP, SOMMELIER

1 South County Road, Palm Beach

561-659-8480

Four Seasons Resort at Palm Beach

DANIEL BRAUN, MANAGER

AND WINE BUYER

2800 South Ocean Boulevard,

Palm Beach

561-582-2800

Gaucho Room at Loews Miami Beach Hotel

THOMAS WRIGHT, RESTAURANT

MANAGER AND WINE BUYER

1601 Collins Avenue, Miami Beach

305-604-5420

The Grill at the Ritz-Carlton Palm Beach

TONY SERVIDEO, SOMMELIER

100 South Ocean Boulevard, Manalapan

561-533-6000

Grove Isle Club and Resort

ALBERT OMEHEN, WINE BUYER

4 Grove Isle Drive, Coconut Grove

305-285-7973

Louie's Backyard

DONNA HASTIE, WINE BUYER
700 Waddell Avenue, Key West
305-294-1061

Mark's Las Olas

THOMAS HILAN, SOMMELIER
1032 East Las Olas Boulevard,
Fort Lauderdale
954-463-1000

Norman's

RODRIGO MARTINEZ, SOMMELIER
21 Almeria Avenue, Coral Gables
305-446-6767

Renato's

BRAD STAPLETON, WINE BUYER
87 Via Mizner, Palm Beach
561-655-9752

Ruth's Chris Steak House

CRAIG CONNLEY, WINE BUYER
661 US Highway 1, North Palm Beach
561-863-0660

Shula's Steak House at the Miami Lakes Golf Resort

CHRISTIAN DAMMERT, GENERAL
MANAGER AND WINE BUYER
7601 North West 154th Street, Miami
305-820-8047

Stefano's

ALEXANDER MAVRIS, DIRECTOR
OF WINE AND SPIRITS
24 Crandon Boulevard, Key Biscayne
305-361-7007

Il Tulipano

RON WAYNE, WINE BUYER
AND SOMMELIER
11052 Biscayne Boulevard, North
Miami
305-893-4811

La Vieille Maison

LEONCE PICOT, WINE BUYER
770 East Palmetto Park, Boca Raton
561-391-6701

Anthony's Restaurant

3109 Piedmont Road Northeast
Atlanta, Georgia 30305-2531
phone 404-262-7379 fax 404-261-6009

Asif Edrish
SOMMELIER

WHAT ARE SOME OF YOUR ULTIMATE FOOD AND WINE PAIRINGS?
Sautéed foie gras served with peaches and peach balsamic sauce paired with
Errazuriz Late Harvest Sauvignon Blanc from Chile. For an entrée, classic Surf
and Turf served with Burgundy sauce paired with Penfolds Bin 707 Cabernet
from South Australia.

DESCRIBE YOUR WINE SELECTIONS.
Our wine list is diverse and dynamic with more than 475 selections. My goal is
to provide quality wines from different parts of the world.

WHAT IS YOUR FAVORITE WINE REGION IN THE WORLD TODAY?
South Australia. I like its big, fat, heavy, fruity, often jammy red wines. I also
like the use of American oak to add flavors.

WHAT LED YOU TO BECOME A SOMMELIER?
I have been involved in the food-service industry since 1991, starting from the
kitchen and then moving to the floor. My passion, interest and, ultimately, the
opportunity pushed me into becoming a sommelier.

IF YOU WERE NOT A SOMMELIER, WHAT WOULD YOU BE DOING?
Definitely in the food service industry, probably as a manager.

Aria

490 East Paces Ferry Road
Atlanta, Georgia 30305
phone 404-233-7673 fax 404-262-5208
website www.aria-atl.com

Christian G. Henderson
WINE DIRECTOR

WHAT ARE SOME OF YOUR ULTIMATE FOOD AND WINE PAIRINGS?
Warm lobster cocktail with butter-braised lobster, broccoli purée and truffled mashed potatoes paired with dry Riesling from Alsace; Hudson Valley foie gras with Sauternes; seared scallops with American Gewürztraminer.

DESCRIBE YOUR WINE SELECTIONS.
We have a strong domestic focus on small or little-known producers, great-value wines, popular premium selections, and California "cult" producers.

WHAT CATEGORY OF WINE IS THE BEST VALUE ON YOUR WINE LIST?
Syrah, Shiraz and Rhône wine.

NAME RECENT WINE DISCOVERIES THAT HAVE EXCITED YOU.
California "port" wines. Extracted, fruit-forward wines for the new generation of wine drinkers. And there are many excellent wines coming from Paso Robles and Edna Valley.

WHAT IS YOUR FAVORITE WINE REGION IN THE WORLD TODAY?
South Australia, especially Barossa Valley and Eden Valley. Virtually any varietal can be found here, wine quality is spectacular, and the wines are often great value.

WHAT LED YOU TO YOUR CURRENT POSITION?
A natural progression from restaurant manager. I was looking for a field where both passion and knowledge were needed to excel.

WHAT IS THE BEST ASPECT OF YOUR JOB?
Staff training. When I see weeks or months of training come together, I know I have passed on knowledge that will never go away.

IF YOU WERE NOT IN THIS PROFESSION, WHAT WOULD YOU BE DOING?
Something in the entertainment business, maybe a talent agent or audio engineer.

Bacchanalia

1198 Howell Mill Road
Atlanta, Georgia 30318
phone 404-365-0410 fax 404-365-8020

Daniel J. Rudiger
SOMMELIER AND FLOOR MANAGER

WHAT ARE SOME OF YOUR ULTIMATE FOOD AND WINE PAIRINGS?
Medjool dates with shaved Parmigiano-Reggiano paired with a Sauternes-style wine; blue crab fritter with avocado, citrus and Thai pepper essence with an off-dry, crisp Mosel Riesling.

DESCRIBE YOUR WINE SELECTIONS.
I maintain a core wine list and seek out different and unfamiliar wines that I promote through our food and wine program.

WHAT CATEGORIES OF WINE ARE THE BEST VALUES ON YOUR WINE LIST?
White and red varietals other than Chardonnay, Merlot, Pinot Noir, etc.

NAME A RECENT WINE DISCOVERY THAT EXCITED YOU.
Drinking a 1980 Riesling from the Barossa Valley with a screw cap. It was a classic, developed Riesling with depth and finesse. Who knew!

WHAT IS YOUR FAVORITE WINE REGION IN THE WORLD TODAY?
Alsace.

WHAT LED YOU TO BECOME A SOMMELIER?
A desire to know about what I was drinking and why it tasted the way it did.

WHAT ARE THE BEST ASPECTS OF YOUR JOB?
Discovering new wines, finding good value/quality wines and having satisfied guests.

Joël Restaurant

The Forum, 3290 Northside Parkway
Atlanta, Georgia 30327
phone 404-233-3500 fax 404-841-0906
website www.joelrestaurant.com

Philippe J. R. Buttin
CHEF, SOMMELIER AND WINE BUYER

WHAT ARE SOME OF YOUR ULTIMATE FOOD AND WINE PAIRINGS?
Tuna and tomato tartare, tomato and olive oil dressing with Sauvignon Blanc; seared foie gras, parsnips and quince with caline sauce with a sweet Chenin Blanc from the Loire Valley; terrine of foie gras "au torchon," fig marmalade with De Bortolli Noble One Semillon 1998; tortellini au duck, mushroom and leek confit, vineuse sauce with Pinotage from South Africa's Warwick Estate.

DESCRIBE YOUR WINE SELECTIONS.
We have a wide selection of wines. We also offer a weekly program of a chef's menu and accompanying wines by the glass and a weekly special consisting of four wines from the wine list.

WHAT CATEGORIES OF WINE ARE THE BEST VALUES ON YOUR WINE LIST?
Whites and reds from South Africa. Also, the wines of Chile and Argentina.

NAME A RECENT WINE DISCOVERY THAT EXCITED YOU.
Klein Constantia Vin de Constance for its history and taste.

WHAT IS YOUR FAVORITE WINE REGION IN THE WORLD TODAY?
South Africa. There are so many microclimates, and the wines have really progressed in quality since the end of apartheid.

WHAT LED YOU TO BECOME A SOMMELIER?
My admiration for Mr. Lepré, former sommelier at the Ritz-Carlton Paris, for his kindness and knowledge.

IF YOU WERE NOT IN THIS PROFESSION, WHAT WOULD YOU BE?
A fighter pilot.

Nikolai's Roof
at the Hilton Atlanta
255 Courtland Street Northeast
Atlanta, Georgia 30303
phone 404-221-6362 fax 404-221-6811

Cristophe Orlarei
ASSISTANT MANAGER AND SOMMELIER

WHAT ARE SOME OF YOUR ULTIMATE FOOD AND WINE PAIRINGS?
Seared scallops and New Zealand Sauvignon Blanc 2000.

DESCRIBE YOUR WINE SELECTIONS.
We have more than 500 wines, emphasizing Californian and French selections, but with some great catches from New Zealand and Australia.

WHAT CATEGORY OF WINE IS THE BEST VALUE ON YOUR WINE LIST?
Australian.

NAME RECENT WINE DISCOVERIES THAT HAVE EXCITED YOU.
Oregon Pinot Gris and Pinot Noir, which both offer superb value.

WHAT IS YOUR FAVORITE REGION OR AREA IN THE WORLD TODAY?
New Zealand, for the refreshing quality of its Sauvignon Blanc and Pinot Noir.

WHAT LED YOU TO BECOME A SOMMELIER?
Love of wine and food.

WHAT IS THE MOST CHALLENGING ASPECT OF YOUR JOB?
Promoting and maintaining an extensive selection of wine by the glass.

IF YOU WERE NOT IN THE WINE PROFESSION, WHAT WOULD YOU BE DOING?
Running my own bar.

1848 House

DUSTIN HANSROTE, HOUSE MANAGER
780 South Cobb Drive, Marietta
770-428-1848

45 South

SANDY HOLANDER, OWNER
AND WINE BUYER
20 East Broad Street, Savannah
912-233-1881

The Abbey

GEORGE GORE, WINE BUYER
163 Ponce De Leon Avenue Northeast,
Atlanta
404-876-8532

BluePointe

ANDY CLARK, GENERAL MANAGER
AND WINE BUYER
3455 Peachtree Road, Atlanta
404-237-9070

Bone's

RON PETERSON, WINE BUYER
3130 Piedmont Road, Atlanta
404-237-2663

Buckhead Life Restaurant Group

EDDIE VALENTE, DIRECTOR OF
OPERATIONS AND WINE BUYER
265 Pharr Road, Atlanta
404-237-2060

Canoe

KEVIN GOOD, MANAGER
AND WINE BUYER
4199 Paces Ferry Road Northwest,
Atlanta
770-432-2663

Chez Philippe's

PHILIPPE HADDAD, OWNER,
CHEF AND WINE BUYER
Ten Kings Circle at Peachtree Hills,
Atlanta
404-231-4113

Chops

TIM STEVENS, GENERAL MANAGER
AND WINE BUYER
70 West Paces Ferry Road Northwest,
Atlanta
404-262-2675

City Grill

DEAN WHITAKER, SOMMELIER
AND BAR MANAGER
55 Hurt Plaza Drive, Atlanta
404-872-2370

The Cloister Sea Island

JOHN CAPOBIANCO, SOMMELIER
Lanier Boulevard, Sea Island
912-638-3611

The Dining Room at the Ritz-Carlton Buckhead

MICHAEL MCNEILL, SOMMELIER
3434 Peachtree Road Northeast, Atlanta
404-237-2700

Elizabeth's On 37th

GARY BUTCH, WINE BUYER
105 East 37th Street, Savannah
912-236-5547

The Food Studio

SAM HOUSTON, WINE BUYER
887 West Marietta Street, Atlanta
404-815-6677

La Grotta

ANTONIO ABIZANDA, CHEF,
OWNER AND WINE BUYER
MICHAEL GLUSKO, SOMMELIER
SERGIO SAVALLI, OWNER
AND SOMMELIER
2637 Peachtree Road Northeast, Atlanta
404-231-1368

Nava

PHIL HANDLEY, BEVERAGE DIRECTOR
3060 Peachtree Road, Atlanta
404-240-1984

Pano's & Paul's

SAM THAN, WINE BUYER
1232 West Paces Ferry Road, Atlanta
404-261-3662

Seeger's Restaurant

STEVEN ROUNDTREE, SOMMELIER
111 West Paces Ferry Road, Atlanta
404-846-9779

South City Kitchen

JOE FERRIS, ASSISTANT MANAGER
AND WINE BUYER
1144 Crescent Avenue Northeast, Atlanta
404-873-7358

Veni, Vidi, Vici

JILL PIPES, BEVERAGE MANAGERI
41 14th Street, Atlanta
404-875-8424

Mariposa at Neiman Marcus Honolulu

1450 Ala Moana Boulevard
Honolulu, Hawaii 96814
phone 808-948-7495 fax 808-951-3409

Roberto E. Viernes
SOMMELIER

WHAT ARE SOME OF YOUR ULTIMATE FOOD AND WINE PAIRINGS?
Our signature dish of lobster katsu with mango-chile-lime dipping sauce paired with New Zealand Sauvignon Blanc; quail wrapped with bacon in a natural jus reduction with full-bodied rosé Champagne.

DESCRIBE YOUR WINE SELECTIONS.
We offer a selection of well-recognized and consistent wines, and great-value wines from little-known producers from around the world.

WHAT CATEGORIES OF WINE ARE THE BEST VALUES ON YOUR WINE LIST?
Southern French Syrah and South American Chardonnay and Malbec.

NAME A RECENT WINE DISCOVERY THAT EXCITED YOU.
Argentinian Malbec is really exciting for its uniqueness and boldness. Most are from old vines and are being made in an international style that is easy to appreciate.

WHAT IS YOUR FAVORITE WINE REGION IN THE WORLD TODAY?
Burgundy. It is so seductive, classy, ethereal and, therefore, irresistible for me.

WHAT LED YOU TO BECOME A SOMMELIER?
I took a course on wine, the Basic Certification course from the Court of Master Sommeliers. Ever since, I have been passionate about wine.

WHAT ARE THE BEST ASPECTS OF YOUR JOB?
Enjoying the company of people at their best. These are people celebrating life, not only the occasions of birthdays and anniversaries, but also enjoying the moment, pleasurable company, dining and imbibing. Where else do you see so many people enjoying themselves and at their best?

IF YOU WERE NOT A SOMMELIER, WHAT WOULD YOU BE?
A chef, or a Michelin Guide critic!

La Mer at the Halekulani Hotel

2199 Kalia Road
Honolulu, Hawaii 96815
phone 808-923-2311 fax 808-931-5039
website www.halekulani.com

Randolph H. Ching
WINE MANAGER

WHAT ARE SOME OF YOUR ULTIMATE FOOD AND WINE PAIRINGS?
Chef Yves Garnier's bouillabaisse and rosé from Provence; crustaceans and Sauvignon Blanc from around the world.

DESCRIBE YOUR WINE SELECTIONS.
We have a wide selection of international wines and a representation of those countries producing world-class wines.

WHAT CATEGORIES OF WINE ARE THE BEST VALUES ON YOUR WINE LIST?
Italian, Australian and South American wines.

NAME RECENT WINE DISCOVERIES THAT HAVE EXCITED YOU.
Domaine Tempier Bandol rouge. This wine has a sense of place. Wonderful terroir. Older vintages are also wonderful and very balanced.

WHAT IS YOUR FAVORITE WINE REGION IN THE WORLD TODAY?
Wherever you can grow good Pinot Noir.

WHAT LED YOU TO BECOME A SOMMELIER?
Wine was my hobby. I have always had a big interest in wine.

WHAT IS THE BEST ASPECT OF YOUR JOB?
I love matching food and wine.

IF YOU WERE NOT IN THE WINE PROFESSION, WHAT WOULD YOU BE?
A chef.

The Anuenue Room at the Ritz-Carlton Kapalua
SHAWN JERVIS, FOOD
AND BEVERAGE DIRECTOR
1 Ritz-Carlton Drive, Kapalua
808-669-6200

Hoku's at the Kahal Mandarin Oriental Hotel
WAYNE WOODS, FOOD
AND BEVERAGE DIRECTOR
5000 Kahala Avenue, Honolulu
808-739-8888

Hy's Steak House
BOB PANTER, GENERAL MANAGER
AND WINE BUYER
2440 Kuhio Avenue, Honolulu
808-922-5555

Lodge at Koele
INGRIDA COUTO, WINE BUYER
1 Keomoku Highway, Lanai City
808-565-7300

Roy's Kahana Bar & Grill
MICHAEL WEBBER, GENERAL
MANAGER AND WINE BUYER
4405 Hanoapiilani Highway, Kahana,
Maui
808-669-6999

Roy's Restaurant
RAINER KUMBROCH, OPERATIONS
DIRECTOR AND WINE BUYER
6600 Kananianaole Highway, Honolulu
808-396-7697

Seasons at the Four Seasons Resort Wailea
KAREN CHRISTENSEN, FOOD
AND BEVERAGE DIRECTOR
3900 Wailea Alanui Drive, Wailea
808-874-8000

Evergreen Restaurant

115 Rivers West
Ketchum, Idaho 83353
phone 208-726-3888 fax 208-726-9365
website www.evergreenbistro.com

Burke Smith
WINE DIRECTOR

WHAT ARE SOME OF YOUR ULTIMATE FOOD AND WINE PAIRINGS?
Chef Chris Kastner's grilled Hawaiian swordfish with artichoke-fennel-
carrot barigoule, roasted sweet pepper and roasted lemon atole with a
Washington Viognier; roasted rack of lamb with a rosemary wine merchant sauce, maitake mushrooms, kale and a butternut squash purée
paired with a Central Coast Pinot Noir or Syrah; hush puppies and Creole
meunière sauce with California Zinfandel.

DESCRIBE YOUR WINE SELECTIONS.
Our wines are from France, California, the Pacific Northwest and Italy
with a balance between celebrated and emerging producers.

WHAT CATEGORY OF WINE IS THE BEST VALUE ON YOUR WINE LIST?
Central Coast Syrah.

WHAT IS YOUR FAVORITE WINE REGION IN THE WORLD TODAY?
Washington. I love the way the wines reflect the diverse personalities of the
winemakers: Chris Camarda, Doug McCrea, Erik Dunham, Matt Loso,
Gary Figgins, Chuck Reininger and Mike Januik.

WHAT LED YOU TO YOUR CURRENT POSITION?
When I was growing up, wine was always on the dinner table. It has been
a part of my life for as long as I can remember.

WHAT IS THE BEST ASPECT OF YOUR JOB?
Facilitating fun on a nightly basis.

IF YOU WERE NOT IN THIS PROFESSION, WHAT WOULD YOU BE
DOING?
I would have a small bed-and-breakfast on a tropical island.

Beverly's at the Coeur D'Alene

SAM LANGE, WINE BUYER

250 Northwest Boulevard,
Coeur D'Alene

208-765-4000

The Capital Grille

633 North St. Clair Street
Chicago, Illinois 60611
phone 312-337-9400 fax 312-337-1259

Paul R. Calzaretta
SOMMELIER

WHAT ARE SOME OF YOUR ULTIMATE FOOD AND WINE PAIRINGS?
Our dry-aged steak au poivre with a Cognac cream sauce paired with
Gigondas; farm-raised bluepoint oysters with Chablis; live, whole Maine
lobsters broiled and steamed, with Chassagne-Montrachet.

DESCRIBE YOUR WINE SELECTIONS.
Our wine program is primarily Cabernet-based because we are a steak-
house, but I am expanding our selections to include more varietals like
Syrah and Zinfandel.

WHAT CATEGORY OF WINE IS THE BEST VALUE ON YOUR WINE LIST?
"Interesting Red," which focuses on less common red varietals and blends.

NAME RECENT WINE DISCOVERIES THAT HAVE EXCITED YOU.
Château Camou, El Gran Vino Tinto from Mexico, a Bordeaux-style red
that offers superior quality for the price.

WHAT IS YOUR FAVORITE WINE REGION IN THE WORLD TODAY?
Spring Mountain District, Napa Valley.

WHAT LED YOU TO BECOME A SOMMELIER?
I have had an avid interest in wine and food since my first restaurant job
in high school.

WHAT IS THE BEST ASPECT OF YOUR JOB?
Being in a profession that is always changing and improving is both challenging and rewarding. It enables me to remain dedicated.

IF YOU WERE NOT IN THIS PROFESSION, WHAT WOULD YOU BE
DOING?
Performing various styles of music. I have been an instrumentalist (trum-
pet/cornet) for nearly twenty years.

Carlos' Restaurant

429 Temple Avenue
Highland Park, Illinois 60035
phone 847-432-0770 fax 847-432-2047
website www.carlos-restaurant.com

Marcello Cancelli

SOMMELIER

WHAT ARE SOME OF YOUR ULTIMATE FOOD AND WINE PAIRINGS?
Escargots in brioche with artichoke hearts and a Roquefort Pernod cream sauce paired with big Merlot; smoked salmon and fresh Maryland crab cake with celery root, organic cucumber, herb salad and sauce aux fines herbes with zingy Sancerre; sautéed John Dory and Hawaiian shrimp on fingerling potatoes and doubloon mushroom ragoût with a shrimp tarragon emulsion paired with Chablis.

DESCRIBE YOUR WINE SELECTIONS.
We have 1,200 selections on our list, emphasizing French and California producers, with a significant presence of Italian, Spanish and German wines. We offer nineteen wines by the glass.

WHAT CATEGORIES OF WINE ARE THE BEST VALUES ON YOUR WINE LIST?
Pinot Noir and our Italian sections.

NAME RECENT WINE DISCOVERIES THAT HAVE EXCITED YOU.
Santa Barbara County wines, especially the Syrahs.

WHAT LED YOU TO BECOME A SOMMELIER?
As a struggling actor working in restaurants, I suddenly realized that my love for wine could become a career.

WHAT ARE YOUR FAVORITE WINE REGIONS IN THE WORLD TODAY?
Santa Barbara County and South America, and vast improvements have been made by both Argentina and Chile.

WHAT ARE THE BEST ASPECTS OF YOUR JOB?
Introducing people to new wines or to their first wine experience. Putting customers at ease and engaging in a friendly, relaxed discussion about their wine selections.

IF YOU WERE NOT IN THIS PROFESSION, WHAT WOULD YOU BE?
A writer.

Nomi at the Park Hyatt Chicago

800 North Michigan Avenue
Chicago, Illinois 60611
phone 312-335-1234 fax 312-239-4000
website www.parkhyattchicago.com

Robert Jovic
SOMMELIER

WHAT ARE SOME OF YOUR ULTIMATE FOOD AND WINE PAIRINGS?
Nomi's chilled cucumber soup with Oregon Pinot or Sancerre. Our sushi is perfect with German Riesling or Sauvignon Blanc.

DESCRIBE YOUR WINE SELECTIONS.
Our wine list represents the entire world, from rare jewels to simple vintages. We are constantly seeking out new wines from small producers that pair well with our cuisine.

WHAT CATEGORIES OF WINE ARE THE BEST VALUES ON YOUR WINE LIST?
Red wines from South Africa and white wines from New Zealand.

NAME RECENT WINE DISCOVERIES THAT HAVE EXCITED YOU.
Darioush Winery Signature Viognier 2001—nice acidity and a wonderful aroma; Vall-Llach from Spain's Priorato region—it's a monster wine, big, bold and intense with a nice finish; Lemelson Pinot Noir Jerome Reserve 1999—just the right combination of spice.

WHAT ARE YOUR FAVORITE WINE REGIONS IN THE WORLD TODAY?
Alsace, Burgundy and Oregon.

WHAT LED YOU TO BECOME A SOMMELIER?
My grandfather was a winemaker, and as a child I worked in his vineyard and became fascinated with wine.

WHAT ARE THE BEST ASPECTS OF YOUR JOB?
I get to taste amazing wines and meet interesting people from all over the world. I also like getting feedback from my customers after making suggestions.

IF YOU WERE NOT A SOMMELIER, WHAT WOULD YOU BE DOING?
Own my own restaurant or be an opera singer.

Le Titi De Paris

1015 West Dundee Road
Arlington Heights, Illinois 60004
phone 847-506-0222 fax 847-506-0474
website www.letitideparis.com

Marcel G. Flori

MAÎTRE D' AND SOMMELIER

WHAT ARE SOME OF YOUR ULTIMATE FOOD AND WINE PAIRINGS?
A Monbazillac with Roquefort cheese; a red Côtes-du-Rhône with bouilla-baisse; an old tawny Port with warm Ambrosia bittersweet chocolate cake.

DESCRIBE YOUR WINE SELECTIONS.
We offer wines from all parts of France and California.

NAME A RECENT WINE DISCOVERY THAT EXCITED YOU.
A red Bellet wine that has the aroma of a wild rose.

WHAT IS YOUR FAVORITE WINE REGION IN THE WORLD TODAY?
I love the wines of Provence. Some are really great. Very underrated.

WHAT LED YOU TO BECOME A SOMMELIER?
I love wine, I love food and I love people.

WHAT IS THE BEST ASPECT OF YOUR JOB?
To be able to make people discover something new again and again.

IF YOU WERE NOT IN THE WINE PROFESSION, WHAT WOULD YOU BE
DOING?
Making fine wood furniture or cheese.

Tuscany

1014 West Taylor Street
Chicago, Illinois 60607
phone 312-829-1990 fax 312-829-8023
website www.stefanirestaurants.com

Peter H. Bovis
GENERAL MANAGER AND WINE BUYER

WHAT ARE SOME OF YOUR ULTIMATE FOOD AND WINE PAIRINGS?
Rack of lamb with a super-Tuscan wine; grilled veal chop with Sassicaia.

DESCRIBE YOUR WINE SELECTIONS.
We specialize in the wines of Italy's Tuscany region.

WHAT CATEGORY OF WINE IS THE BEST VALUE IN YOUR RESTAU-
RANT?
Chianti, by the glass or bottle.

NAME RECENT WINE DISCOVERIES THAT HAVE EXCITED YOU.
The improvement of wines from the country of Greece.

WHAT IS YOUR FAVORITE WINE REGION IN THE WORLD TODAY?
The Tuscany region in Italy.

WHAT LED YOU TO YOUR CURRENT POSITION?
The love of wine.

WHAT IS THE BEST ASPECT OF YOUR JOB?
Serving new and different people every day.

IF YOU WERE NOT IN THE WINE PROFESSION, WHAT WOULD YOU BE
DOING?
I would be in the medical profession.

Ambria

BOB BANSBERG, SOMMELIER
2300 North Lincoln Park West, Chicago
773-472-5959

Angelo's Ristorante

ANGELO BATTAGLIA, OWNER
AND WINE BUYER
247 North York Road, Elmhurst
630-833-2400

Arun's

VIVIAN LEVINE, WINE BUYER
AND SOMMELIER
4156 North Kedzie Avenue, Chicago
773-539-1909

Bin 36

BRIAN DUNCAN, SOMMELIER
339 North Dearborn Street, Chicago
312-755-9463

Blackbird

EUARD SEITAN, SOMMELIER
619 West Randolph Street, Chicago
312-715-0708

Cab's Wine Bar & Bistro

ALIXE LISCHETT, WINE BUYER
430 North Main Street, Glen Ellyn
630-942-9463

Cape Cod Room

KAREN NAGY, WINE BUYER
140 East Walton, Chicago
312-787-2200

Carlton Club and Four Seasons at the Ritz-Carlton

PIERRE LASSERRE, SOMMELIER
160 East Pearson Street, Chicago
312-266-1000

Charlie Trotter's

BELINDA CHANG, SOMMELIER
816 West Armitage Avenue, Chicago
773-248-6228

Cité

MANUEL LOPEZ, DINING ROOM MANAGER
505 North Lake Shore Drive, Chicago
312-644-4050

The Dining Room at the Ritz-Carlton

STEVEN LANDE, SOMMELIER
160 East Pearson Street, Chicago
312-573-5223

Edgewood Valley Country Club

CHRISSIE CONLEY, ASSISTANT
MANAGER AND WINE BUYER
7500 South Willow Springs Road, LaGrange
708-246-2800

Everest

ALPANA SINGH, SOMMELIER
440 La Salle, 40th Floor, Chicago
312-663-8920

Froggy's French Café

PASCAL ROCHELEMAGNE, WINE BUYER
306 Green Bay Road, Highwood
847-433-7080

Harry Carry's Restaurant

MICHELLE ANDERSON, SOMMELIER
33 West Kinzie, Chicago
312-828-0966

Hyatt Hotel

ANDREW DAVIDSON, FOOD
AND BEVERAGE DIRECTOR
200 West Madison, Chicago
312-750-8424

Italian Village

RON BALTER, WINE DIRECTOR
71 West Monroe, 2nd Floor, Chicago
312-332-7005

Knightsbridge Wine Shop & Epicurean Centre

KEVIN MOHALLEY, WINE DIRECTOR
824 Sunset Ridge Road, Northbrook
847-498-9300

Maggiano's Little Italy

DAVID PENNACHETTI, WINE AND
BEVERAGE MANAGER
101 West Grand, Suite 400, Chicago
312-644-7766

MK

GRANT HOUGH, BEVERAGE MANAGER
868 North Franklin, Chicago
312-482-9179

Nine

LARRY FLAM, MANAGER AND WINE BUYER
440 West Randolph Street, Chicago
312-575-9900

One Sixty Blue

MYRON MARKEWYCZ, SOMMELIER
160 North Loomis Street, Chicago
312-850-0303

Printers Row Restaurant

PHILIP GAVEN, WINE BUYER
550 South Dearborn Street, Chicago
312-461-0780

Pump Room

EVRIM ORALKAN, BEVERAGE MANAGER
1301 North State Parkway, Chicago
312-266-0360

Shaw's Crab House & Blue Crab Lounge

STEVE SHERMAN, WINE BUYER
1900 East Higgins Road, Schaumbourg
847-517-2722

Spago

SPIRO BOYAZIS, SOMMELIER
520 North Dearborn, Chicago
312-527-3704

Spiaggia Restaurant

HENRY BISHOP, SOMMELIER
980 North Michigan Avenue, Chicago
312-280-2750

Tallgrass

TOM ALVES, WINE BUYER
1006 South State Street, Lockport
815-838-5566

Thyme

JOHN BUBALA, CHEF AND SOMMELIER
464 North Halstead, Chicago
312-226-4300

Tru

AARON ELLIOT, ASSISTANT SOMMELIER
R. SCOTT TYREE, WINE DIRECTOR AND
SOMMELIER
676 North Saint Clair Street, Chicago
312-202-0001

Va Pensiero

TOM GORHAM, WINE BUYER
PATRICK HANLEY, SOMMELIER
1566 Oak Avenue, Evanston
847-475-7779

Vivere

RON BALTER, WINE BUYER
71 West Monroe Street, Chicago
312-332-4040

Zinfandel

DREW GOSS, OWNER AND WINE BUYER
59 West Grand Avenue, Chicago
312-527-1818

The Carriage House Dining Room

24460 Adams Road
South Bend, Indiana 46628
phone 574-272-9220 fax 574-272-6179

Judith L. Cote
PRESIDENT

WHAT ARE SOME OF YOUR ULTIMATE FOOD AND WINE PAIRINGS?
Balsamic-roasted pear, chèvre and lavender honey with a California
Gewürztraminer; grilled Mississippi quail, sweet potato pancake and cran-
berry Cumberland sauce with a 1997 California Cabernet; white chocolate
mousse cake with apricot sauce with a tawny Port; rabbit sausage with red
Burgundy of some age, preferably a 1990.

DESCRIBE YOUR WINE SELECTIONS.
We have 600 wines on our list, which includes the most comprehensive
offering of domestic and French wines in our state.

WHAT CATEGORY OF WINE IS THE BEST VALUE IN YOUR RESTAURANT?
Bordeaux.

NAME RECENT WINE DISCOVERIES THAT HAVE EXCITED YOU.
1997 Langtry red Meritage. Incredible style and quality, great complexity
from start to finish.

WHAT IS YOUR FAVORITE WINE REGION IN THE WORLD TODAY?
California, because it embodies the American spirit and dream that hard
work, determination and diligence equals success.

WHAT LED YOU TO YOUR CURRENT POSITION?
A twenty-five-year "apprenticeship" with my mother that was at times
casual in nature and very formal at others.

WHAT ARE THE BEST ASPECTS OF YOUR JOB?
Direct interface with our guests and the ability to ensure complete satisfaction and enjoyment in their dining experience.

IF YOU WERE NOT IN THE WINE PROFESSION, WHAT WOULD YOU BE?
Involved in fine art and antiques.

INDIANA

LaSalle Grill
115 West Colfax Avenue
South Bend, Indiana 46601
phone 574-288-1155 fax 219-288-2012
website www.lasallegrille.com

Joseph R. Wilfing
BEVERAGE DIRECTOR AND SOMMELIER

DESCRIBE YOUR WINE SELECTIONS.
Our wine program is geared toward wines that are drinkable now. We have 350 wines on our list from the finest vineyards around the world. We also have a great selection of wines by the glass and half-bottle.

WHAT CATEGORY OF WINE IS THE BEST VALUE ON YOUR WINE LIST?
The Rhône Valley.

NAME RECENT WINE DISCOVERIES THAT HAVE EXCITED YOU.
Wines from the Loire Valley and New Zealand.

WHAT ARE YOUR FAVORITE WINE REGIONS IN THE WORLD TODAY?
The Russian River Valley. Most of the Chardonnay is produced to the Burgundy standard, and the scenery is to die for. Secondly, Pomerol. The wine is exquisite and the land is remarkable.

WHAT LED YOU TO BECOME A SOMMELIER?
It is based on my own enjoyment. I personally enjoy talking to and educating people about wine and its production.

WHAT ARE THE BEST ASPECTS OF YOUR JOB?
The people I serve. Customers seem to enjoy and engage in conversation about wine, not only because it is pertinent to the evening, but also because wine is a wonderful beverage. I am also able to gain a personal knowledge of culture and regions of the world through travel and study, something I would not be doing if I were not in the wine business.

IF YOU WERE NOT IN THE WINE PROFESSION, WHAT WOULD YOU BE DOING?
Public speaking.

Le Relais Restaurant
ANTHONY DIKE, WINE BUYER
Bowman Field, Taylorsville Road,
Louisville
502-451-9020

The Oakroom
JERRY SLATER, MAÎTRE'D
500 Fourth Avenue, Louisville
502-807-3463

Vincenzo's
PAULA FISCHER, WINE BUYER
150 South Fifth Street, Louisville
502-580-1350

Andrea's Restaurant

3100 19th Street at Ridgelake
Metairie, Louisiana 70002
phone 504-834-8583 fax 504-834-6698
website www.andreasrestaurant.com

Andrea Apuzzo
PROPRIETOR AND SOMMELIER

WHAT IS ONE OF YOUR ULTIMATE FOOD AND WINE PAIRINGS?
Red snapper with Fontanelle Chardonnay.

DESCRIBE YOUR WINE SELECTIONS.
I select wines from around the world and then try to share my passion for wine with friends, family and guests.

WHAT CATEGORIES OF WINE ARE THE BEST VALUES ON YOUR WINE LIST?
Zinfandel, red Bordeaux.

NAME RECENT WINE DISCOVERIES THAT HAVE EXCITED YOU.
Ca' Montini Pinot Grigio L'Aristocratico and Bastianich Vespa Bianco.

WHAT IS YOUR FAVORITE WINE REGION IN THE WORLD TODAY?
Tuscany.

WHAT LED YOU TO BECOME A SOMMELIER?
Love of wine. I made wine in my home in Capri.

WHAT ARE THE BEST ASPECTS OF YOUR JOB?
Being able to create a fine wine list from wines around the world; encouraging my guests to have discriminating taste.

IF YOU WERE NOT IN THE WINE PROFESSION, WHAT WOULD YOU BE?
A doctor or musician.

Bayona Restaurant

430 Dauphine Street
New Orleans, Louisiana 70112
phone 504-525-4455 fax 504-522-0589

Dan Brown
WINE STEWARD

WHAT ARE SOME OF YOUR ULTIMATE FOOD AND WINE PAIRINGS?
Banyuls with plum-based desserts; Champagne with fish and rabbit entrées;
Sauternes with foie gras; Champagne and oysters; Port and chocolate.

DESCRIBE YOUR WINE SELECTIONS.
European focus, broad selection, known for eclectic geek juice.

WHAT CATEGORY OF WINE IS THE BEST VALUE ON YOUR WINE LIST?
Rhône Valley.

NAME RECENT WINE DISCOVERIES THAT HAVE EXCITED YOU.
1999 Bourgogne blanc; Spanish wines; Palmina Sangiovese; and Terry Theise
Champagnes.

WHAT IS YOUR FAVORITE WINE REGION IN THE WORLD TODAY?
Rhône for the flavors, value, style and rustic nature.

WHAT LED YOU TO BECOME A SOMMELIER?
Love of wine.

WHAT ARE THE BEST ASPECTS OF YOUR JOB?
Contact with customers and helping them to have a special evening.

IF YOU WERE NOT IN THE WINE PROFESSION, WHAT WOULD YOU BE
DOING?
I am a working preservation contractor and am finishing a master's degree in
preservation architecture at Tulane University. I renovate historic structures and
buy and sell 18th- and early-19th-century glass and silver.

Bistro at Maison de Ville Hotel

727 Rue Toulouse
New Orleans, Louisiana 70130
phone 504-528-9206 fax 504-528-9939
website www.mdv-ac.com

Patrick P. Van Hoorebeek
"Master of Ceremonies"

WHAT ARE SOME OF YOUR ULTIMATE FOOD AND WINE PAIRINGS?
Our cream cheese, pecan torte, dark chocolate ganache with Pierre Ferrand five-year-old Pineau des Charentes; bread pudding du jour with Bonny Doon Muscat Vin de Glacière; red Bordeaux with fish; Zinfandel with chocolate.

DESCRIBE YOUR WINE SELECTIONS.
Our wine program is inclusive, active and very diverse. All wines are available by the glass. We also offer special selections in the sections "Best Kept Secret," "Cork of the Month" and "Patrick's Connoisseur's Corner." The Bistro strives to satisfy the diverse palates and "noses" that grace our establishment.

WHAT CATEGORY OF WINE IS THE BEST VALUE ON YOUR WINE LIST?
Our "Best Kept Secret" section, which consists of handpicked wines selected during my visits to various wineries.

NAME RECENT WINE DISCOVERIES THAT HAVE EXCITED YOU.
Lawson's Sauvignon Blanc from New Zealand with its aroma of lime, grapefruit, gooseberries and hints of quince and dried flowers.

WHAT IS YOUR FAVORITE WINE REGION IN THE WORLD TODAY?
Rhône River Valley wines from France, for their complexity and aroma.

WHAT LED YOU TO YOUR CURRENT POSITION?
"Son like father" and my love of wine.

WHAT IS THE MOST CHALLENGING ASPECT OF YOUR JOB?
It's challenging to teach and learn something new every day.

IF YOU WERE NOT IN THE WINE PROFESSION, WHAT WOULD YOU BE?
A television anchor.

Café Margaux

765 Bayou Pines Drive East
Lake Charles, Louisiana 70601
phone 337-433-2902 fax 337-494-0606

D. C. Flynt

MASTER OF WINE, OWNER
AND EXECUTIVE CHEF

WHAT ARE SOME OF YOUR ULTIMATE FOOD AND WINE PAIRINGS?
Classical cuisine and wine created from the regional varietals that come from the same area as the food, but the wine does not have to come from the same region.

DESCRIBE YOUR WINE SELECTIONS.
Our list features 450 wines, which are arranged by varietal, region and appellation and are listed from fullest to lightest body in each category.

WHAT IS YOUR FAVORITE WINE REGION IN THE WORLD TODAY?
Australia. No other region in the world is as successful in providing the greatest quality wines at the best price.

WHAT LED YOU TO YOUR CURRENT POSITION?
The love of the world's most natural fermented beverage.

WHAT IS THE MOST CHALLENGING ASPECT OF YOUR JOB?
Training the wait staff to understand that their role is to add value at every level (wine, food and pleasure) and that wine is not a trophy hunt, but part of a pleasurable lifestyle.

IF YOU WERE NOT IN THE WINE PROFESSION, WHAT WOULD YOU BE DOING?
If I was not involved in wine, I would not be involved in life.

The Grill Room at the Windsor Court Hotel

300 Gravier Street
New Orleans, Louisiana 70130
phone 504-523-6000 fax 504-596-4649
website www.windsorcourthotel.com

David Singer
SOMMELIER D'HOTEL
Team: Dwayne Savole, Sommelier

WHAT ARE SOME OF YOUR ULTIMATE FOOD AND WINE PAIRINGS?
Veal ribeye with hedgehog mushrooms, veal sausage and carrot-sage sauce with Sonoma Pinot Noir; risotto with white truffles with old Barolo.

DESCRIBE YOUR WINE SELECTIONS.
Right now I'm concentrating on acquiring more verticals of producers who have single vineyards that show different expressions of terroir.

WHAT CATEGORY OF WINE IS THE BEST VALUE ON YOUR WINE LIST?
My "Recommended" page, which has somewhat esoteric wines, including little-known southern Italian reds and outstanding garagistes from Bordeaux.

NAME RECENT WINE DISCOVERIES THAT HAVE EXCITED YOU.
Some of the "kinky" blends from Australia and California. Who else would put Tempranillo, Sangiovese, and Cabernet together?

WHAT IS YOUR FAVORITE WINE REGION IN THE WORLD TODAY?
Burgundy. No other wine reaches such extremes.

WHAT LED YOU TO BECOME A SOMMELIER?
To help put me through school, I was a waiter in fine dining restaurants. Wine had a mystique about it, so I started asking questions. The person in charge of the wine program where I was working told me to start reading. After that I was "bitten" by the grape and here I am.

WHAT ARE THE BEST ASPECTS OF YOUR JOB?
Tasting some of the great wines of the world. Introducing a completely new wine to a client.

IF YOU WERE NOT IN THE WINE PROFESSION, WHAT WOULD YOU BE DOING?
I have no idea.

Bacco at W Hotel of New Orleans

RICHARD KRUMM, SOMMELIER

310 Chartres Street, New Orleans

504-522-2426

Brennan's Restaurant

HARRY HILL, WINE BUYER

417 Royal Street, New Orleans

504-525-9711

Broussard's Restaurant

MARC PREUSS, WINE BUYER

819 Conti Street, New Orleans

504-581-3866

Commander's Palace

RICHARD SHAKESPEARE, SOMMELIER

1403 Washington Avenue, New Orleans

504-899-8221

Delmonico Restaurant & Bar

RICHARD FLETCHER, SOMMELIER

1300 Saint Charles Avenue, New Orleans

504-525-4937

Dominique's at Maison Depuy Hotel

WALTER BERTOD, SOMMELIER

1001 Rue Toulouse, New Orleans

504-522-8800

Emeril's

MATT LIRETTE, SOMMELIER

800 Tchoupitoulas Street, New Orleans

504-528-9393

The Grill Room at the Windsor Court Hotel

HEATHER SCHNEIDER, SOMMELIER

300 Gravier Street, New Orleans

504-523-6000

Lafittes Landing

PATRICIA TATE, BEVERAGE MANAGER

10275 Highway 70, New Orleans

225-473-1232

The White Barn Inn

CHRISTOPHER BAILEY, SOMMELIER

37 Beech Street, Kennebunkport

207-967-2321

Antrim 1844 Country Inn
RICHARD MOLLETT, SOMMELIER
30 Trevanion Road, Taneytown
410-756-6812

Brass Elephant
JACK ELSBY, WINE BUYER
924 North Charles Street, Baltimore
410-547-8480

The Crossing at Casey Jones
LISA BALES, WINE BUYER
417 Charles Street, La Plata
301-932-6226

The Inn at Perry Cabin
THAD HOY, WINE BUYER
308 Watkins Lane, St. Michaels
410-745-2200

The Prime Rib
JOHN KLAUS, WINE BUYER
David Derewicz, Wine Buyer
1101 North Calvert Street, Baltimore
410-539-1804

Roccoco
SUZI O'BOYLE, BAR MANAGER
AND WINE BUYER
20 West Washington Street, Hagerstown
301-790-3331

Tragara
SHELLEY AMSELLEM, WINE BUYER
4935 Cordell Avenue, Bethseda
301-951-4935

Boston College Club

100 Federal Street, 36th Floor
Boston, Massachusetts 02110
phone 617-946-2828 fax 617-345-9172

Shaun P. Hubbard
BEVERAGE MANAGER

WHAT IS ONE OF YOUR ULTIMATE FOOD AND WINE PAIRINGS?
Artichoke terrine with warm foie gras and truffle vinaigrette with Château
Mont-Redon Châteuneuf-du-Pape blanc 1998.

DESCRIBE YOUR WINE SELECTIONS.
It is a collaboration of efforts, staff input and exposure to outside influence
such as local wine tastings, reading materials and dining experiences.

WHAT ARE SOME OF YOUR FAVORITE WINE REGIONS IN THE WORLD
TODAY?
From Italy, the Piedmont region for reds, the Veneto for some floral whites. But
I also truly enjoy the Châteauneuf-du-Pape region of France for both red and
white wines.

WHAT LED YOU TO YOUR CURRENT POSITION?
The excitement and passion of experiencing and learning about the world of
wine and the pleasure of sharing that knowledge with family, friends, co-workers and guests.

WHAT ARE THE BEST ASPECTS OF YOUR JOB?
Expanding the horizons of others, getting people to try something new, which
is sometimes a challenge.

IF YOU WERE NOT IN THE WINE PROFESSION, WHAT WOULD YOU BE?
Captain of my own charter fishing boat.

Grille 23 & Bar

161 Berkeley Street
Boston, Massachusetts 02116
phone 617-542-2255 fax 617-542-5114
website www.grille23.com

Alicia R. Towns Franken
WINE DIRECTOR

DESCRIBE YOUR WINE SELECTIONS.
Our wine list has a selection of 900 wines with a focus on America and France.
On any given night, there are two to three sommeliers working the floor.

WHAT CATEGORIES OF WINE ARE THE BEST VALUES ON YOUR WINE LIST?
California Zinfandel, southern Rhône and South America.

WHAT IS YOUR FAVORITE WINE REGION IN THE WORLD TODAY?
Burgundy. It is so sensual. If I had to choose only one thing to drink for the
rest of my life, Burgundy would be it.

WHAT LED YOU TO YOUR CURRENT POSITION?
A bottle of Penfolds Grange.

WHAT IS THE BEST ASPECT OF YOUR JOB?
The relationships that are developed with vintners, peers and customers.

Lala Rokh on Beacon Hill

97 Mount Vernon Street
Boston, Massachusetts 02108
phone 617-720-5511 fax 617-720-0489

Babak Bina
GENERAL MANAGER AND CO-OWNER

WHAT ARE SOME OF YOUR ULTIMATE FOOD AND WINE PAIRINGS?
A German Riesling (von Hövel) with our pâté of olive and walnuts; Chalk Hill Estate Vineyard Selection Pinot Gris 1997 with our spinach, caramelized onion, yogurt and walnuts.

DESCRIBE YOUR WINE SELECTIONS.
Particular, concise and ever-changing.

WHAT IS YOUR FAVORITE WINE REGION IN THE WORLD TODAY?
Sonoma County. Dedication, while being relaxed about it.

WHAT LED YOU TO YOUR CURRENT POSITION?
The love of wine and food.

WHAT IS THE MOST CHALLENGING ASPECT OF YOUR JOB?
Keeping up with the vintages as well as new winemakers from around the world.

IF YOU WERE NOT IN THE WINE PROFESSION, WHAT WOULD YOU BE?
A professional polo player.

No. 9 Park
9 Park Street
Boston, Massachusetts 02108-4804
phone 617-742-9991 fax 617-742-9993

Catherine Silirie
WINE DIRECTOR

WHAT IS ONE OF YOUR ULTIMATE FOOD AND WINE PAIRINGS?
Wellfleet oysters and Louis Michel, Grossot or Raveneau Chablis.

DESCRIBE YOUR WINE SELECTIONS.
Our wine list is mostly French, Italian and American wines because our menu is based in these traditions. We pride ourselves on staff wine training (ten sommeliers are better than one).

WHAT IS YOUR FAVORITE WINE REGION IN THE WORLD TODAY?
Tuscany, for its natural and man-made beauty and for its straightforward cooking that goes so well with Chianti and Brunello.

WHAT LED YOU TO YOUR CURRENT POSITION?
Bacchus spoke to me in a dream and I was then determined to find my way in the trade.

WHAT IS THE MOST CHALLENGING ASPECT OF YOUR JOB?
Continued staff training; trying to keep servers constantly involved and enthusiastic.

IF YOU WERE NOT IN THIS PROFESSION, WHAT WOULD YOU BE DOING?
I would still find a way to be involved with wine, as it is my ultimate interest.

Olives

90 Main Street
Charlestown, Massachusetts 02129
phone 617-242-9715 fax 617-242-1333
website www.toddenglish.com

Glenn A. Tanner
WINE DIRECTOR AND SOMMELIER

WHAT ARE SOME OF YOUR ULTIMATE FOOD AND WINE PAIRINGS?
Todd's tuna tartare with Grüner Veltliner; soft-shell crab with big California Chardonnay; beef with Argentine Malbec.

DESCRIBE YOUR WINE SELECTIONS.
We offer a broad variety of wines, which we try to make user-friendly and accessible.

WHAT CATEGORY OF WINE IS THE BEST VALUE ON YOUR WINE LIST?
The "Other Red" section of the Olives' wine lists offers funky, delicious stuff that doesn't fit into mainstream varietal categories.

NAME A RECENT WINE DISCOVERY THAT EXCITED YOU.
Frank Potts' 1999 by Bleasdale Vineyards in South Australia. Delicious stuff and a ridiculous bargain.

WHAT IS YOUR FAVORITE WINE REGION IN THE WORLD TODAY?
Austria. I love Austrian wines.

WHAT LED YOU TO BECOME A SOMMELIER?
Love of food, wine and people. I enjoy turning people on to new tastes and flavors.

WHAT ARE THE BEST ASPECTS OF YOUR JOB?
Training staff, guest interaction and the theater of the floor.

IF YOU WERE NOT IN THIS PROFESSION, WHAT WOULD YOU BE DOING?
Teaching and writing.

75 Chestnut
F. GOODE, WINE BUYER
75 Chestnut Street, Boston
617-227-2175

Anthonys Pier 4
PETER HOLT, SOMMELIER
140 Northern Avenue, Boston
617-482-6262

Aujourd'hui at the Four Seasons Hotel
ALEX RIVEROS, MANAGER
AND WINE BUYER
200 Boylston Street, Boston
617-451-1392

The Bay Tower
ROBERT CZAJAK, WINE BUYER
60 State Street, Boston
617-723-1666

Biba
HEIDI MARCOULLIER, MANAGER
AND WINE BUYER
272 Boylston Street, Boston
617-426-7878

Black Rhino
MATT ROSSI, BAR MANAGER
21 Broad Street, Boston
617-263-0101

The Blue Room
DEANNA BRIGGS, WINE BUYER
1 Kendall Square, Cambridge
617-494-9034

Boston Harbor Hotel
DAVID LOWER, BEVERAGE MANAGER
70 Rowes Wharf, Boston
617-439-7000

Café Louis
PAUL LANG, WINE BUYER
234 Berkeley Street, Boston
617-266-4680

The Capital Grille
STEFANIE GERKEN, MANAGER
AND WINE BUYER
359 Newbury Street, Boston
617-262-8900

Clio at the Elliot Hotel
ED PETERSON, WINE BUYER
370 A Commonwealth Avenue, Boston
617-536-7200

L'Espalier
ERIK JOHNSON, SOMMELIER
30 Gloucester Street, Boston
617-262-3023

The Fairmont Copley Plaza
THOMAS MEDING, FOOD
AND BEVERAGE DIRECTOR
138 St. James Avenue, Boston
617-267-5300

The Federalist at Fifteen Beacon Hill
JAMES FLYNN, SOMMELIER
BRUNO MELLINI, WINE BUYER
AND SOMMELIER
Fifteen Beacon Street, Boston
617-670-1500

Four Seasons Hotel
PETER SZENDE, ASSISTANT FOOD
AND BEVERAGE DIRECTOR
200 Boylston Street, Boston
617-338-4400

Icarus

RACQUEL SCHWOLLOW, WINE STEWARD
3 Appleton Street, Boston
617-426-1790

Julien at the Meridien Boston

MAX COMPAGNON, WINE BUYER
250 Franklin Street, Boston
617-451-1900

Maison Robert

MONDETH PHAN, WINE BUYER
45 School Street, Boston
617-227-3370

Mistral

PAMELA SORBELLO, WINE BUYER
223 Columbus Avenue, Boston
617-867-9300

Plaza III

PAUL MCKEEVER, SOMMELIER
101 South Market Boulevard, Boston
617-720-5570

Prezza

DAVID PETRILLI, GENERAL MANAGER
AND WINE BUYER
24 Fleet Street, Boston
617-227-1577

Radius

MARCO DEARY, SOMMELIER
8 High Street, Boston
617-426-1234

Rialto

PATRICK DUBSKY, WINE BUYER
1 Bennett Street, Cambridge
617-661-5050

Salamander Restaurant

MORIYA BODIE, WINE BUYER
1 Huntington Avenue, Boston
617-451-2150

Seaport Hotel Boston

STEVE WOOD, WINE BUYER
1 Seaport Lane, Boston
617-385-4000

Seasons Restaurant at the Millennium Bostonian Hotel

SEAN WILCOX, FOOD
AND BEVERAGE DIRECTOR
6 Faneuil Hall Marketplace, Boston
617-523-3600

Somerset Club

A. DENNIS MICHEL, GENERAL
MANAGER AND WINE BUYER
42 Beacon Street, Boston
617-227-1731

Top of the Hub at the Prudential Center

RAPHAEL OLIVER, GENERAL MANAGER
AND WINE BUYER
800 Boylston Street, Boston
617-536-1775

True

KAREN DENSMORE, OWNER
AND WINE BUYER
560 Tremont Street, Boston
617-338-8070

The Vault Bistro & Wine Bar

PETER GREERTY, SOMMELIER
105 Water Street, Boston
617-292-9966

21 Federal

21 Federal Street
Nantucket, Massachusetts 02554
phone 508-228-2121 fax 508-228-2962
website www.21federal.net

Amber Stevens
FLOOR MANAGER AND WINE DIRECTOR

WHAT ARE SOME OF YOUR ULTIMATE FOOD AND WINE PAIRINGS?
Portobella mushroom with parmesan pudding served with Burgundy; grilled swordfish with mole, corn pudding and Pinot Noir; lamb and Pinot Noir; steak and Cabernet.

DESCRIBE YOUR WINE SELECTIONS.
Our selection consists of wines from classic vineyards of France, Italy and California, as well as selections from lesser-known wine regions in Spain, South Africa, New Zealand and Australia.

WHAT CATEGORIES OF WINE ARE THE BEST VALUES ON YOUR WINE LIST?
Spanish reds and South African Cabernets.

NAME RECENT WINE DISCOVERIES THAT HAVE EXCITED YOU.
California Meritages! It has been exciting to taste new styles and combinations of my favorite grapes.

WHAT IS YOUR FAVORITE WINE REGION IN THE WORLD TODAY?
Willamette Valley, Oregon, for its expanding Pinot Noirs and good value.

WHAT LED YOU TO YOUR CURRENT POSITION?
After years of managing 21 Federal, the opportunity arose to expand my position to include wine. My position is unique and now complete.

WHAT IS THE BEST ASPECT OF YOUR JOB?
Ensuring a pleasant experience for more than 200 customers nightly, from food to wine service.

IF YOU WERE NOT IN THE WINE PROFESSION, WHAT WOULD YOU BE DOING?
I would be involved in other aspects of the restaurant business.

Il Capriccio

888 Main Street
Waltham, Massachusetts 02453
phone 781-894-2234 fax 781-891-3227

Jeannie Rogers
CO-OWNER AND WINE BUYER

WHAT ARE SOME OF YOUR ULTIMATE FOOD AND WINE PAIRINGS?
Tagliatelle with white truffles and egg and Barolo; clam-stuffed calamari with 1999 Renato Keber Bianco Bel Grici, a blend from Collio; Tocai Friulano with mussels; calamaretti with Ribolla Gialla; white bean crostini with Chianti Classico.

DESCRIBE YOUR WINE SELECTIONS.
We specialize in northern Italian wines and offer wines from smaller wineries at realistic prices. Our selections are changed frequently.

WHAT CATEGORY OF WINE IS THE BEST VALUE IN YOUR RESTAURANT?
Chianti Classico.

NAME A RECENT WINE DISCOVERY THAT EXCITED YOU.
1999 Tenuta Migliavacca Barbera d'Asti: biodynamic, authentic, with incredible fruit.

WHAT IS YOUR FAVORITE WINE REGION IN THE WORLD TODAY?
Piedmont, because of its diversity and proximity to the Alps.

WHAT LED YOU TO BECOME A SOMMELIER?
I was waiting tables and became a sommelier because of my love for wine and travel.

WHAT IS THE BEST ASPECT OF YOUR JOB?
The interaction with customers and wine producers year after year.

IF YOU WERE NOT IN THIS PROFESSION, WHAT WOULD YOU BE DOING?
Working in a winery.

Cioppino's Restaurant

20 Broad Street
Nantucket, Massachusetts 02554
phone 508-228-4622 fax 508-228-2152
website www.cioppinos.com

Tracy W. Root
PROPRIETOR AND SOMMELIER

WHAT ARE SOME OF YOUR ULTIMATE FOOD AND WINE PAIRINGS?
Lobster tail and jumbo prawns over pesto linguini paired with Pinot Blanc from Alsace or California; braised lamb shanks and Syrah; ossobuco with Dolcetto d'Alba.

DESCRIBE YOUR WINE SELECTIONS.
Our selections are weighted to California wines.

WHAT CATEGORIES OF WINE ARE THE BEST VALUES ON YOUR WINE LIST?
California Cabernets and Syrahs.

WHAT IS YOUR FAVORITE WINE REGION IN THE WORLD TODAY?
Champagne. The people are just like their product, very bubbly.

WHAT LED YOU TO YOUR CURRENT POSITION?
I have been involved with wine since 1976. I was very interested in the wines from different regions, and the customs and styles of wines from Europe and America.

WHAT IS THE BEST ASPECT OF YOUR JOB?
Meeting all different types of people.

IF YOU WERE NOT IN THIS PROFESSION, WHAT WOULD YOU BE DOING?
Running a small Caribbean island!

Le Soir
51 Lincoln Street
Newton Highlands, Massachusetts 02461
phone 617-965-3100 fax 617-964-5069
website www.lesoirbistro.com

Paul Westerkamp
SOMMELIER

WHAT ARE SOME OF YOUR ULTIMATE FOOD AND WINE PAIRINGS?
Lobster and fennel profiterole with wine from Alsace or Chalk Hill Pinot Gris;
pan-roasted monkfish with red Burgundy; rabbit pot pie with Sonoma old vine
Zinfandel; crispy napoleon of panna cotta with caramelized cherries and cherry
sorbet with a late-harvest Riesling.

DESCRIBE YOUR WINE SELECTIONS.
We specialize in and focus on red Burgundy and American Pinot Noir.

WHAT CATEGORIES OF WINE ARE THE BEST VALUES ON YOUR WINE LIST?
Red Burgundy and Pinot Noir from California.

NAME RECENT WINE DISCOVERIES THAT HAVE EXCITED YOU.
Italian wines from established Italian grapes being made with modern techniques.

WHAT IS YOUR FAVORITE WINE REGION IN THE WORLD TODAY?
Italy.

WHAT LED YOU TO BECOME A SOMMELIER?
Love of food and wine.

WHAT IS THE BEST ASPECT OF YOUR JOB?
The most challenging and rewarding aspects are one and the same; introducing
guests to a food and wine match and then to see the excitement in their faces.

IF YOU WERE NOT IN THIS PROFESSION, WHAT WOULD YOU BE?
A cheesemaker.

Topper's at The Wauwinet

120 Wauwinet Road
Nantucket, Massachusetts 02584
phone 508-228-0145 fax 508-228-6712
website www.wauwinet.com

Craig R. Hanna
CELLAR MASTER

MASSACHUSETTS, OTHER

WHAT ARE SOME OF YOUR ULTIMATE FOOD AND WINE PAIRINGS?
Seared foie gras with peach-pepper jam with sweet Loire white wine; Beluga caviar with tête-de-cuvée Champagne.

DESCRIBE YOUR WINE SELECTIONS.
We have a 1,400-item wine list, specializing in Burgundy, the Rhône, Champagne and half-bottles. We also feature a six-course wine tasting menu.

WHAT CATEGORIES OF WINE ARE THE BEST VALUE ON YOUR WINE LIST?
Provence, southern France, Alsace and Spain.

NAME RECENT WINE DISCOVERIES THAT HAVE EXCITED YOU.
The wines of Austria, Switzerland and the French mountainside for their great pairing with indigenous cuisine.

WHAT IS YOUR FAVORITE WINE REGION IN THE WORLD TODAY?
The northern Rhône Valley for the history of the region, the beauty of the city of Lyon and the fabulous dining. The severe vineyards which yield great wines.

WHAT LED YOU TO BECOME A SOMMELIER?
Love of wine, love of restaurant guests and love of matching food and wine.

WHAT ARE THE BEST ASPECTS OF YOUR JOB?
Finding new (or old) and exciting wines for knowledgeable guests to try. Also, I enjoy the personal contact with everyone involved in the wine business.

IF YOU WERE NOT IN THE WINE PROFESSION, WHAT WOULD YOU BE?
A chef—or doing car restoration.

Brant Point Grill at the White Elephant

TERRY JOHNSON, SOMMELIER

50 Easton Street, Nantucket Island

508-325-1320

The Chantecleer Inn

JEAN-CHARLES BERRUET, WINE BUYER

9 New Street, Siasconset

508-257-6231

The Daniel Webster Inn

RICHARD CATANIA, WINE BUYER

WALLY BLANCHETTE, SOMMELIER

149 Main Street, Sandwich

508-888-3622

Flora

JOE ANTOUN, WINE BUYER

190 Massachusetts Avenue, Arlington

781-641-1664

The Pearl

DAVID LOWER, SOMMELIER

12 Federal Street, Nantucket

508-228-9622

Silks at Stonehedge Inn

MICHAEL OTAKA, SOMMELIER

160 Pawtucket Boulevard, Tyngsboro

978-649-4400

Skipjack's

JEFFREY SENIOR, WINE BUYER

154 Wells Avenue, Newton

617-232-8887

Wheatleigh

NICOLAS BAUDIC, SOMMELIER

Hawthorne Road, Lenox

413-637-0610

Big Rock Chop House

245 South Eton
Birmingham, Michigan 48009
phone 248-647-7774 fax 248-647-2103
website www.bigrockchophouse.com

Keith R. Walsh
FLOOR MANAGER AND SOMMELIER

WHAT ARE SOME OF YOUR ULTIMATE FOOD AND WINE PAIRINGS?
Beef Wellington with southern Rhône; a fourteen-ounce, bone-in filet with Cabernet Sauvignon; calamari with Chardonnay; potato-encrusted salmon with Pinot Noir; walnuts and Roquefort with Sauternes; veal Marsala with Barolo; sushi with Alsace Riesling or German Spätlese Riesling; consommé with Fino Sherry; dark chocolate with high-end California Cabernet Sauvignon.

DESCRIBE YOUR WINE SELECTIONS.
A modern chophouse wine list with a large selection of California Cabernets, Merlots and Chardonnays supplemented with a reserve list of more traditional Bordeaux, Burgundy, Italian and up-and-coming West Coast varietal wines.

WHAT CATEGORY OF WINE IS THE BEST VALUE ON YOUR WINE LIST?
Older vintages of Burgundy, Bordeaux, Champagne and California wine.

NAME RECENT WINE DISCOVERIES THAT HAVE EXCITED YOU.
Australian Shiraz, for its depth and complexity in top releases; California Port-style wine made from Cabernet.

WHAT IS YOUR FAVORITE WINE REGION IN THE WORLD TODAY?
France, because of the history and culture behind the wines.

WHAT LED YOU TO BECOME A SOMMELIER?
A serious hobby became a profession when a great opportunity to become involved in an aggressive restaurant wine program became a reality.

WHAT ARE THE BEST ASPECTS OF YOUR JOB?
Personal interaction with the guests, the opportunity to taste great wines, the ongoing education and the knowledge gained from working with some of the area's best professionals.

IF YOU WERE NOT IN THIS PROFESSION, WHAT WOULD YOU BE?
A singer and songwriter.

Café Cortina

30715 West Ten Mile Road
Farmington Hills, Michigan 48025
phone 248-474-3033 fax 248-474-9064
website www.cafecortina.com

Adriano L. Tonon
OWNER, MAÎTRE D' AND SOMMELIER

WHAT ARE SOME OF YOUR ULTIMATE FOOD AND WINE PAIRINGS?
Gnocchetti con funghi selvatici with Pinot Grigio or Chalk Hill Chardonnay; Amarone with meats; Barolo with pasta; Chardonnay or Pinot Grigio with fish.

DESCRIBE YOUR WINE SELECTIONS.
We specialize in Italian wines, but offer some wonderful American (California, Michigan) wines, as well.

WHAT CATEGORIES OF WINE ARE THE BEST VALUES ON YOUR WINE LIST?
Sangiovese and California Cabernet Sauvignon.

NAME A RECENT WINE DISCOVERY THAT EXCITED YOU.
Carpineto Chianti Classico. I am not an avid Chianti connoisseur, but Carpineto is a delightful discovery.

WHAT IS YOUR FAVORITE WINE REGION IN THE WORLD TODAY?
We are very biased toward Italian wines, but California wines are my personal favorites.

WHAT LED YOU TO BECOME A SOMMELIER?
A passion for food, wine and Italian hospitality.

WHAT IS THE BEST ASPECT OF YOUR JOB?
Creating lifelong memories for our cherished clientele.

IF YOU WERE NOT IN THE WINE PROFESSION, WHAT WOULD YOU BE?
An actor or rock star. I enjoy the art of entertainment.

The Lark

6430 Farmington Road
West Bloomfield, Michigan 48322
phone 248-661-4466 fax 248-661-8891
website www.thelark.com

James D. Lark

PROPRIETOR, MAÎTRE D' AND SOMMELIER

WHAT ARE SOME OF YOUR ULTIMATE FOOD AND WINE PAIRINGS?
Rich Alsace Gewürztraminer with foie gras; Banyuls Grand Cru with chocolate; top Pouilly-Fuissé with soft-shell crab; red Bordeaux with rack of lamb; great Sauternes with foie gras or Roquefort cheese; Chablis with oysters on the half shell; Pinot Noir with pheasant; Barolo with venison; Cabernet Sauvignon with beef.

DESCRIBE YOUR WINE SELECTIONS.
More than 1,000 selections from Australia, France, Germany, Italy, Portugal, Spain and the United States; a carefully chosen selection of classic wines such as Bordeaux, Burgundies, Champagnes, Barolos and Portos, and a collection of the most sought-after wines.

WHAT CATEGORIES OF WINE ARE THE BEST VALUES IN YOUR RESTAURANT?
Red Côtes-du-Rhône and the white wines of Alsace.

NAME RECENT WINE DISCOVERIES THAT HAVE EXCITED YOU.
Australian Shirazs, for their quality and pricing; Oregon Pinot Noirs from 1998 and 1999 are good quality and reasonably priced.

WHAT IS YOUR FAVORITE WINE REGION IN THE WORLD TODAY?
Burgundy, because of the unique and unsurpassed wines, the beauty of the countryside, its fine restaurants and the hospitality of its vintners.

WHAT LED YOU TO YOUR CURRENT POSITION?
My love of food and wine led me to open my own restaurant in 1981.

WHAT IS THE BEST ASPECT OF YOUR JOB?
Matching a fine wine to the taste of our patrons, the food they have ordered and their pocket-book.

IF YOU WERE NOT IN THIS PROFESSION, WHAT WOULD YOU BE DOING?
Travel writing.

No. VI Chophouse at the Hotel Baronette

27790 Novi Road
Novi, Michigan 48377
phone 248-305-5210 fax 248-646-0379
website www.uniquerestaurants.com

Richard G. Rubel
WINE MANAGER AND SOMMELIER

WHAT ARE SOME OF YOUR ULTIMATE FOOD AND WINE PAIRINGS?
Austrian Grüner Veltliner and seviche; medium-rare New York strip au poivre and Châteauneuf-du-Pape or Gigondas.

DESCRIBE YOUR WINE SELECTIONS.
Our list focuses on California Cabernet, but we offer 275 choices from several countries, including France, Italy, Australia, Argentina, Chile and New Zealand, as well as from Washington, Oregon and Michigan in the USA.

WHAT CATEGORY OF WINE IS THE BEST VALUE ON YOUR WINE LIST?
Red Burgundy. A favorite category, but not one that gets tremendous attention in a steakhouse, which I try to change by offering them at wonderful prices.

NAME RECENT WINE DISCOVERIES THAT HAVE EXCITED YOU.
Southern Rhône Valley. Every time I taste the wines in groups, the values are stunning, considering the quality and how food-friendly they are!

WHAT IS YOUR FAVORITE WINE REGION IN THE WORLD TODAY?
Alsace. I was smitten while looking down at the villages from the steep vineyards of Rangen. And it has such "pure" wines.

WHAT LED YOU TO BECOME A SOMMELIER?
Meeting Master Sommelier Madeline Triffon and seeing how a passion can become a career.

WHAT ARE THE BEST ASPECTS OF YOUR JOB?
Holding special event dinners and going so far beyond our guests' expectations that they are mesmerized.

IF YOU WERE NOT IN THIS PROFESSION, WHAT WOULD YOU BE DOING?
Building handcrafted wooden sailboats.

Northern Lakes Seafood

39475 North Woodward Avenue
Bloomfield Hills, Michigan 48305
phone 248-646-7900 fax 248-646-8148
website www.uniquerestaurants.com

Michelle DeHayes

GENERAL MANAGER AND SOMMELIER

WHAT ARE SOME OF YOUR ULTIMATE FOOD AND WINE PAIRINGS?
Seared rare ahi tuna with grilled portobella mushrooms paired with Pinot Noir; grilled George's Banks sea scallops paired with Sauvignon Blanc; oysters and Grüner Veltliner.

DESCRIBE YOUR WINE SELECTIONS.
The menu has the wine list on the back and changes daily. The list is focused on quality wines to pair with our seafood. The selection is international; a grouping of quality wines from Europe, the USA, South America, New Zealand and Australia.

WHAT CATEGORY OF WINE IS THE BEST VALUE ON YOUR WINE LIST?
We strive to have great values in every category.

NAME RECENT WINE DISCOVERIES THAT HAVE EXCITED YOU.
Austrian Grüner Veltliner—it presents great value and unique qualities; Old World and New World Rhône-style wines.

WHAT IS YOUR FAVORITE WINE REGION IN THE WORLD TODAY?
Burgundy. I love the differences and complexities among its wines.

WHAT LED YOU TO BECOME A SOMMELIER?
Working with a restaurant owner who has an informal, eclectic approach to wine and a great palate.

WHAT ARE THE BEST ASPECTS OF YOUR JOB?
Every day is different. Tasting wine with new guests or familiar faces makes my day.

IF YOU WERE NOT IN THIS PROFESSION, WHAT WOULD YOU BE DOING?
I studied biology in college but stayed with restaurants to avoid the nine-to-five lab job!

Tapawingo

9502 Lake Street
Ellsworth, Michigan 49729
phone 231-588-7971 fax 231-588-6175
website www.tapawingo.net

Ron Edwards

MANAGER AND SOMMELIER

WHAT ARE SOME OF YOUR ULTIMATE FOOD AND WINE PAIRINGS?
Sushi-style fish paired with German Riesling; spice-cured salmon with
Grüner Veltliner; artichoke and tomato broth with dry French rosé; foie gras
and cherry reduction with Black Muscat; morel mushrooms with Mosel Riesling;
tuna with red wine veal reduction and Syrah; aged ewes' milk cheese with Shiraz.

DESCRIBE YOUR WINE SELECTIONS.
We have committed to a large wine list of both esoteric and mainstream wines
from leading wine regions of the world. Our challenge to the guests is to never
drink a wine that they already know.

WHAT CATEGORIES OF WINE ARE THE BEST VALUES IN YOUR RESTAURANT?
Spanish wines and German Riesling.

NAME RECENT WINE DISCOVERIES THAT HAVE EXCITED YOU.
German Riesling—there's no better value in white wine; Red Burgundy from
Bernard Dugat-Py; dry reds of Douro Valley.

WHAT IS YOUR FAVORITE WINE REGION IN THE WORLD TODAY?
Burgundy. The elegance and finesse of great Burgundy is awe-inspiring. Trying
to grasp the region is daunting.

WHAT LED YOU TO BECOME A SOMMELIER?
I worked as a waiter through engineering school and fell in love with wine.
Then I met Madeline Triffon, M.S., at a tasting.

WHAT ARE THE BEST ASPECTS OF YOUR JOB?
Watching that "lightbulb" go on in people's eyes when they have a new wine
experience.

IF YOU WERE NOT IN THE WINE PROFESSION, WHAT WOULD YOU BE?
An engineer, but I sure hope it never comes to that.

Bravo! Restaurant & Bar

STEPHANIE LARSEN, SOMMELIER

5402 Portage, Portage

616-344-7700

Giovanni's Ristorante

RANDY TRUANT, WINE BUYER

330 South Oakwood Boulevard, Detroit

313-841-0122

Golden Mushroom

BRIAN CISLO, SOMMELIER

18100 West Ten Mile Road, Southfield

248-559-4230

Morel's

MADELINE TRIFFON, MASTER
SOMMELIER

30100 Telegraph Road, Bingham Farms

248-642-1094

Opus One

CHARLES FATER, MAÎTRE D'
AND WINE STEWARD

565 East Larned Street, Detroit

313-961-7766

Rattlesnake Club

KIRBY POPE, SOMMELIER
JIMMY SCHMIDT, OWNER
AND WINE BUYER
David Mazella, Sommelier

300 River Place, Detroit

313-567-4400

Rowe Inn

KURT VAN SUMEREN, WINE BUYER
AND SOMMELIER

6303 Country Road, Ellsworth

231-588-7351

La Belle Vie
312 South Main Street
Stillwater, Minnesota 55082
phone 651-430-3545 fax 651-430-3519

Sean Q. Meyer
SOMMELIER

WHAT IS ONE OF YOUR ULTIMATE FOOD AND WINE PAIRINGS?
Seared foie gras with Roquefort bread pudding, Port and cherries with Au Bon Climat 1998 Pinot Mondeuse (Pinot Noir, Mondeuse blend).

DESCRIBE YOUR WINE SELECTIONS.
Our list reflects the regional focus of the cuisine. Currently, I am striving for more vintage depth throughout the Rhône and Spain. We also offer wine flights with the chef's tasting menus.

WHAT IS YOUR FAVORITE WINE REGION IN THE WORLD TODAY?
The northern Rhône, because of the wonderful variety of the wines. I don't think I could ever tire of Condrieu or Hermitage blanc for whites, or the power and finesse of Côte Rôtie.

WHAT LED YOU TO BECOME A SOMMELIER?
Simply, a passion for wine. I also love the interaction with people. Pairing wine and food is an all-consuming passion.

WHAT IS THE MOST CHALLENGING ASPECT OF YOUR JOB?
Creating vintage depth in our wine program while maintaining a very tight inventory.

IF YOU WERE NOT IN THE WINE PROFESSION, WHAT WOULD YOU DO?
Sing professionally or go into holistic health.

Goodfellow's

40 South Seventh Street
Minneapolis, Minnesota 55402
phone 612-332-4800 fax 612-332-1274
website www.goodfellowsrestaurant.com

Martina M. Priadka
MANAGER AND SOMMELIER

WHAT ARE SOME OF YOUR ULTIMATE FOOD AND WINE PAIRINGS?
Marsanne/Viognier blends with our poke (a sushi-grade fish, diced and tossed with sesame oil and other seasonings) and carpaccios; Pinot Noirs with our game consommé with rabbit Wellington and truffles.

DESCRIBE YOUR WINE SELECTIONS.
With more than 800 selections, we offer one of the largest exclusively domestic wine lists in the world, which complements the restaurant's American menu. Our eight-course chef's tasting menu has a flight of wines chosen to match each course.

WHAT CATEGORIES OF WINE ARE THE BEST VALUES ON YOUR WINE LIST?
Any of the blending grapes, such as Mourvèdre, Marsanne, Cabernet Franc and the Rhône blends.

NAME RECENT WINE DISCOVERIES THAT HAVE EXCITED YOU.
David Bruce wines. They are consistent, high quality and affordable.

WHAT IS YOUR FAVORITE WINE REGION IN THE WORLD TODAY?
Spain. It is producing not only great wines but also great wines at reasonable prices.

WHAT LED YOU TO BECOME A SOMMELIER?
I had a career in writing in mind, but my passion for food and wine pairing took over.

WHAT ARE THE BEST ASPECTS OF YOUR JOB?
Putting together our monthly wine dinners and choosing wines to pair with our tasting menus. It is rewarding to watch people enjoy the flavor interaction and know that I have created a memorable experience.

IF YOU WERE NOT IN THE WINE PROFESSION, WHAT WOULD YOU BE DOING?
Writing, both fiction and articles on food and wine.

Lord Fletcher's

3746 Sunset Drive
Spring Park, Minnesota 55384-0446
phone 952-471-8513 fax 952-471-8937
website www.lordfletchers.com

Steve M. Michalski
SOMMELIER

WHAT ARE SOME OF YOUR ULTIMATE FOOD AND WINE PAIRINGS?
Jumbo diver sea scallops with pancetta bacon, Yukon gold potatoes and bell peppers with Dijon mustard paired with Rhône white wine or New World Chardonnay; cast iron–seared beef tenderloin medallions with lobster meat ravioli and ricotta cheese, grilled asparagus spears and hollandaise sauce paired with Bordeaux or California Cabernet; vine-ripened tomatoes and goat cheese salad with Sancerre; Dijon-encrusted lamb and Yukon gold potatoes with Rhône red; barbecued ribs with California Zinfandel or Australian Shiraz; Argentina steak with Argentina Malbec.

DESCRIBE YOUR WINE SELECTIONS.
We have two wine lists: a short list which is well-stocked with familiar wines, and a reserve list for our Chart Room which is literally a book.

WHAT CATEGORIES OF WINE ARE THE BEST VALUES ON YOUR WINE LIST?
"Periphery" French wine regions, such as the Loire Valley, Provence and Beaujolais.

NAME RECENT WINE DISCOVERIES THAT HAVE EXCITED YOU.
Cassis from Provence, Malbec from Argentina and Saumur-Champigny rouge from the Loire Valley.

WHAT IS YOUR FAVORITE WINE REGION IN THE WORLD TODAY?
France, because of the tremendous diversity of its wines and their exceptional compatibility with food.

WHAT LED YOU TO BECOME A SOMMELIER?
Wine became a passion.

WHAT ARE THE BEST ASPECTS OF YOUR JOB?
Encouraging conservative customers to try new and unfamiliar wines.

IF YOU WERE NOT IN THE WINE PROFESSION, WHAT WOULD YOU BE DOING?
Something in international business.

D'Amico Cucina
BILL SUMMERVILLE, WINE BUYER
100 North Sixth Street, Minneapolis
612-338-2401

St. Paul Grill
at St. Paul Hotel
SCOTT IDA, WINE BUYER
350 Market Street, St. Paul
651-224-7455

Bravo! Restaurant and Bar

LESLEY TOLAR, SOMMELIER
244 Highland Village, Jackson
601-982-8111

American Restaurant

2450 Grand Boulevard
Kansas City, Missouri 64108
phone 816-426-1133 fax 816-426-1190

James A. Andrews
SOMMELIER AND
ASSISTANT GENERAL MANAGER

WHAT IS ONE OF YOUR ULTIMATE FOOD AND WINE PAIRINGS?
Dark bittersweet chocolate desserts with Brachetto d'Acqui.

DESCRIBE YOUR WINE SELECTIONS.
Our list offers 1,500 selections with an emphasis on California Cabernets and Bordeaux. We also really focus on education. The wine list opens with a section that covers wine basics, and we offer wine classes to our guests. Our staff attends weekly wine training sessions.

WHAT IS YOUR FAVORITE WINE REGION IN THE WORLD TODAY?
Italy. The variety of wines produced there is astounding. Italian wines are some of the world's most distinctive and pair well with food.

WHAT LED YOU TO BECOME A SOMMELIER?
After twenty-two years in fine dining, I fell in love with wine and began to study it. I was hired to run the first wine program here eight years ago.

WHAT IS THE MOST CHALLENGING ASPECT OF YOUR JOB?
Keeping up with current developments in the industry and educating my staff about them. The world of wine is constantly evolving and always changing.

IF YOU WERE NOT IN THE WINE PROFESSION, WHAT WOULD YOU BE DOING?
Making art and running a gallery.

Annie Gunn's
16806 Chesterfield Airport Road
Chesterfield, Missouri 63005
phone 636-532-7684 fax 636-532-0561

Patricia D. Wamhoff
ADVANCED SOMMELIER
Team: Glenn Bardgett, Wine Director

WHAT ARE SOME OF YOUR ULTIMATE FOOD AND WINE PAIRINGS?

Fresh seafood with Pinot Noir; dry-aged prime beef selections with Cabernet Sauvignon or Bordeaux-style red; loin of venison with huckleberry sauce paired with Châteauneuf-du-Pape; foie gras with several late-harvest wines; fresh berries and crème brûlée with demi-sec Champagne; freshly grilled John Dory with white Rhône; lamb shanks or foie gras with 1998 Dolce; house-cured smoked salmon with Veuve Clicquot Yellow Label Brut Champagne.

DESCRIBE YOUR WINE SELECTIONS.

We feature 623 wines, both American and imported, on our wine list and nearly forty wines by the glass.

WHAT CATEGORY OF WINE IS THE BEST VALUE ON YOUR WINE LIST?

Bordeaux petits châteaux, classified growths and second-label wines. In every category of our list we offer values as well as highly respected wines.

NAME RECENT WINE DISCOVERIES THAT HAVE EXCITED YOU.

Spanish wines, which have an exciting and impressive mix of New World and Old World characteristics; and Australian wines, which are incredibly food-friendly.

WHAT IS YOUR FAVORITE WINE REGION IN THE WORLD TODAY?

Spain, because of the innovation and quality improvements within the industry.

WHAT LED YOU TO BECOME A SOMMELIER?

A career change and my love of food and wine.

WHAT IS THE BEST ASPECT OF YOUR JOB?

Turning a customer onto something new.

IF YOU WERE NOT IN THE WINE PROFESSION, WHAT WOULD YOU BE DOING?

I have no idea.

The Blue Heron
Highway HH
Lake Ozark, Missouri 65049
phone 573-365-4646 fax 573-365-5743

Joseph H. Boer
OWNER AND OPERATOR

WHAT ARE SOME OF YOUR ULTIMATE FOOD AND WINE PAIRINGS?
Abalone with late-harvest Riesling; smoked lamb rack with old vine Zinfandel.

DESCRIBE YOUR WINE SELECTIONS.
We have more than 1,600 wines from all over the world, in vintages from 1935 to 2001. We strive to have a well-informed and knowledgeable staff.

WHAT CATEGORY OF WINE IS THE BEST VALUE ON YOUR WINE LIST?
Beaujolais.

NAME A RECENT WINE DISCOVERY THAT EXCITED YOU.
Lava Cap 1997 Zinfandel, because of its depth.

WHAT IS YOUR FAVORITE WINE REGION IN THE WORLD TODAY?
Napa Valley. The wines have depth, dependability and marketability. Its labels are appealing and informative.

WHAT LED YOU TO YOUR CURRENT POSITION?
My father and brother both were in the restaurant business in Holland. My father was sommelier at the Hotel des Indes in Den Haag, Holland.

WHAT IS THE BEST ASPECT OF YOUR JOB?
Meeting and pleasing many different types of customers. Sometimes it is a challenge, but I am rewarded with each response.

IF YOU WERE NOT IN THIS PROFESSION, WHAT WOULD YOU BE?
A dentist or architect.

The Grill at the Ritz-Carlton Saint Louis

100 Carondelet Plaza
Clayton, Missouri 63105
phone 314-863-6300 fax 314-863-7486
website www.ritzcarlton.com

Jonathan J. Burge
SOMMELIER
Team: Adriane Lawlor, Wine Buyer

WHAT ARE SOME OF YOUR ULTIMATE FOOD AND WINE PAIRINGS?
Thai spiced lobster bisque and Champagne; foie gras and Sauternes; spicy dishes and Champagne; blue cheese and Port.

DESCRIBE YOUR WINE SELECTIONS.
We offer 1,000 selections, and our strength is in California and Bordeaux. We have twenty-five wines by the glass and fifty half-bottles.

WHAT CATEGORY OF WINE IS THE BEST VALUE ON YOUR WINE LIST?
German Riesling.

NAME RECENT WINE DISCOVERIES THAT HAVE EXCITED YOU.
Australian Riesling, Sauvignon Blanc and Semillon.

WHAT IS YOUR FAVORITE WINE REGION IN THE WORLD TODAY?
Rhône Valley for its constant quality.

WHAT LED YOU TO BECOME A SOMMELIER?
My love of wine and the pairing of food and wine.

IF YOU WERE NOT IN THIS PROFESSION, WHAT WOULD YOU BE?
A used car salesman.

Saint Louis Club

7701 Forsyth Boulevard
St. Louis, Missouri 63105
phone 314-726-1964 fax 314-862-5528

John E. Sears
SOMMELIER

WHAT ARE SOME OF YOUR ULTIMATE FOOD AND WINE PAIRINGS?
Daube de marcassin (wild boar in red wine) and fine red Bordeaux, Brunello di
Montalcino or mature Châteauneuf-du-Pape; batata cinnamon-rubbed duck
breast, fresh cherry and Pinot Noir sauce and molasses johnnycakes with savory
ricotta filling, paired with California Pinot Noir.

DESCRIBE YOUR WINE SELECTIONS.
We have an excellent, worldly representation with very extensive selections from
France and California.

WHAT CATEGORY OF WINE IS THE BEST VALUE ON YOUR WINE LIST?
Spanish wines.

WHAT IS YOUR FAVORITE WINE REGION IN THE WORLD TODAY?
Alsace, for its outstanding Rieslings and Pinot Gris.

WHAT LED YOU TO BECOME A SOMMELIER?
I have been interested in cuisine and beverages from an early age.

WHAT ARE THE BEST ASPECTS OF YOUR JOB?
Interaction with clientele and gratification from well-received wine recommendations.

IF YOU WERE NOT A SOMMELIER, WHAT WOULD YOU BE DOING?
Exclusive, private, upscale catering, specializing in very small, exotic dinner
parties.

Trattoria Marcella
3600 Watson Road
St. Louis, Missouri 63109-1232
phone 314-352-7706 fax 314-352-0848

Blake Shelton
SOMMELIER

WHAT ARE SOME OF YOUR ULTIMATE FOOD AND WINE PAIRINGS?
Braised veal cheeks with semolina gnocchi and Italian parsley salad paired with
Claudio Alario Dolcetto di Diano d'Alba "Costa Fiore"; pan-seared sweetbreads
with Champagne; ossobuco with Barolo or Barbaresco; foie gras with Pinot
Noir or Sauternes.

DESCRIBE YOUR WINE SELECTIONS.
We have a broad selection of Italian wines and a strong emphasis on California
wine from Monterey to Lake County.

WHAT CATEGORY OF WINE IS THE BEST VALUE ON YOUR WINE LIST?
Piedmont wines, especially Dolcetto and Barbera. They offer great quality and
are not yet overpriced.

NAME A RECENT WINE DISCOVERY THAT EXCITED YOU.
Falesco Merlot from Umbria. The wine has the complexity of a Pomerol, with
good extraction, for less than forty dollars.

WHAT IS YOUR FAVORITE WINE REGION IN THE WORLD TODAY?
Vosne-Romanée in Burgundy. It is a magical place that produces the world's
most majestic wines.

WHAT LED YOU TO BECOME A SOMMELIER?
When I discovered Burgundy, it changed my whole perspective on wine and
the industry. A passion arose.

WHAT IS THE BEST ASPECT OF YOUR JOB?
Being able to introduce common restaurant diners to new wines that they per-
haps have never seen or tasted.

IF YOU WERE NOT IN THE WINE PROFESSION, WHAT WOULD YOU BE
DOING?
Something in the music business or radio, unless I was on the PGA tour.

630 North and South Restaurant
JOSEPH KING, WINE BUYER
630 North and South, University City
314-863-6013

Café Allegro
STEVE COLE, WINE BUYER
1815 West 39th Street, Kansas City
816-561-3663

Eau
TOM SUTLIFF, WINE BUYER
212 North Kings Highway, St. Louis
314-454-9000

Grand St. Café
DENNIS DICKEY, WINE BUYER
4740 Grand Street, Kansas City
816-561-8000

JJ's
MATT NICHOLS, GENERAL MANAGER
AND WINE BUYER
910 West 48th Street, Kansas City
816-561-7136

The Potted Steer Restaurant
JOSEPH BOER, OWNER AND OPERATOR
5085 Highway 54, Osage Beach
573-348-5053

Starker's Restaurant
CLIFF BATH, OWNER
AND WINE BUYER
201 West 47th Street, Kansas City
816-753-3565

Tony's Restaurant
VINCENT BOMMARITO, OWNER
AND WINE BUYER
410 Market Street, St. Louis
314-231-7007

Buck's T-4 Lodge

46621 Gallatin Road
Big Sky, Montana 59716
phone 406-995-4111 fax 406-995-2191
website www.buckst4.com

David R. O'Connor
GENERAL MANAGER

WHAT ARE SOME OF YOUR ULTIMATE FOOD AND WINE PAIRINGS?
Pheasant consommé and Sauvignon Blanc; smoked Montana trout with Burgundy; New Zealand red deer and Petite Sirah.

DESCRIBE YOUR WINE SELECTIONS.
Our list focuses on rich and full reds that match our menu's emphasis on wild game. We also regularly offer winemaker dinners and special tastings.

WHAT CATEGORIES OF WINE ARE THE BEST VALUES ON YOUR WINE LIST?
California Zinfandel and Syrah.

NAME RECENT WINE DISCOVERIES THAT HAVE EXCITED YOU.
Ribera del Duero Arzuaga Reserva, for its tremendous complexity and richness at the price; Bonny Doon Malvasia, for its intriguing flavor profile.

WHAT IS YOUR FAVORITE WINE REGION IN THE WORLD TODAY?
Spain, for the richness, depth, complexity and personality of the wines.

WHAT LED YOU TO BECOME A SOMMELIER?
Wine was always part of dinner growing up. I've always had a love of wine.

WHAT IS THE BEST ASPECT OF YOUR JOB?
I most enjoy conducting classes and leading tastings.

IF YOU WERE NOT IN THIS PROFESSION, WHAT WOULD YOU BE DOING?
I'd be part of the wine industry, on the production side.

Greenlee's at the Pollard

DARCY KELLY, MANAGER
AND WINE BUYER
2 North Broadway, Red Lodge
406-446-0001

Alizé at the Top of the Palms
4321 West Flamingo Road
Las Vegas, Nevada 89103
phone 702-951-7000 fax 702-951-7002

Hank Maglia
WINE DIRECTOR

WHAT ARE SOME OF YOUR ULTIMATE FOOD AND WINE PAIRINGS?
Rack of lamb with Pommard; Dover sole with Alsatian white; veal cheeks or bison with Rhône varietals.

DESCRIBE YOUR WINE SELECTIONS.
We have an extensive wine list, with a range of prices. We try our best to give customers the best wines for the money.

WHAT CATEGORY OF WINE IS THE BEST VALUE ON YOUR WINE LIST?
Burgundy.

WHAT ARE THE BEST ASPECTS OF YOUR JOB?
Introducing a customer to a new wine or a new region and having them return to tell me what a great discovery that was.

WHAT ARE THE MOST CHALLENGING ASPECTS OF YOUR JOB?
Wines are always changing and new wines are always coming out.

IF YOU WERE NOT DOING WHAT YOU ARE, WHAT WOULD YOU DO?
Operating a combination of a small bistro and wine cellar.

André's French Restaurant at the Monte Carlo

3770 Las Vegas Boulevard South
Las Vegas, Nevada 89109
phone 702-798-7151 fax 702-798-7175

Steve Pregman
SOMMELIER

WHAT ARE SOME OF YOUR ULTIMATE FOOD AND WINE PAIRINGS?
Foie gras with Sauternes; steak with red Bordeaux.

DESCRIBE YOUR WINE SELECTIONS.
World-class, with an emphasis on French and California wines.

WHAT CATEGORIES OF WINE ARE THE BEST VALUES ON YOUR WINE LIST?
Bordeaux and Burgundy reds.

NAME RECENT WINE DISCOVERIES THAT HAVE EXCITED YOU.
Big Australian Cabernet Sauvignons and Shirazs. They have huge, lush fruit and are relative bargains for their intensity.

WHAT IS YOUR FAVORITE WINE REGION IN THE WORLD TODAY?
Tuscany, for its beauty and its part in my heritage. The wines are rich, elegant and complex.

WHAT LED YOU TO BECOME A SOMMELIER?
A career change and love of wine led me from being a patron to a performer.

WHAT IS THE BEST ASPECT OF YOUR JOB?
Providing people with a grand experience.

IF YOU WERE NOT IN THE WINE PROFESSION, WHAT WOULD YOU BE?
A movie star.

Aureole at the Mandalay Bay Resort

3950 Las Vegas Boulevard South
Las Vegas, Nevada 89119
phone 702-632-7401 fax 702-632-7425
website www.ewinetower.com

Andrew Bradbury
WINE DIRECTOR
Team: Jason Wade, Sommelier

WHAT IS ONE OF YOUR ULTIMATE FOOD AND WINE PAIRINGS?
Pizza and Zinfandel.

DESCRIBE YOUR WINE SELECTIONS.
We have an international wine list on the world's first Internet-based web tablet.

WHAT CATEGORY OF WINE IS THE BEST VALUE ON YOUR WINE LIST?
German Riesling.

NAME RECENT WINE DISCOVERIES THAT HAVE EXCITED YOU.
Spain and Italy. They're making some great wine that are also great wine values.

WHAT IS YOUR FAVORITE WINE REGION IN THE WORLD TODAY?
Austria. It can compete with the great wines of the world at sensible prices.

WHAT LED YOU TO YOUR CURRENT POSITION?
I have been in the "biz" since I was twelve. I kind of stumbled into it.

WHAT ARE THE BEST ASPECTS OF YOUR JOB?
Learning (always), great customers, and committed staff.

IF YOU WERE NOT IN THIS PROFESSION, WHAT WOULD YOU BE DOING?
Scuba diving in warm, tropical waters.

Charlie Palmer Steak House at Four Seasons Hotel

3960 Las Vegas Boulevard South
Las Vegas, Nevada 89119
phone 702-632-5000 fax 702-632-5195

Tamir Shanel

FOOD AND BEVERAGE DIRECTOR
Team: Jason Wade, Wine Director and Sommelier

WHAT ARE SOME OF YOUR ULTIMATE FOOD AND WINE PAIRINGS?
Lamb carpaccio centered with confit of leg of lamb balanced with a sauce of wine and micro greens paired with de Montille's 1997 Pommard Les Pezerolles. A selection from the cheese cart paired with 1977 Dow's vintage Port.

DESCRIBE YOUR WINE SELECTIONS.
Our wine list offers a New World vs. Old World approach. Because our food is French, so are many of our wines, including an extensive range of Bordeaux. We have forty-five Ports by the glass.

WHAT CATEGORIES OF WINE ARE THE BEST VALUES ON YOUR WINE LIST?
Australian and Washington state wines.

NAME A RECENT WINE DISCOVERY THAT EXCITED YOU.
I tasted an Oregon wine that I had helped make. It was great to be a part of the process; almost addictive.

WHAT IS YOUR FAVORITE WINE REGION IN THE WORLD TODAY?
I've been most impressed with the quality of wine coming from Australia.

WHAT LED YOU TO YOUR CURRENT POSITION?
I found wine to be the most interesting expression of biology and chemistry, along with a little alchemy.

WHAT IS THE BEST ASPECT OF YOUR JOB?
Being part of the process, when a guest recognizes quality in wine and gets really excited. I am often asked to write down the name of the wine and where to find more wines like it.

IF YOU WERE NOT IN THIS PROFESSION, WHAT WOULD YOU BE DOING?
Biodynamic farming, in the Pacific Northwest, probably in vineyards.

China Grill at Mandalay Bay Resort

3950 Las Vegas Boulevard South
Las Vegas, Nevada 89119
phone 702-632-7404 fax 702-632-6906

Steve M. Moberly
RESTAURANT MANAGER AND SOMMELIER
Team: Steve Torgason, Wine Buyer

WHAT ARE SOME OF YOUR ULTIMATE FOOD AND WINE PAIRINGS?
Grilled, dry-aged Szechuan beef with three- to five-year-old California Cabernet Sauvignon; ginger and panko–crusted Chilean sea bass with South Australian Chardonnay; sizzling striped bass with California Sauvignon Blanc; five spice–blackened tenderloin with California Zinfandel.

DESCRIBE YOUR WINE PROGRAM.
Wine is fun and we want our guests to feel comfortable making their selections.

WHAT CATEGORY OF WINE IS THE BEST VALUE IN YOUR RESTAURANT?
California Cabernet Sauvignon.

NAME RECENT WINE DISCOVERIES THAT HAVE EXCITED YOU.
Australian Cabernet Sauvignon and Shiraz, blockbusters without blockbuster prices.

WHAT IS YOUR FAVORITE WINE REGION IN THE WORLD TODAY?
Australia. It is producing high-quality Cabernet Sauvignon and Shiraz (two of our favorite varietals) with modest prices.

WHAT LED YOU TO YOUR CURRENT POSITION?
Wine began as a hobby. Eventually, I decided it would be nice to be paid for my hobby.

WHAT ARE THE BEST ASPECTS OF YOUR JOB?
Getting paid to do something I love and being able to taste many different kinds of wines as part of my work.

IF YOU WERE NOT IN THIS PROFESSION, WHAT WOULD YOU BE?
A professional guide for rock climbing, hiking, mountaineering and mountain biking.

Delmonico's Steakhouse at the Venetian Hotel

3355 Las Vegas Boulevard South
Las Vegas, Nevada 89109
phone 702-414-3737 fax 702-414-3838

Kevin M. Vogt
MASTER SOMMELIER

WHAT IS ONE OF YOUR ULTIMATE FOOD AND WINE PAIRINGS?
Delmonico's bone-in rib steak with Chave Hermitage 1990. The light Creole seasoning pairs exceptionally with this Rhône Valley wonder. Sometimes the simplest pairings are the best.

DESCRIBE YOUR WINE SELECTIONS.
We currently have more than 850 selections on our list, which is heavily weighted toward big California, French and Spanish wines.

WHAT IS YOUR FAVORITE WINE REGION IN THE WORLD TODAY?
The Rhône Valley in France has such a diverse range of wines that can suit almost any palate. Several of my favorite wines are Rhône Valley selections.

WHAT LED YOU TO BECOME A SOMMELIER?
My assumption was that if I chose a career doing something I love, that I would perform better than doing something less desirable. So far, so good.

WHAT ARE THE MOST CHALLENGING ASPECTS OF YOUR JOB?
Keeping wines in stock. We sell 300–400 cases a month. We have to reprint and update our wine list weekly to keep up with out-of-stock wines and new selections.

IF YOU WERE NOT IN THIS PROFESSION, WHAT WOULD YOU BE DOING?
A computer software engineer. It was my first degree plan. At the time, I didn't have the patience to sit in front of a keyboard all day.

Emeril's New Orleans Fish House at the MGM Grand

3799 Las Vegas Boulevard South
Las Vegas, Nevada 89109
phone 702-891-7777 fax 702-891-7338
website www.emerils.com

James T. O'Neil
SOMMELIER

WHAT ARE SOME OF YOUR ULTIMATE FOOD AND WINE PAIRINGS?
Emeril's barbecue shrimp with German Rieslings; scallops and foie gras sauce with Pinot Gris from Alsace.

DESCRIBE YOUR WINE SELECTIONS.
We have more than 700 rare and eclectic wines from all over the world on our wine list. Most of these wines are from small producers. More than half the selections are wines priced from $25 to $100.

WHAT CATEGORIES OF WINE ARE THE BEST VALUES ON YOUR WINE LIST?
German whites and Spanish reds.

NAME RECENT WINE DISCOVERIES THAT HAVE EXCITED YOU.
Red Riojas from the 1994 vintage. They can be as exciting as great, aged red Burgundy at a fraction of the price.

WHAT IS YOUR FAVORITE WINE REGION IN THE WORLD TODAY?
The Mosel River region in Germany. No other wines display terroir like those from the Mosel.

WHAT LED YOU TO BECOME A SOMMELIER?
I felt that combining my favorite pastime with a career choice would help lead me to success in life.

IF YOU WERE NOT A SOMMELIER, WHAT WOULD YOU BE?
An attorney or chef.

Galena Forest Inn

17025 Mount Rose Highway
Reno, Nevada 89503
phone 775-849-2100 fax 775-786-1314
website www.galenaforestrestaurant.com

Craig S. Cunningham
OWNER AND WINE MANAGER

WHAT ARE SOME OF YOUR ULTIMATE FOOD AND WINE PAIRINGS?
Wild boar with blackberries and golden chanterelles paired with Syrah
(Hermitage); black walnuts and Roquefort cheese paired with Sauternes.

DESCRIBE YOUR WINE SELECTIONS.
We have approximately 250 wines on our list. Most of our wines are from
California, but we also have representations from France, Italy, Spain, Australia
and Oregon.

WHAT CATEGORIES OF WINE ARE THE BEST VALUES IN YOUR RESTAU-
RANT?
Australian and Spanish wines.

NAME A RECENT WINE DISCOVERY THAT EXCITED YOU.
Karly's Sadie Upton Zinfandel, which demonstrates the full potential of
Zinfandel from the Shenandoah Valley of Amador County. Great intensity of
fruit and a good value.

WHAT IS YOUR FAVORITE WINE REGION IN THE WORLD TODAY?
The Rhône Valley in France, for its earthy Syrahs and Grenache-based wines
with their jammy flavors and great pricing.

WHAT LED YOU TO BECOME A SOMMELIER?
A love of wine and food, and my role in the front of the house in this restaurant.

WHAT ARE THE BEST ASPECTS OF YOUR JOB?
Interacting with great people on a nightly basis and sending them away with a
new favorite food and wine pairing.

IF YOU WERE NOT IN THIS PROFESSION, WHAT WOULD YOU BE DOING?
Architecture and design (commercial and residential buildings).

Hugo's Cellar at the Four Queens Hotel

202 Fremont Street
Las Vegas, Nevada 89101
phone 702-385-4011 fax 702-387-5120
website www.fourqueens.com

Vincent K. Wiggins
SOMMELIER

WHAT ARE SOME OF YOUR ULTIMATE FOOD AND WINE PAIRINGS?

"Queens Lobster" with sun-dried tomatoes and mushrooms, beurre blanc, and crushed red peppers with Pinot Blanc; salmon with herb butter and classic Chardonnay; grilled veal chop with Pinot Noir; a thick New York strip steak with crushed peppercorn and garlic paired with Sangiovese.

DESCRIBE YOUR WINE SELECTIONS.

Our 250-item wine list concentrates on an array of Californian, French and Italian wines, with selections from several other countries, as well.

WHAT CATEGORY OF WINE IS THE BEST VALUE ON YOUR WINE LIST?

South American wines. They offer a huge variety of wines and styles at great prices.

WHAT IS YOUR FAVORITE WINE REGION IN THE WORLD TODAY?

Burgundy, for its Pinot Noir grape, which come in a wide variety of styles. Pinot Noir is one of the most food-friendly varietals.

WHAT LED YOU TO BECOME A SOMMELIER?

I have a food and beverage management background, and while living in Northern California, I was surrounded by avid wine enthusiasts.

WHAT ARE THE BEST ASPECTS OF YOUR JOB?

Turning guests on to new varietals and then, on later visits, having them tell me those varietals have become their favorites.

IF YOU WERE NOT IN THE WINE PROFESSION, WHAT WOULD YOU BE DOING?

Music. I was a drummer and singer in a Bay Area rock and funk band and I still sit in with a few local bands. How does it go? "Wine, women and song!"

Lone Eagle Grille at Lake Tahoe Hyatt Regency Hotel

111 Country Club Drive
Incline Village, Nevada 89451
phone 775-832-1234 fax 775-831-7508
website www.hyatttahoe.com

Robert Vicale
SENIOR SOMMELIER

WHAT ARE SOME OF YOUR ULTIMATE FOOD AND WINE PAIRINGS?
Lamb with Pinot Noir; certified Angus filet with peppercorn demi-glace with Cabernet Sauvignon; rack of venison with lingonberry demi-glace with Pinot Noir; grilled ahi with Pinot Noir; fresh oysters with Sauvignon Blanc; veal chop with Merlot.

DESCRIBE YOUR WINE SELECTIONS.
Our selections are exclusively from North America, except for "bubbles," where we also have some Champagnes. We are known for our Cabernets, Merlots and blends, with extensive selections from Napa Valley, Sonoma County and Carneros.

WHAT CATEGORY OF WINE IS THE BEST VALUE IN YOUR RESTAURANT?
Napa Cabernet Sauvignon.

NAME RECENT WINE DISCOVERIES THAT HAVE EXCITED YOU.
The red varietals of Amador County, California.

WHAT IS YOUR FAVORITE WINE REGION IN THE WORLD TODAY?
Napa Valley, California. The wines are food-friendly, evolving and made from a wide range of varieties.

WHAT LED YOU TO BECOME A SOMMELIER?
Wine was my father's only hobby. He imparted his love for it to me.

WHAT ARE THE BEST ASPECTS OF YOUR JOB?
Introducing our guests to new and different wines, keeping the list at its best with all the new competition and watching the enjoyment on the part of the guests.

IF YOU WERE NOT IN THIS PROFESSION, WHAT WOULD YOU BE?
A teacher of Greek and Roman mythology.

MGM Grand Hotel

3799 Las Vegas Boulevard South
Las Vegas, Nevada 89109
phone 702-891-7116 fax 702-891-7330
website www.mgmgrand.com

Patricia Beck
HOTEL SOMMELIER

WHAT IS ONE OF YOUR ULTIMATE FOOD AND WINE PAIRINGS?
Steak with big reds from California and Australia.

DESCRIBE YOUR WINE SELECTIONS.
The wine selections in each restaurant are geared to each menu. The wine lists
vary greatly, but include mainstream, well-known wines with a range of exciting, eclectic choices.

WHAT CATEGORY OF WINE IS THE BEST VALUE ON YOUR WINE LISTS?
California Zinfandel. The flavors can be so full and rich or deliciously subtle.
No Cabernet can touch it at the price.

NAME RECENT WINE DISCOVERIES THAT HAVE EXCITED YOU.
Chile and Argentina are producing knockout reds. Malbec is one of my new
favorites.

WHAT IS YOUR FAVORITE WINE REGION IN THE WORLD TODAY?
Spain. The diversity of styles and grapes can match any style of food or any
mood.

WHAT LED YOU TO BECOME A SOMMELIER?
I became obsessed with wine while I was a bartender at a major casino. My
manager at the time challenged me to become a sommelier.

WHAT IS THE BEST ASPECT OF YOUR JOB?
I love taking people who are uncomfortable with wine to the point where their
fear turns into curiosity and inspiration.

IF YOU WERE NOT IN THIS PROFESSION, WHAT WOULD YOU BE?
A singer, specializing in oldies rock and roll.

MGM Grand Hotel

3799 Las Vegas Boulevard South
Las Vegas, Nevada 89109
phone 702-891-7777 fax 702-891-7330
website www.mgmgrand.com

Kim Beto
DIRECTOR OF BEVERAGE

WHAT ARE SOME OF YOUR ULTIMATE FOOD AND WINE PAIRINGS?
Banyuls and chocolate; Sauternes and Stilton.

DESCRIBE YOUR WINE SELECTIONS.
We have various programs at MGM. Individual restaurants have different wine programs. There are some amazing wines on the hotel's reserve list.

NAME RECENT WINE DISCOVERIES THAT HAVE EXCITED YOU.
Priorat in Spain. Insane wines! Alvaro Palacios is awesome.

WHAT IS YOUR FAVORITE WINE REGION IN THE WORLD TODAY?
Champagne. Incredible history and great food and wine. Also, both Alsace and Burgundy, which produce phenomenal wines.

WHAT LED YOU TO YOUR CURRENT POSITION?
I've loved wine since I was very young. My father introduced me to wine and Fred Dame got me "hooked."

WHAT ARE THE BEST ASPECTS OF YOUR JOB?
Seeing someone selling or talking about something you showed them. Developing people.

IF YOU WERE NOT IN THIS PROFESSION, WHAT WOULD YOU BE?
A tennis player.

Morton's of Chicago Las Vegas

400 East Flamingo Road
Las Vegas, Nevada 89109
phone 702-893-0703 fax 702-893-3020

Pierre A. Gendebien
ASSISTANT MANAGER AND SOMMELIER

WHAT ARE SOME OF YOUR ULTIMATE FOOD AND WINE PAIRINGS?
Filet Oskar with a well-defined Cabernet; scallops wrapped in bacon with a spicy apricot chutney paired with Zinfandel.

DESCRIBE YOUR WINE SELECTIONS.
We offer a very diverse selection of wines to our guests. Red wines dominate our offerings, since we are a steakhouse.

WHAT CATEGORY OF WINE IS THE BEST VALUE ON YOUR WINE LIST?
Pinot Noirs.

NAME RECENT WINE DISCOVERIES THAT HAVE EXCITED YOU.
Australian wines. They offer quality for great value.

WHAT IS YOUR FAVORITE WINE REGION IN THE WORLD TODAY?
France. It offers so many different terroirs and wines that pair well with food.

WHAT LED YOU TO BECOME A SOMMELIER?
I grew up in a European family and wine was always part of our lives. It grew into a passion.

WHAT IS THE BEST ASPECT OF YOUR JOB?
People. From guests to vendors, people make my job challenging and very rewarding.

IF YOU WERE NOT IN THIS PROFESSION, WHAT WOULD YOU DO?
Become a pilot and travel the world.

Olives at the Bellagio Resort

3600 Las Vegas Boulevard South
Las Vegas, Nevada 89109
phone 702-693-1111 fax 702-693-8511

Tammie W. Ruesenberg
SOMMELIER

WHAT IS ONE OF YOUR ULTIMATE FOOD AND WINE PAIRINGS?
Spicy tuna tartare with Domaines Schlumberger 1998 Pinot Gris from Alsace.

DESCRIBE YOUR WINE SELECTIONS.
We pour twenty premier wines by the glass and have a 300-item wine list, which includes wines from around the world. We also have access to the Bellagio master list of another 900 wines.

WHAT IS YOUR FAVORITE WINE REGION IN THE WORLD TODAY?
California. I love the New World style of the wines, as do most of our guests.

WHAT LED YOU TO BECOME A SOMMELIER?
I had worked both in the restaurant industry and as a sales rep for a wine distributor.

WHAT IS THE MOST CHALLENGING ASPECT OF YOUR JOB?
Being able to buy wines I want to keep on our list. Many are in short supply.

IF YOU WERE NOT IN THIS PROFESSION, WHAT WOULD YOU BE DOING?
I just can't imagine doing anything else.

Osteria Del Circo at the Bellagio Resort

3600 Las Vegas Boulevard South
Las Vegas, Nevada 89109
phone 702-693-8150 fax 702-693-8512

Joseph P. Phillips
SOMMELIER
Team: Paolo Barbieri, Sommelier; Patrick Pretz, Sommelier

WHAT IS ONE OF YOUR ULTIMATE FOOD AND WINE PAIRINGS?
A cold glass of Gewürztraminer from Alsace with a 110-degree summer day in Las Vegas.

DESCRIBE YOUR WINE SELECTIONS.
We have many selections from several of the world's great wine regions, but our Italian section really shines, especially the Piedmont and Tuscany selections.

WHAT IS YOUR FAVORITE WINE REGION IN THE WORLD TODAY?
Alsace. I find the aromatics and body of Alsace whites intriguing. I've also got my eyes (and nose) on Austria.

WHAT LED YOU TO BECOME A SOMMELIER?
Early in my restaurant career, in order to answer the many wine questions I received from guests, I bought a book about wine. One book led to another.

WHAT IS THE BIGGEST CHALLENGE IN YOUR JOB?
Finding just the right wine to match a customer's taste and dining needs.

Pamplemousse

400 East Sahara Avenue
Las Vegas, Nevada 89104-2612
phone 702-733-2066 fax 702-739-7885
website www.pamplemousserestaurant.com

Reggie King
SOMMELIER
Team: Georges La Forge, Wine Buyer

WHAT ARE SOME OF YOUR ULTIMATE FOOD AND WINE PAIRINGS?
Roast duckling with a green peppercorn sauce and California Cabernet; salmon with an orange and curry recipe with Loire Valley white wine; shrimp diablo with California Chardonnay; veal medallions and sauce moutarde with California Sauvignon Blanc.

DESCRIBE YOUR WINE SELECTIONS.
I select primarily California and French wines to match our French menu. Currently, we offer more than sixty French and seventy California wines.

WHAT CATEGORY OF WINE IS THE BEST VALUE ON YOUR WINE LIST?
California Cabernet Sauvignon.

NAME A RECENT WINE DISCOVERY THAT EXCITED YOU.
Robert Sinskey Pinot Noir Reserve. An excellent value for such fine quality.

WHAT IS YOUR FAVORITE WINE REGION IN THE WORLD TODAY?
Burgundy. White Burgundies are simply my favorite.

WHAT LED YOU TO BECOME A SOMMELIER?
We don't serve spirits in this restaurant, so it was imperative to develop my wine knowledge if I wanted to advance.

WHAT IS THE BEST ASPECT OF YOUR JOB?
Trying to create and improve upon new wine pairings for our unique menu items.

IF YOU WERE NOT A SOMMELIER, WHAT WOULD YOU BE DOING?
Bartending or management.

Renoir at the Mirage Hotel

3400 Las Vegas Boulevard South
Las Vegas, Nevada 89109
phone 702-791-7353 fax 702-791-7437
website www.mirage.com

Stewart G. Patchefsky
WINE DIRECTOR AND SOMMELIER

WHAT ARE SOME OF YOUR ULTIMATE FOOD AND WINE PAIRINGS?
Sautéed foie gras with Tokaji Aszú; salads that combine fresh apples or pears
with Roquefort cheese and German Kabinett Riesling.

DESCRIBE YOUR WINE SELECTIONS.
We have a classical wine list, with approximately 650 selections, that focuses on
quality French and Californian wines.

WHAT CATEGORY OF WINE IS THE BEST VALUE ON YOUR WINE LIST?
German wines. Germany offers some perfectly balanced wines that are also
modestly priced.

NAME A RECENT WINE DISCOVERY.
I have come to realize that the wine industry, or shall I say community, is much
smaller than I had first anticipated.

WHAT IS YOUR FAVORITE WINE REGION IN THE WORLD TODAY?
Champagne. I love the history, the people and, most of all, the wine.

WHAT LED YOU TO BECOME A SOMMELIER?
When I was a waiter at The Phoenician Resort in Arizona, I became fascinated
with the sommelier position. It was obviously the best job in the resort. After
attending an organized wine trip to Napa Valley, I knew that I would become a
sommelier.

WHAT IS THE BEST ASPECT OF YOUR JOB?
The exposure I have to such a wide range of interesting people. I learn so much
about life from other people's experiences.

IF YOU WERE NOT IN THIS PROFESSION, WHAT WOULD YOU BE DOING?
Real estate.

Rosemary's Restaurant

8125 West Sahara Avenue
Las Vegas, Nevada 89117
phone 702-869-2251 fax 702-869-2283
website www.rosemarysrestaurant.com

Amy D. Smith

SOMMELIER

WHAT ARE SOME OF YOUR ULTIMATE FOOD AND WINE PAIRINGS?
Prosciutto-wrapped figs stuffed with goat cheese with Gewürztraminer; pan-seared honey glazed salmon with Pinot Gris from Alsace; crispy-skin striped bass, potato hash, hush puppies and Creole meunière sauce with California Zinfandel.

DESCRIBE YOUR WINE SELECTIONS.
We focus on American wines, predominantly California wines. But we also have a very good half-bottle list, and are broadening our imported wine selections.

WHAT CATEGORIES OF WINE ARE THE BEST VALUES ON YOUR WINE LIST?
Sauvignon Blanc and nontraditional red varietals such as Petite Sirah and Dolcetto.

NAME RECENT WINE DISCOVERIES THAT HAVE EXCITED YOU.
Wines from southern France and areas of the United States such as New York, Virginia and Texas, because of their value and unique styles.

WHAT ARE YOUR FAVORITE WINE REGIONS IN THE WORLD TODAY?
Northern Italy and the Rhône. Both have a wide variety of varietals and styles, and the wines go so well with food.

WHAT LED YOU TO BECOME A SOMMELIER?
A dining experience at Emeril's in New Orleans. The sommelier paired a wine with every course and opened a whole new world to me.

WHAT ARE THE BEST ASPECTS OF YOUR JOB?
Meeting people from all walks of life, educating myself and others about wine, debunking misconceptions, and meeting and working with people who love what they do.

IF YOU WERE NOT IN THIS PROFESSION, WHAT WOULD YOU BE DOING?
Three-day eventing, gemologist, enologist.

Valentino Las Vegas at the Venetian

3355 Las Vegas Boulevard South
Las Vegas, Nevada 89109
phone 702-414-3000 fax 702-414-3099

Steven Hua
SOMMELIER

WHAT ARE SOME OF YOUR ULTIMATE FOOD AND WINE PAIRINGS?
Truffle and super-Piedmont red (Barbera, Nebbiolo, Dolcetto blend); cheese and Amarone.

DESCRIBE YOUR WINE SELECTIONS.
We have a large selection of Italian wines (800 labels on a 1,700-label list). We are working on becoming the second-best list in this country, after Valentino Ristorante in Santa Monica.

WHAT CATEGORY OF WINE IS THE BEST VALUE ON YOUR WINE LIST?
Piedmont red, especially the blends.

NAME A RECENT WINE DISCOVERY THAT EXCITED YOU.
Super-Piedmont blends. Nebbiolo and Barbera yield wines of great character and balance.

WHAT IS YOUR FAVORITE WINE REGION IN THE WORLD TODAY?
California, and Napa in particular. The opulence of fruit and body is unequaled anywhere else.

WHAT LED YOU TO BECOME A SOMMELIER?
After fifteen years of working as a captain and server, I decided to concentrate on wine in order to maximize my knowledge.

WHAT ARE THE BEST ASPECTS OF YOUR JOB?
Tasting and talking about wine that most people have only heard or read about.

IF YOU WERE NOT IN THIS PROFESSION, WHAT WOULD YOU BE?
A computer geek.

Andre's

HANK MAGLIA, WINE DIRECTOR
401 South Sixth Street, Las Vegas
702-385-5016

Aqua at the Bellagio Resort

CALEB DIAL, SOMMELIER
OLIVER WHARTON, WINE BUYER
CHRISTOPHE ROLLAND, SOMMELIER
3600 Las Vegas Boulevard South,
Las Vegas
702-693-7111

Caesars Palace

LISA LEROUX, BEVERAGE DIRECTOR
3570 Las Vegas Boulevard South,
Las Vegas
702-731-7110

Caesars Tahoe

DIANE DOMINGUEZ,
PROPERTY SOMMELIER
55 Highway 50, Lake Tahoe
775-588-3515

Chinois Las Vegas at the Forum Shops at Caesars

LUIS DE SANTOS, MASTER SOMMELIER
AND DIRECTOR OF WINE
3500 Las Vegas Boulevard South,
Las Vegas
702-737-9700

Crown Point Restaurant at Gold Hill Hotel

NICK FAIN, BEVERAGE MANAGER
1540 South Main, Gold Hill
775-847-0111

Del Frisco's Double Eagle Steak House

STEPHEN WALKER, SOMMELIER
3925 Paradise Road, Las Vegas
702-796-0063

Eiffel Tower Restaurant at the Paris Resort

DEANA ERICKSON, SOMMELIER
GULNARA JANZ, SOMMELIER
3655 Las Vegas Boulevard, Las Vegas
702-948-6937

Ferraro's

MICHAEL SCHWAB, WINE STEWARD
5900 West Flamingo Road, Las Vegas
702-364-5300

Fiore Rotisserie & Grille

DAVID EVERETT, SOMMELIER
3700 West Flamingo Road, Las Vegas
702-252-7702

Llewellyn's at Harvey's

CHERYL ATTANASIO, WINE BUYER
GREG PSILOPOULOS, SOMMELIER
U.S. Highway 50 & Stateline Avenue,
Stateline
775-588-2411

Mayflower Cuisinier

THERESA WOO, MANAGER
AND WINE BUYER
4750 West Sahara, Suite 27, Las Vegas
702-870-8432

The Mirage

BART MAHONEY, VICE PRESIDENT
FOOD AND BEVERAGE
3400 Las Vegas Boulevard South,
Las Vegas
702-791-7370

Picasso at the Bellagio Resort

JAY JAMES, MASTER SOMMELIER
AND WINE DIRECTOR
ROBERT SMITH, SOMMELIER
3600 Las Vegas Boulevard South, Las Vegas
702-693-7111

Pinot Brasserie at the Venetian Resort

RICHARD DOUGLAS, SOMMELIER
LUIS DE SANTOS, MASTER SOMMELIER
3355 Las Vegas Boulevard South, Las Vegas
702-735-8888

Postrio at the Venetian Resort

LUIS DE SANTOS, MASTER SOMMELIER
AND WINE DIRECTOR
3377 Las Vegas Boulevard South, Las Vegas
702-796-1110

Prime at the Bellagio Resort

JASON QUINN, ASSISTANT SOMMELIER
JOHN BURKE, SOMMELIER
3600 Las Vegas Boulevard South, Las Vegas
702-693-7223

Rio Suite Hotel & Casino

KEN MEHAN, BEVERAGE DIRECTOR
3700 West Flamingo Road, Las Vegas
702-252-7777

Roxy's at the El Dorado Hotel

ALAIN GREGOIRE, MAÎTRE D'
345 North Virginia Street, Reno
800-648-5966

Smith & Wollensky

MICHAEL KENNEDY, CELLAR MASTER
3767 Las Vegas Boulevard South, Las Vegas
702-862-4100

Spago Las Vegas at the Forum Shops at Caesars

LUIS DE SANTOS, DIRECTOR OF WINE
AND MASTER SOMMELIER
3500 Las Vegas Boulevard South, Las Vegas
702-369-6300

Trattoria del Lupo at the Mandalay Bay Resort

LUIS DE SANTOS, MASTER SOMMELIER
AND WINE DIRECTOR
3950 Las Vegas Boulevard South, Las Vegas
702-740-5522

Treasure Island at the Mirage

RICK GOLDSTEIN, FOOD AND
BEVERAGE DIRECTOR
3400 Las Vegas Boulevard South, Las Vegas
702-894-7111

White Orchid

JIM MORITZ, FOOD AND
BEVERAGE DIRECTOR
JOHN SANDERS, MAÎTRE D'
AND WINE BUYER
2707 South Virginia Street, Reno
775-689-7300

The 1785 Inn Restaurant

CHARLES MALLAR, OWNER
AND SOMMELIER
Route 16 at the Scenic Vista,
North Conway
603-356-9025

Kingston 1686 House

MARLENE GILLESPIE, OWNER
AND WINE BUYER
127 Main Street, Kingston
603-642-3637

Ya Mama's

MICHELLE FERRAZANNI, OWNER
AND WINE BUYER
75 Daniel Webster Highway, Merrimack
603-578-9201

The Bernards Inn

27 Mine Brook Road
Bernardsville, New Jersey 07924
phone 908-766-0002 fax 908-766-4604
website www.bernardsinn.com

Terri A. Baldwin
WINE DIRECTOR AND SOMMELIER

WHAT ARE SOME OF YOUR ULTIMATE FOOD AND WINE PAIRINGS?

New York dry-aged sirloin with a Bordeaux Cabernet blend; roast squab with Pinot Noir; oysters with spinach and saffron with Sauvignon Blanc; sautéed tuna with Pinot Noir; lobster with cream sauce and Chardonnay; chocolate raspberry torte with raspberry dessert wine or sweet Brachetto; roast duck and red Meritage.

DESCRIBE YOUR WINE SELECTIONS.

We feature more than 655 selections from around the world on our wine list and another twenty-five choices by the glass. We also have a large selection of half-bottles and large-format bottles.

WHAT CATEGORY OF WINE IS THE BEST VALUE ON YOUR WINE LIST?

New Zealand Sauvignon Blancs. Great juice that pairs extremely well with food.

NAME RECENT WINE DISCOVERIES THAT HAVE EXCITED YOU.

Grüner Veltliners and Zweigelts from Austria; New Zealand Sauvignon Blancs and Pinot Noirs.

WHAT IS YOUR FAVORITE WINE REGION IN THE WORLD TODAY?

Burgundy, especially the Côte de Nuits.

WHAT LED YOU TO BECOME A SOMMELIER?

While working in restaurants, I became interested in wine and began attending tastings.

WHAT IS THE BEST ASPECT OF YOUR JOB?

Moving customers away from what they normally drink and turning them on to new and exciting wines.

IF YOU WERE NOT A SOMMELIER, WHAT WOULD YOU BE DOING?

Affiliated with the restaurant business as I love food, wine and people.

Fromagerie

26 Ridge Road
Rumson, New Jersey 07760
phone 732-842-8088 fax 732-842-6625

Markus Peter

OWNER AND SOMMELIER

WHAT ARE SOME OF YOUR ULTIMATE FOOD AND WINE PAIRINGS?
Seared foie gras and vanilla compote with Alois Kracher 1997 Beerenauslese
from Austria.

DESCRIBE YOUR WINE SELECTIONS.
Our wine list has many selections from California and reflects my interest in
white and red Burgundies, but the rest of the world can be tasted here, too.

WHAT IS YOUR FAVORITE WINE REGION IN THE WORLD TODAY?
Alsace. I love the food and the wines, and the towns and villages are beautiful.

WHAT LED YOU TO BECOME A SOMMELIER?
Winery visits to Burgundy, Germany, Alsace, Bordeaux and California.

WHAT IS THE MOST CHALLENGING ASPECT OF YOUR JOB?
Not being able to help every customer with his wine selection. I want everyone
to get the most enjoyment from their experience here.

IF YOU WERE NOT IN THE WINE PROFESSION, WHAT WOULD YOU BE?
Travel writer.

Diamond's

TOMMY ZACHETTI, WINE BUYER

132 Kent Street, Trenton

609-393-1000

The Dining Room at Hilton Short Hills

ISAAC ALEXANDER, SOMMELIER

41 JFK Parkway, Short Hills

973-379-0100

Grand Café

DESMOND LLOYD, WINE BUYER

42 Washington Street, Morristown

973-540-9444

The Manor

MIKE CAMARANO, WINE BUYER

KURT KNOWLES, WINE BUYER

111 Prospect Avenue, West Orange

973-731-2360

Panico's

JOSE SOLANO, WINE BUYER

103 Church Street, New Brunswick

732-545-6100

Park and Orchard

BUDDY GEBHARDT, OWNER
AND WINE BUYER

240 Hackensack Street, East Rutherford

201-939-9292

The Ryland Inn

CRAIG SHELTON, CHEF, OWNER
AND WINE BUYER

Route 22, Whitehouse

908-534-4011

Verve American Bar & Restaurant

EDWARD WALSH, SOMMELIER

18 East Main Street, Somerville

908-707-8655

Billy Crews Dining Room

1200 Country Club Road
Santa Teresa, New Mexico 88008
phone 505-589-2071 fax 505-589-9463
website www.billycrews.com

Billy Crews
OWNER AND WINE BUYER

WHAT IS ONE OF YOUR ULTIMATE FOOD AND WINE PAIRINGS?
Great steak with a great wine.

DESCRIBE YOUR WINE SELECTIONS.
We have 2,200 wines on our list, including many of the world's finest, with an emphasis on Cabernet Sauvignon and Bordeaux.

WHAT CATEGORIES OF WINE ARE THE BEST VALUES ON YOUR WINE LIST?
Wines from Australia and Chile.

NAME RECENT WINE DISCOVERIES THAT HAVE EXCITED YOU.
Many small French châteaus are now producing quality wines at good prices.

WHAT IS YOUR FAVORITE WINE REGION IN THE WORLD TODAY?
All regions are making great wines now. It is really hard to choose one.

WHAT LED YOU TO YOUR CURRENT POSITION?
I inherited the family restaurant. Because of my love for wine, I wanted to learn more about food and wine pairing and build a more extensive wine list.

WHAT IS THE BIGGEST CHALLENGE IN YOUR JOB?
Keeping the wine list current and the waitstaff informed.

IF YOU WERE NOT IN THIS PROFESSION, WHAT WOULD YOU BE DOING?
Hunting, fishing, and drinking good wine.

Coyote Café

QUINN STEPHENSON,
BEVERAGE MANAGER
132 West Water Street, Santa Fe
505-983-1615

Hilton Inn Albuquerque

LORETTA GUZMAN, GENERAL MANAGER
AND WINE BUYER
1901 University Boulevard East,
Albuquerque
505-884-2500

Alain Ducasse
at Essex House

155 West 58th Street
New York, New York 10019
phone 212-265-5535 fax 212-265-5200

Pieter J. Verheyde

CHEF AND SOMMELIER
Team: Gerard Margeon, Wine Director

DESCRIBE YOUR WINE SELECTIONS.
Three-dimensional: age, country and style in a harmonized presentation.

WHAT ARE YOUR FAVORITE WINE REGIONS IN THE WORLD TODAY?
Northern Italy, Switzerland and Austria.

WHAT LED YOU TO BECOME A SOMMELIER?
Perfumes.

WHAT IS THE MOST CHALLENGING ASPECT OF YOUR JOB?
A complete and correct wine list that is balanced in age and taste and proportion.

IF YOU WERE NOT A SOMMELIER, WHAT WOULD YOU BE?
A chef.

Le Bernardin
155 West 51st Street
New York, New York 10019
phone 212-489-1515 fax 212-265-1615

Michel R. Couvreux
WINE DIRECTOR
Team: Oliver Dufeu, Sommelier

WHAT IS ONE OF YOUR ULTIMATE FOOD AND WINE PAIRINGS?
Sautéed scallops with foie gras and truffle sauce with Chambolle-Musigny Les Fuées, Ghislaine Barthod 1997.

DESCRIBE YOUR WINE SELECTIONS.
A large selection of international wines, which is very strong in Burgundy (white and red), followed by Bordeaux (red), and California wines (white and red). We also feature wines from the rest of France, and other countries like Spain, Italy and New Zealand.

WHAT IS YOUR FAVORITE WINE REGION IN THE WORLD TODAY?
The Rhône Valley in France, especially Côte Rôtie and Hermitage. I love the spices of the Syrah and the character of the terroir.

WHAT LED YOU TO BECOME A SOMMELIER?
The pleasure of opening a bottle of wine without knowing what will be inside.

WHAT IS THE BIGGEST CHALLENGE IN YOUR JOB?
Making sure every customer is satisfied with his wine selection and that it matches the food.

IF YOU WERE NOT WINE DIRECTOR, WHAT WOULD YOU BE DOING?
Cooking, because my pleasure in life is eating and drinking well.

Café Boulud at the Surrey Hotel

20 East 76th Street
New York, New York 10021
phone 212-772-2600 fax 212-772-9372

Olivier Flosse
CHEF AND SOMMELIER

WHAT ARE SOME OF YOUR ULTIMATE FOOD AND WINE PAIRINGS?
Salade de crab (from Maine) with Sauvignon Blanc from New Zealand; côte de boeuf with a full-bodied Hermitage.

DESCRIBE YOUR WINE SELECTIONS.
We have a good balance, but focus on traditional French wines, notably Bordeaux, Burgundy and the Rhône Valley. But we don't forget about Italy, Spain, the United States and Australia.

WHAT CATEGORY OF WINE IS THE BEST VALUE ON YOUR WINE LIST?
White Burgundies like Pernand-Vergelesses and Savigny-les-Beaune.

NAME A RECENT WINE DISCOVERY THAT EXCITED YOU.
Penfolds Grange Hermitage 1988, an unforgettable wine.

WHAT IS YOUR FAVORITE WINE REGION IN THE WORLD TODAY?
Rhône Valley. I love the character and complexity of the region.

WHAT LED YOU TO BECOME A SOMMELIER?
The owner at the first restaurant I worked at took a personal interest in my future and introduced me to the beautiful world of wine.

WHAT ARE THE BEST ASPECTS OF YOUR JOB?
Discovering new wines and introducing them to my clients while expanding their palates.

IF YOU WERE NOT IN THIS PROFESSION, WHAT WOULD YOU BE?
The number one tennis player in the world.

Chanterelle

2 Harrison Street
New York, New York 10013
phone 212-966-6960 fax 212-966-6143

Roger Dagorn
MASTER SOMMELIER AND MAÎTRE D'

WHAT ARE SOME OF YOUR ULTIMATE FOOD AND WINE PAIRINGS?
Viognier with seafood sausages; southern Rhônes with lamb with Moroccan spices.

DESCRIBE YOUR WINE SELECTIONS.
Diversity of wines from different appellations, varietals and styles that go with David Waltuck's intense food, but mostly that satisfy the needs of the customer.

WHAT CATEGORY OF WINE IS THE BEST VALUE IN YOUR RESTAURANT?
The flight of wines that go with our tasting menu.

NAME RECENT WINE DISCOVERIES THAT HAVE EXCITED YOU.
The wines of the Wachau and Burgenland in Austria; the Veneto and Umbria in Italy; and Priorat, Rioja and Ribera del Duero in Spain.

WHAT IS YOUR FAVORITE WINE REGION IN THE WORLD TODAY?
Burgundy. Great wines, yet often elusive.

WHAT LED YOU TO BECOME A SOMMELIER?
Love of people.

WHAT ARE THE BEST ASPECTS OF YOUR JOB?
Working (playing) in a beautiful environment, surrounded by fun people, enjoying great food and great wines to match.

IF YOU WERE NOT IN YOUR CURRENT POSITION, WHAT WOULD YOU BE?
Assistant to a sommelier.

Le Cirque 2000

455 Madison Avenue
New York, New York 10022
phone 212-303-7788 fax 212-303-7712

Paul Altuna
SOMMELIER

WHAT IS ONE OF YOUR ULTIMATE FOOD AND WINE PAIRINGS?
Pétrus 1986 with a New York steak served with french fries and ketchup on the side.

DESCRIBE YOUR WINE SELECTIONS.
It's a door that opens to the legendary wines of the world.

WHAT IS YOUR FAVORITE WINE REGION IN THE WORLD TODAY?
Bordeaux. I grew up near this area. I know the terroir, châteaus, families and the history of these wines.

WHAT LED YOU TO BECOME A SOMMELIER?
My father's passion for wine.

WHAT ARE THE MOST CHALLENGING ASPECTS OF YOUR JOB?
Understanding my customers, selecting the right wines and waiting for big smiles on their faces.

IF YOU WERE NOT IN THIS PROFESSION, WHAT WOULD YOU BE?
A professional golfer.

Le Cirque 2000
455 Madison Avenue
New York, New York 10022
phone 212-303-7788 fax 212-303-7712

Ralph Hersom
WINE DIRECTOR
Team: Jeff Puccine, Assistant Sommelier

WHAT IS ONE OF YOUR ULTIMATE FOOD AND WINE PAIRINGS?
Krug rosé with a hamburger.

DESCRIBE YOUR WINE SELECTIONS.
We have 710 selections, which represent some of the best quality and most reasonably priced wines from around the world.

WHAT IS YOUR FAVORITE WINE REGION IN THE WORLD TODAY?
Piedmont, Italy. Barbaresco and Barolo are wonderful, and Dolcetto and Barbera are great wines for quality and price.

WHAT LED YOU TO BECOME A SOMMELIER?
While working as a waiter at Legal Sea Foods during college, I had the chance to taste some exciting wines.

WHAT IS THE MOST CHALLENGING ASPECT OF YOUR JOB?
Demanding clientele.

IF YOU WERE NOT IN THE WINE PROFESSION, WHAT WOULD YOU BE DOING?
A & R (Artist and Repertoire) for Sire Records.

La Côte Basque

60 West 55th Street
New York, New York 10019
phone 212-688-6525 fax 212-258-2493
website www.lacotebasqueny.com

Jean-Paul Zaremba
GENERAL MANAGER

WHAT ARE SOME OF YOUR ULTIMATE FOOD AND WINE PAIRINGS?
Baby back barbecue pork ribs with our homemade sauce paired with
Gewürztraminer from California or Alsace; shrimp cocktail with German
Kabinett Riesling; lamb with Châteauneuf-du-Pape rouge.

DESCRIBE YOUR WINE SELECTIONS.
We have approximately 1,300 selections from all over the world on our wine
list. The majority of our wines come from California and France.

WHAT CATEGORY OF WINE IS THE BEST VALUE ON YOUR WINE LIST?
Chilean wines, especially the reds.

NAME RECENT WINE DISCOVERIES THAT HAVE EXCITED YOU.
South African wines have come around in terms of quality and are reasonably
priced. Wines from the Languedoc-Roussillon in France and Madeira are also
great values.

WHAT IS YOUR FAVORITE WINE REGION IN THE WORLD TODAY?
The Rhône Valley. The wines, red and white, are such great food wines.

WHAT LED YOU TO YOUR CURRENT POSITION?
I began working at the Angus Barn. I fell in love with the restaurant, its owner
and the wine list.

WHAT ARE THE MOST CHALLENGING ASPECTS OF YOUR JOB?
Three things: picking out the perfect wine for a guest that matches the food
beautifully; convincing a guest to try a new wine that he has never had before;
and keeping our wine list new and exciting for our customers.

IF YOU WERE NOT IN THIS PROFESSION, WHAT WOULD YOU BE DOING?
Working with mentally handicapped children.

Daniel

60 East 65th Street
New York, New York 10021
phone 212-288-0033 fax 212-396-9014
website www.danielnyc.com

Jean Luc S. Le Du

CHEF AND SOMMELIER

WHAT ARE SOME OF YOUR ULTIMATE FOOD AND WINE PAIRINGS?
Black sea bass in potato crust with red wine sauce paired with Saumur-Champigny "Les Poyeux" 1996 from Clos Rougeard; Fourme d'Ambert and pear tart with rich Coteaux du Layon.

DESCRIBE YOUR WINE SELECTIONS.
We have a comprehensive list with more than 1,500 selections. Sixty percent of these are French wines, but we are also strong in wines from the United States, Spain, Italy and Australia. We also pour twenty wines by the glass.

WHAT CATEGORY OF WINE IS THE BEST VALUE IN YOUR RESTAURANT?
Languedoc-Roussillon.

NAME RECENT WINE DISCOVERIES THAT HAVE EXCITED YOU.
Barrique-aged Barbera from Piedmont; 1998 St.-Émilions, for their richness and early drinkability.

WHAT IS YOUR FAVORITE WINE REGION IN THE WORLD TODAY?
Burgundy, for the charm and aromas of its wines.

WHAT LED YOU TO BECOME A SOMMELIER?
A chance encounter with a great bottle of wine (Cheval Blanc, 1964).

WHAT ARE THE BEST ASPECTS OF YOUR JOB?
Interacting with customers and winemakers.

La Goulue

746 Madison Avenue
New York, New York 10021
phone 212-988-8169 fax 212-396-2552

James E. Cawdron
MANAGER AND SOMMELIER

WHAT IS YOUR FAVORITE WINE REGION IN THE WORLD TODAY?
Australia. It is rich in history and the wines offer great quality at great prices.

WHAT LED YOU TO BECOME A SOMMELIER?
A job change to a French restaurant with more exposure to wine.

WHAT ARE THE BEST ASPECTS OF YOUR JOB?
Matching wine with the personalities of businessmen, rock stars, actors and beautiful ladies.

IF YOU WERE NOT IN THIS PROFESSION, WHAT WOULD YOU BE DOING?
Rolls-Royce or Bentley car sales!

Grand Central Oyster Bar

Grand Central Terminal
New York, New York 10017
phone 212-490-6650 fax 212-949-5210
website www.oysterbarny.com

Michael J. Garvey
GENERAL MANAGER

WHAT ARE SOME OF YOUR ULTIMATE FOOD AND WINE PAIRINGS?

Belon (or other briny) oysters on the half shell with Sauternes or Eiswein; bouillabaisse with red Meursault or Oregon Pinot Noir; Florida stone crab with Vouvray demi-sec; rare steak with Old World–style Pinot Noir; foie gras with Tokaji Aszú (4, 5 or 6 puttonyos); turkey sandwich with cold climate California Chardonnay.

DESCRIBE YOUR WINE SELECTIONS.

We have a diverse selection of wines, with something for everybody, from the novice to the pro.

WHAT CATEGORIES OF WINE ARE THE BEST VALUES ON YOUR WINE LIST?

Loire whites or reds, dessert wines and expensive wines, which are marked up less than at other establishments.

NAME RECENT WINE DISCOVERIES THAT HAVE EXCITED YOU.

A 1987 white Rioja, which held together magnificently; Long Island wines, whose quality-to-price ratio recently has improved markedly.

WHAT IS YOUR FAVORITE WINE REGION IN THE WORLD TODAY?

Loire Valley. The wines of the region are very diverse and reasonably priced

WHAT LED YOU TO YOUR CURRENT POSITION?

Personal interest. I realized the more I learned about wine, the less I knew about it.

WHAT ARE THE BEST ASPECTS OF YOUR JOB?

Being a tour guide. I'm happy to take the standard tour through our list, but going off road is much more fun.

IF YOU WERE NOT IN THIS PROFESSION, WHAT WOULD YOU BE?

A Sherpa.

I Trulli

122 East 27th Street
New York, New York 10010
phone 212-481-7372 fax 212-481-5785

Charles R. Scicolone
WINE DIRECTOR AND SOMMELIER

WHAT IS ONE OF YOUR ULTIMATE FOOD AND WINE PAIRINGS?
Steak with a Chianti Classico Riserva or Chianti Rùfina Riserva.

DESCRIBE YOUR WINE SELECTIONS.
We have an all-Italian wine list, with wines from all twenty regions of Italy.
There are 400 listings and fifty wines by the glass.

WHAT IS YOUR FAVORITE WINE REGION IN THE WORLD TODAY?
Italy is one vast wine region. This is the moment for Italian wine.

WHAT LED YOU TO BECOME A SOMMELIER?
Interest in Italian wine.

WHAT ARE THE MOST CHALLENGING ASPECTS OF YOUR JOB?
Keeping a balanced wine list; finding good, low-priced wines; and matching
customers' food with wine.

IF YOU WERE NOT IN THE WINE PROFESSION, WHAT WOULD YOU BE?
A pizza maker.

March Restaurant

405 East 58th Street
New York, New York 10022
phone 212-754-6272 fax 212-838-5108
website www.marchrestaurant.com

Joseph D. Scalice
CO-PROPRIETOR, WINE DIRECTOR
AND SOMMELIER

WHAT ARE SOME OF YOUR ULTIMATE FOOD AND WINE PAIRINGS?
Confit de foie gras (de canard) au tourchon with almonds, garam masala and
Sauternes glaze served with a Bodegas Dios Baco Oloroso Sherry; white asparagus on sweet pea purée with Château d'Auviernier Neuchâtel Blanc 2000; rack
of Colorado lamb with carrot and potato purée and Abadia Retuerta 1997.

DESCRIBE YOUR WINE SELECTIONS.
Our list consists primarily of boutique wines, both known and unknown, from
the United States, France and a selection of other international wines. Our
wine program is based on taste, not pretension.

WHAT CATEGORY OF WINE IS THE BEST VALUE ON YOUR WINE LIST?
The lesser known communes of Burgundies, red and white.

NAME RECENT WINE DISCOVERIES THAT HAVE EXCITED YOU.
The wines of Chile and Argentina have gotten better and better while still
remaining great values.

WHAT IS YOUR FAVORITE WINE REGION IN THE WORLD TODAY?
Rioja, Spain. I love the elegance and food-friendliness of the wines.

WHAT LED YOU TO BECOME A SOMMELIER?
I have always loved wine.

WHAT ARE THE BEST ASPECTS OF YOUR JOB?
My "fun" begins when the guests arrive and I get to find, share and pour the
crowning jewels to their dining experiences.

IF YOU WERE NOT IN THIS PROFESSION, WHAT WOULD YOU BE?
A teacher.

March Restaurant

405 East 58th Street
New York, New York 10022
phone 212-754-6272 fax 212-838-5108

Brett A. Feore
ASSISTANT WINE DIRECTOR

WHAT IS ONE OF YOUR ULTIMATE FOOD AND WINE PAIRINGS?
Peter Michael 1997 Pinot Noir "Le Moulin Rouge" paired with roasted
California squab with sauce foie gras, garnished with cherry relish.

DESCRIBE YOUR WINE SELECTIONS.
Small-production boutique wineries predominantly from the United States,
France, Spain and several other nations.

WHAT IS YOUR FAVORITE WINE REGION IN THE WORLD TODAY?
Spain. The exciting blends produced, using Tempranillo, Cabernet Sauvignon
and Garnacha, keep me coming back for more.

WHAT LED YOU TO BECOME A SOMMELIER?
My passion for food, wine and people.

WHAT ARE THE BEST ASPECTS OF YOUR JOB?
Keeping abreast of all trends and different products out on the market, and
delivering March's customers great product at a fair price.

IF YOU WERE NOT IN YOUR CURRENT POSITION, WHAT WOULD YOU BE?
A chef-owner.

Mark's Restaurant
at The Mark Hotel

25 East 77th Street
New York, New York 10021
phone 212-744-4300 fax 212-744-4584

Richard E. Dean

MASTER SOMMELIER AND BEVERAGE MANAGER

DESCRIBE YOUR WINE SELECTIONS.

Extensive selection of quality wines. An extensive, ongoing program of wine dinners and wine classes.

WHAT IS YOUR FAVORITE WINE REGION IN THE WORLD TODAY?

Saar, Germany.

WHAT LED YOU TO BECOME A SOMMELIER?

The retail business and working in restaurants.

WHAT IS THE MOST CHALLENGING ASPECT OF YOUR JOB?

Staying informed about all the world's wine regions.

IF YOU WERE NOT IN THE WINE PROFESSION, WHAT WOULD YOU BE?

A stockbroker.

Montrachet

239 West Broadway
New York, New York 10013
phone 212-219-2777 fax 212-274-9508

Daniel A. Johnnes
WINE DIRECTOR

WHAT ARE SOME OF YOUR ULTIMATE FOOD AND WINE PAIRINGS?
Volnay and grilled salmon; Sauternes and Roquefort.

DESCRIBE YOUR WINE SELECTIONS.
We are committed to providing wines from top growers and wines that are great values.

WHAT IS YOUR FAVORITE WINE REGION IN THE WORLD TODAY?
Burgundy, because of my passion for the wines.

WHAT LED YOU TO BECOME A SOMMELIER?
Love of wine and sharing knowledge with consumers.

WHAT IS THE MOST CHALLENGING ASPECT OF YOUR JOB?
Finding great value in wine.

Nobu
105 Hudson Street
New York, New York 10013
phone 212-219-0500 fax 212-219-1441

Orlando L. Ramos
BEVERAGE MANAGER AND SOMMELIER

WHAT ARE SOME OF YOUR ULTIMATE FOOD AND WINE PAIRINGS?
Our sashimi salad with Viognier; yellowtail jalapeño with crisp Pinot Blanc; Kobe beef flamed with saki soy with red Bordeaux or Zinfandel.

DESCRIBE YOUR WINE SELECTIONS.
Ours is an international list of 150 wines, categorized by style. We also have a large half-bottle program, with about thirty-five selections to choose from.

WHAT CATEGORY OF WINE IS THE BEST VALUE ON YOUR WINE LIST?
New Zealand wines. Sauvignon Blanc and Riesling are stellar, with Pinot Noir on the way.

NAME RECENT WINE DISCOVERIES THAT HAVE EXCITED YOU.
Chilean wines. There are many great values in Merlot, Cabernet Sauvignon and Malbec that are Old World in style.

WHAT IS YOUR FAVORITE WINE REGION IN THE WORLD TODAY?
Burgundy. It produces both red and white wines that range in style from crisp and acidic to full and rich.

WHAT LED YOU TO BECOME A SOMMELIER?
A total love of wine.

WHAT ARE THE BEST ASPECTS OF YOUR JOB?
Being able to make wine suggestions to customers and producing a wine list that is very approachable. Let's face it, the days of the pretentious sommelier are over.

IF YOU WERE NOT IN THIS PROFESSION, WHAT WOULD YOU BE DOING?
A landscape architect.

Oceana Restaurant

55 East 54th Street
New York, New York 10022
phone 212-759-5941 fax 212-759-6076
website www.oceanarestaurant.com

Douglas W. Bernthal
WINE DIRECTOR

WHAT ARE SOME OF YOUR ULTIMATE FOOD AND WINE PAIRINGS?
Wild striped bass with chive-whipped potatoes, mushrooms, black truffle
vinaigrette paired with Pinot Noir from Burgundy or Oregon; salmon tartare
wrapped with smoked salmon, garnished with rainbow trout caviar, with rosé
Champagne.

DESCRIBE YOUR WINE SELECTIONS.
We have 1,100 selections from around the world that are geared to our seafood
menu. A main focus is Burgundy; we feature more than 225 of them.

WHAT CATEGORY OF WINE IS THE BEST VALUE IN YOUR RESTAURANT?
Australian Shiraz. Great, forward fruit, highly extracted, accessible at an early
age and a great value compared to wines from other regions.

NAME RECENT WINE DISCOVERIES THAT HAVE EXCITED YOU.
Australian-style Ports. Seductive, elusive, unique and a perfect way to finish a
meal. The quality is amazing as well.

WHAT IS YOUR FAVORITE WINE REGION IN THE WORLD TODAY?
Burgundy. I visited the region four times and fell in love with its history, traditions and great wines.

WHAT LED YOU TO YOUR CURRENT POSITION?
I was attending a Swiss hotel school and fell in love with food and wine after
visiting various vineyards and châteaus.

WHAT ARE THE BEST ASPECTS OF YOUR JOB?
Working with my staff captains and being fortunate enough to have a wine-
savvy clientele who appreciate fine wine.

IF YOU WERE NOT IN THIS PROFESSION, WHAT WOULD YOU BE?
Either a NASCAR or offshore powerboat driver.

Patroon

160 East 46th Street
New York, New York 10017
phone 212-883-7373 fax 212-883-1118

Thierry M. Bruneau
SOMMELIER

WHAT IS ONE OF YOUR ULTIMATE FOOD AND WINE PAIRINGS?
Niman Ranch pork loin, ginger potato, cockles and pancetta with a bottle of
Cobos Malbec 1999 from Argentina.

DESCRIBE YOUR WINE SELECTIONS.
We feature a selection of wines from all over the world.

WHAT IS YOUR FAVORITE WINE REGION IN THE WORLD TODAY?
Priorat, in Spain. Some of the world's best wine values come from there, and its
vineyards are some of the oldest in the world.

WHAT LED YOU TO BECOME A SOMMELIER?
I was born and raised in a winery in Loire Valley.

WHAT ARE THE MOST CHALLENGING ASPECTS OF YOUR JOB?
Making a great wine list with a small budget; trying to encourage customers to
try new and different wines.

IF YOU WERE NOT A SOMMELIER, WHAT WOULD YOU BE?
A chef de cuisine, winemaker or conductor.

San Pietro Restaurant

18 East 54th Street
New York, New York 10022-4203
phone 212-753-9015 fax 212-371-2337
website www.sanpietro.net

Cosimo Bruno
SOMMELIER

WHAT IS ONE OF YOUR ULTIMATE FOOD AND WINE PAIRINGS?
A dish from antiquity from southern Italy, now served at San Pietro: branzino al sale, sea bass baked in a sea salt crust and served with a great bottle of white wine.

DESCRIBE YOUR WINE SELECTIONS.
We offer top wines, with an emphasis on value, from California, Washington, France, Germany, Chile, Spain and Italy, with special attention given to the south.

WHAT IS YOUR FAVORITE WINE REGION IN THE WORLD TODAY?
Burgundy, for its remarkable white wines.

WHAT LED YOU TO BECOME A SOMMELIER?
I love wine.

WHAT IS THE MOST CHALLENGING ASPECT OF YOUR JOB?
Educating my clients.

IF YOU WERE NOT IN THIS PROFESSION, WHAT WOULD YOU BE?
A music engineer.

Tavern on the Green

1 West 67th Street, Central Park West
New York, New York 10023
phone 212-673-3200 fax 212-875-8051

Daniel I. Hartenstein
WINE AND BEVERAGE DIRECTOR

WHAT ARE SOME OF YOUR ULTIMATE FOOD AND WINE PAIRINGS?

Wild mushroom blintz or borscht with red Burgundy; caviar and Champagne;
beef stroganoff with Cabernet Sauvignon; foie gras and Sauternes; duck and
Pinot Noir; seafood and Grüner Veltliner.

DESCRIBE YOUR WINE SELECTIONS.

We have a range of international wines that complement our menu. We have a
variety of food-friendly wines, like Riesling and Pinot Noir, as well as many
interesting Champagnes and Bordeaux-style wines.

WHAT CATEGORIES OF WINE ARE THE BEST VALUES ON YOUR WINE LIST?

German Rieslings; grower-producer Champagnes; Australian Grenache and
Shiraz; California Zinfandel.

NAME RECENT WINE DISCOVERIES THAT HAVE EXCITED YOU.

Grüner Veltliner can be a great value and is excellent with food (great acidity);
Pinot Noirs from New Zealand and British Columbia for their good quality
and low prices.

WHAT IS YOUR FAVORITE WINE REGION IN THE WORLD TODAY?

For red wine, Burgundy. Its variety and quality is unmatched. For white,
Austria or Alsace. Both of these have a huge range of interesting and food-
friendly wines.

WHAT LED YOU TO YOUR CURRENT POSITION?

I've always loved food and beverages. I love to cook. All the flavors excite me. I
wanted to share this with others.

WHAT ARE THE BEST ASPECTS OF YOUR JOB?

I love to teach. I want to help develop in my staff the same passion that I have
for wine and food.

Tribeca Grill

375 Greenwich Street
New York, New York 10013
phone 212-941-3900 fax 212-941-3915

David Gordon
WINE DIRECTOR

WHAT ARE SOME OF YOUR ULTIMATE FOOD AND WINE PAIRINGS?
Herb-crusted rack of lamb with cauliflower purée served with California
Cabernet Sauvignon; honey mustard–glazed quail with choucroute with Alsace
Gewürztraminer; foie gras with Alsace Pinot Gris Vendange Tardive.

DESCRIBE YOUR WINE SELECTIONS.
We have 1,400 selections on our list, with concentrations in California
Cabernet and Châteauneuf-du-Pape. We offer more than eighty different
Zinfandels, dozens of wines from 1990 (the year the restaurant opened), and a
page of rare wines titled "Wines of the Century."

WHAT CATEGORY OF WINE IS THE BEST VALUE ON YOUR WINE LIST?
Southern Rhône reds, specifically Gigondas, Côtes-du-Rhône and
Châteauneuf-du-Pape.

NAME A RECENT WINE DISCOVERY THAT EXCITED YOU.
Vega de Toro, Numanthia, from Spain; a Tempranillo-based wine from an up-
and-coming region. It is concentrated and delicious, a world-class effort.

WHAT IS YOUR FAVORITE WINE REGION IN THE WORLD TODAY?
The southern Rhône Valley, where the wines are the best values in the market
today, after three great vintages (1998, 1999, 2000).

WHAT LED YOU TO YOUR CURRENT POSITION?
While working as a restaurant manager I tasted Grange Hermitage 1971 and
decided to pursue wine as a career.

WHAT ARE THE BEST ASPECTS OF YOUR JOB?
It is very rewarding when our customers are knowledgeable about wine, appreciate the scope and value of our list, and order accordingly.

IF YOU WERE NOT IN THIS PROFESSION, WHAT WOULD YOU BE?
Point guard for the New York Knicks.

Union Pacific

111 East 22nd Street
New York, New York 10010
phone 212-995-8570 fax 212-460-5881
website www.unionpacificrestaurant.com

Fred Price
WINE DIRECTOR

WHAT ARE SOME OF YOUR ULTIMATE FOOD AND WINE PAIRINGS?
Taylor Bay scallops with mustard oil paired with lighter Grüner Veltliner;
Copper River salmon with rhubarb and fava beans with Oregon Pinot Noir;
wild mushroom bouillon with Prosecco; braised short ribs of beef with Frick
Cinsaut; lamb with sour cherry mustard glaze with Sonoma Zinfandel.

DESCRIBE YOUR WINE SELECTIONS.
We have around 250 wine selections from many different regions. We are
known for our Riesling, Pinot Gris, Gewürztraminer and Grüner Veltliner
offerings because of their affinity with Chef Rocco DiSpirito's food. We also
recommend a wine by the glass with each appetizer, entrée and dessert.

**WHAT CATEGORIES OF WINE ARE THE BEST VALUES IN YOUR RESTAU-
RANT?**
Riesling and Gewürztraminer. They are priced aggressivly to encourage people
to try them.

NAME RECENT WINE DISCOVERIES THAT HAVE EXCITED YOU.
Washington Cabernet Sauvignon, Merlot and Syrah; German Riesling.

WHAT IS YOUR FAVORITE WINE REGION IN THE WORLD TODAY?
Washington. Its wine exhibits New World fruit and Old World subtlety and
refinement.

WHAT LED YOU TO YOUR CURRENT POSITION?
After graduating from the Culinary Institute of America in Hyde Park, I took
the "Windows on the World" wine course.

WHAT IS THE BEST ASPECT OF YOUR JOB?
I get to taste the best of the best from all over the world.

IF YOU WERE NOT IN THIS PROFESSION, WHAT WOULD YOU BE?
A jazz drummer.

Union Square Café

21 East 16th Street
New York, New York 10003
phone 212-243-4020 fax 212-627-2673

Karen A. King
WINE DIRECTOR

WHAT ARE SOME OF YOUR ULTIMATE FOOD AND WINE PAIRINGS?
Lemon pepper duck and spicy reds (Rhône or California Zins); foie gras with
Sauternes; mushroom dishes with earthy red Burgundy; truffles with Barolo.

DESCRIBE YOUR WINE SELECTIONS.
Eclectic with an emphasis on French, Italian and Californian wines. We have
about 340 selections of tasty, interesting wines that are well priced.

WHAT CATEGORY OF WINE IS THE BEST VALUE ON YOUR WINE LIST?
Red Bordeaux (because we cellar wines).

NAME RECENT WINE DISCOVERIES THAT HAVE EXCITED YOU.
Older vintages of white Rioja from Lopez de Heredia. I love the family history.

WHAT IS YOUR FAVORITE WINE REGION IN THE WORLD TODAY?
Piedmont. I love old Barolos and Barbarescos.

WHAT LED YOU TO YOUR CURRENT POSITION?
Working at this restaurant introduced me to wine, which I grew to love. Then I
was "forced" to help with inventory and ordering. Eventually, I began tasting
and buying the wines.

WHAT ARE THE BEST ASPECTS OF YOUR JOB?
I love educating the staff.

IF YOU WERE NOT IN THIS PROFESSION, WHAT WOULD YOU BE DOING?
I went to school to be a teacher, so I would probably be doing something in
education.

Veritas Restaurant
43 East 20th Street
New York, New York 10003
phone 212-353-3700 fax 212-353-1632

Tim Kopec
WINE DIRECTOR

WHAT IS ONE OF YOUR ULTIMATE FOOD AND WINE PAIRINGS?
Roasted artichokes with Manzanilla Sherry.

DESCRIBE YOUR WINE SELECTIONS.
We believe it is the greatest wine list in America, including more than 2,800
well-selected and fairly priced wines, including all the classics from California,
France, Italy, Spain and Australia.

WHAT IS YOUR FAVORITE WINE REGION IN THE WORLD TODAY?
Burgundy. So few varietals expressing such diversity based on soil and winemaking.

WHAT LED YOU TO BECOME A SOMMELIER?
Passion for food and wine.

WHAT IS THE BEST ASPECT OF YOUR JOB?
Great wine directors and sommeliers work the floor.

21 Club
CHRISTOPHER SHIPLEY,
BEVERAGE DIRECTOR
PHILIP PRATT, SOMMELIER
21 West 52nd Street, New York
212-582-7200

An American Place in the Benjamin Hotel
MARK MAGNOTTA, GENERAL
MANAGER AND WINE BUYER
565 Lexington Avenue, New York
212-888-5650

Aureole
NED BENEDICT, SOMMELIER
34 East 61st Street, New York
212-319-1660

Babbo
JOSEPH BASTIANICH, OWNER
AND WINE BUYER
DAVID LYNCH, DIRECTOR OF WINE
110 Waverly Place, New York
212-777-0303

Barbetta
DANIEL ZWICKE, SOMMELIER
LEO FROKIC, SOMMELIER
321 West 46th Street, New York
212-246-9171

Ben Benson's Steak House
BRIAN JANTOW, SOMMELIER
123 West 52nd Street, New York
212-581-8888

Beppe Trattoria
TOMMY BENNEDICT, BAR MANAGER
45 East 22nd Street, New York
212-982-8422

Carmine's
ROBERT CASTLEBERRY,
BEVERAGE DIRECTOR
200 West 44th Street, New York
212-221-3800

Cent'Anni
GARY DIVINCENZI, WINE BUYER
50 Carmine Street, New York
212-989-9494

Chiam Restaurant
DAVID NG, WINE BUYER
160 East 48th Street, New York
212-371-2323

Ciao Europa Ristorante
RAUL SORIA, WINE BUYER
63 West 54th Street, New York
212-247-1200

Cité
MICHAEL MCCANN,
BEVERAGE MANAGER
BOB DEGROAT, SOMMELIER
120 West 51st Street, New York
212-956-7100

Club Guastavino
ARTAN GJONI, SOMMELIER
409 East 59th Street, New York
212-421-6644

Danube
WALTER KRANJC, MAÎTRE D'
30 Hudson Street, New York
212-791-3771

DB Bistro Moderne
RYAN BUTTNER, WINE BUYER
55 West 44th Street, New York
212-391-1616

Del Frisco's Double Eagle Steak House

DAVID O'DAY, WINE DIRECTOR

1221 Avenue of the Americas, New York

212-575-5129

Dock's

PETER GOLDWATER, WINE BUYER

2427 Broadway, New York

212-724-5588

Dylan Prime

PETER KLEIN, WINE DIRECTOR

62 Laight Street, New York

212-334-2274

Felidia Ristorante

RICHARD LUFTIG, SOMMELIER

243 East 58th Street, New York

212-758-1479

Four Seasons Hotel

JULIAN NICCOLINI, SOMMELIER

57 East 52nd Street, New York

212-754-9494

Gotham Bar & Grill

MICHAEL GREENLEE, SOMMELIER

12 East 12th Street, New York

212-620-4020

Jean Georges

KURT ECKHERT, SOMMELIER

1 Central Park West, New York

212-299-3900

Judson Grill

BETH VON BENZ, WINE BUYER

152 West 52nd Street, New York

212-582-5252

Lenox Room

TONY FORTUNA, OWNER

AND WINE BUYER

1278 Third Avenue at 73rd, New York

212-772-0404

Lespinasse at the St. Regis Hotel

DANIELLE NALLY, WINE BUYER

2 East 55th Street, New York

212-339-6719

Lutèce

RAIMUNDO GABY, MAÎTRE D'

249 East 50th Street, New York

212-752-2225

Maloney & Porcelli

JERRY CHIMENTI, MANAGER

AND WINE BUYER

37 East 50th Street, New York

212-750-2233

Manhattan Ocean Club

PETER KING, BEVERAGE MANAGER

57 West 58th Street, New York

212-371-7777

The Melrose Restaurant

FRANCOIS TROUVE, MANAGER

AND SOMMELIER

995 Fifth Avenue, New York

212-650-4737

Michael's New York

EVAN TURNER, WINE BUYER

24 West 55th Street, New York

212-767-0555

Milos Restaurant

RENO CHRISTOU, SOMMELIER

125 West 55th Street, New York

212-245-7400

New York Palace Hotel

JEFFREY SELDEN, EXECUTIVE
DIRECTOR, CATERING
455 Madison Avenue, New York
212-888-7000

Olica

CHRISTOPHE LAHAPHILIO,
WINE BUYER
145 East 50th Street, New York
212-888-1220

One If By Land, Two If By Sea

MICHEL FLORANC, WINE BUYER
17 Barrow Street, New York
212-228-0822

Park Avenue Café

EDWARD KENNELLY, WINE BUYER
100 East 63rd Street, New York
212-644-1900

The Post House

JOSEPH FUGHINI, WINE DIRECTOR
28 East 63rd Street, New York
212-935-2888

Rihga Royal Hotel

RICK HORRIGAN, RESTAURANT
DIRECTOR AND WINE PURCHASER
151 West 54th Street, New York
212-468-8858

Rock Center Café

DAVID GORDON, SOMMELIER
600 Fifth Avenue, Building 17, New York
212-332-7621

San Domenico NY

GIORGIO LINGERO, WINE BUYER
PIERRO TROTTA, SOMMELIER
240 Central Park South, New York
212-265-5959

Smith & Wollensky

PAT COLTON, BEVERAGE MANAGER
MIKE BYRNE, TASTING MANAGER
797 Third Avenue, New York
212-753-1530

Spark's Steakhouse

MIKE CETTA, WINE BUYER
210 East 46th Street, New York
212-687-4855

The Tonic Restaurant and Bar

TIM VLAHOPOULOS, MANAGING
PARTNER AND WINE PURCHASER
108 West 18th Street, New York
212-929-9755

Verbena

AARON VON ROCK, WINE DIRECTOR
54 Irving Place, New York
212-260-5454

Waldorf Astoria Hotel

CHARLIE SHEIL, DIRECTOR
OF BEVERAGES
301 Park Avenue, New York
212-355-3000

The Water Club

SAM CORRENTI, BEVERAGE DIRECTOR
500 East 30th Street, New York
212-683-3333

Friends Lake Inn

963 Friends Lake Road
Chestertown, New York 12817
phone 518-494-4751 fax 518-494-4616
website www.friendslake.com

Thomas P. Burke
SOMMELIER

WHAT ARE SOME OF YOUR ULTIMATE FOOD AND WINE PAIRINGS?
Pan-seared lobster and scallops, mousseline cake with a macadamia nut
quenelle and vanilla bean beurre blanc paired with a California Chardonnay;
Broken Arrow Ranch venison chop with caramelized potato tian and creamy
leek fondue with Grenache; blue cheese and Bonnezeaux; a grilled flatiron or
hanger steak with rosemary paired with Gigondas.

DESCRIBE YOUR WINE SELECTIONS.
We have more than 2,400 selections from around the world. We try to hit all
the bases in depth and breadth while trying to be cutting edge in regions, grape
variety, and quality.

WHAT CATEGORIES OF WINE ARE THE BEST VALUES ON YOUR WINE LIST?
Wines from the south of France and Spain, as well as Zinfandel.

NAME RECENT WINE DISCOVERIES THAT HAVE EXCITED YOU.
Gavi and Albariño. They are delicious white wines.

WHAT IS YOUR FAVORITE WINE REGION IN THE WORLD TODAY?
Italy, with its indigenous varieties like Prugnolo and Aglianico.

WHAT LED YOU TO BECOME A SOMMELIER?
My interest in wine led me to work a harvest with Preston of Dry Creek Valley.
It spurred my curiosity into finding out about wines from around the world
and how they are made.

WHAT IS THE BEST ASPECT OF YOUR JOB?
Recommending wine to guests who want to break out of their comfort zone.

IF YOU WERE NOT IN THE WINE PROFESSION, WHAT WOULD YOU BE?
An organic farmer.

The Grill at Strathallan

550 East Avenue
Rochester, New York 14607
phone 585-454-1880 fax 585-461-2845
website www.grill175.com

Milisav Tadich
OWNER AND WINE DIRECTOR

WHAT ARE SOME OF YOUR ULTIMATE FOOD AND WINE PAIRINGS?
Carpaccio of Kobe beef over soft polenta, drizzled with white truffle oil, paired with 1998 Gaja Sauvignon Blanc, "Alteni di Brassica."

DESCRIBE YOUR WINE SELECTIONS.
Our wine list has more than 1,200 selections, with a focus on California, Italy (Toscana, Piemonte and Friuli) and France (Bourgogne and Champagne), but most wine regions in the world are also represented, from Croatia to Lebanon.

WHAT IS YOUR FAVORITE WINE REGION IN THE WORLD TODAY?
Austria. Rieslings and Grüner Veltliners produced in Austria's Wachau Valley and Burgenland's Neusiedlersee dessert wines are simply world-class.

WHAT LED YOU TO YOUR CURRENT POSITION?
I grew up in Europe tasting wines and being involved in the process, from vineyard to the table. It was captivating. Later, the "mystery" became a passion.

IF YOU WERE NOT IN THIS PROFESSION, WHAT WOULD YOU BE?
Worldwide food and wine tour guide.

River Café

1 Water Street
Brooklyn, New York 11201
phone 718-522-5200 fax 718-875-0037
website www.therivercafe.com

Katherine M. Klymyshyn
SOMMELIER

WHAT ARE SOME OF YOUR ULTIMATE FOOD AND WINE PAIRINGS?
Pistachio-dusted foie gras, caramelized ruby red grapefruit with a Ste-Croix-du-Mont (Sauternes-style); lamb and Rioja; short ribs and Barolo; goat cheese and Viognier; ceviche and Albariño; veal and Burgundy.

DESCRIBE YOUR WINE SELECTIONS.
The list is classic, representing many countries and regions.

WHAT CATEGORY OF WINE IS THE BEST VALUE ON YOUR WINE LIST?
The list has hidden values in every section. We believe there is a value for everyone.

NAME RECENT WINE DISCOVERIES THAT HAVE EXCITED YOU.
The south of France has been making very exciting wines.

WHAT IS YOUR FAVORITE WINE REGION IN THE WORLD TODAY?
Champagne. It can turn a meal into a celebration.

WHAT LED YOU TO BECOME A SOMMELIER?
I had a great wine director who mentored me.

WHAT IS THE BIGGEST CHALLENGE YOU FACE AS SOMMELIER?
Tailoring and refining the dining experience to personal tastes for each table and, sometimes, to each person.

Yono's Restaurant

64 Colvin Avenue
Albany, New York 12206
phone 518-436-7747 fax 518-437-3410
website www.yonosrestaurant.com

Dominick H. Purnomo
MAÎTRE D'HOTEL AND SOMMELIER

WHAT ARE SOME OF YOUR ULTIMATE FOOD AND WINE PAIRINGS?
Pork tenderloin with orange rind and Indonesian spices with California Zinfandel. Nearly everything on our menu with German Riesling. The complex flavors of our Indonesian cuisine goes great with German Riesling.

DESCRIBE YOUR WINE SELECTIONS.
We have a large selection of wines with good depth and breadth. Wine dinners are held monthly.

WHAT CATEGORY OF WINE IS THE BEST VALUE ON YOUR WINE LIST?
Our markups are very moderate, but there are very good values to be found in wines from the southern hemisphere.

NAME A RECENT WINE DISCOVERY THAT EXCITED YOU.
Rudd 2000 Sauvignon Blanc, Napa Valley, is one of the best wines I've had recently.

WHAT IS YOUR FAVORITE WINE REGION IN THE WORLD TODAY?
I can't narrow it down to one because I get excited about so many wines from all over the world.

WHAT LED YOU TO BECOME A SOMMELIER?
While working in the restaurant, wine just seemed to be a fascinating topic. You can know a lot, but you can't know it all!

WHAT ARE THE BEST ASPECTS OF YOUR JOB?
Teaching the public about something it is unfamiliar with and absorbing wine knowledge from those around me.

IF YOU WERE NOT IN THIS PROFESSION, WHAT WOULD YOU BE DOING?
Something in education, a spin-off of what I do now.

American Hotel
TED CONKLIN, OWNER
AND WINE BUYER
Main Street, Sag Harbor
631-725-3535

La Caravelle Restaurant
ANDRE AND RITA JAMMET,
PROPRIETORS AND WINE BUYERS
46 Bedford-Banksville Road, Bedford
212-586-4252

Crabtree's Kittle House Inn
DON CASTALDO, SOMMELIER
11 Kittle Road, Chappaqua
914-666-8044

Culinary Institute of America
STEVE KOLPAN, WINE BUYER
433 Albany Post Road, Hyde Park
845-471-6608

Depuy Canal House
LEE HARRINGTON, SOMMELIER
Route 213, High Fallas
845-687-7700

Eastchester Fish Gourmet
RICK ROSS, WINE BUYER
837 White Plains Road, Scarsdale
914-725-3450

Equus at the Castle at Tarrytown
JOHN AGUIRRE, MANAGER
AND WINE BUYER
400 Benedict Avenue, Tarrytown
914-631-1980

Lake Placid Lodge
MARK STEBBINGS, SOMMELIER
Whiteface Inn Road, Lake Placid
518-523-2700

Mirabelle
JULIE PASQUIER, SOMMELIER
404 North Country Road, St. James
631-584-5999

Pascale Wine Bar
CHUCK PASCALE, WINE BUYER
204 West Fayette Street, Syracuse
315-471-3040

Pierce's 1894 Restaurant
JOE PIERCE, WINE BUYER
228 Oakwood Avenue, Elmira Heights
607-734-2022

Xaviar's
WILLIAM RATTNER, SOMMELIER
506 Piermont Avenue, Piermont
845-359-7007

The Angus Barn

9401 Glenwood Avenue
Raleigh, North Carolina 27617
phone 919-787-3505 fax 919-783-5568
website www.angusbarn.com

Hendrik P. Schuitemaker
WINE AND BEVERAGE DIRECTOR

WHAT ARE SOME OF YOUR ULTIMATE WINE AND FOOD PAIRINGS?
Baby back barbecued pork ribs with our homemade sauce are perfect with
Gewürztraminer from California or Alsace. Shrimp cocktail with a Kabinet
Riesling from Germany and lamb with a Chateauneuf-du-Pape rouge.

DESCRIBE YOUR WINE PROGRAM AND WINE SELECTIONS.
We have approximately 1,300 selections and 24,000 bottles of wine from all
over the world, with a majority from California and France. Our wait staff goes
through extensive wine training.

WHAT CATEGORY OF WINE IS THE BEST VALUE ON YOUR WINE LIST OR
IN YOUR RESTAURANT?
Chilean wines, especially the reds, tend to be better values these days. However,
there are great values throughout our wine list. We believe in fair pricing.

NAME RECENT WINE DISCOVERIES THAT HAVE EXCITED YOU AND TELL WHY.
African wines are really coming on the scene with great quality at good prices.
The wines from the French Languedoc region are also great values.

WHAT IS YOUR FAVORITE REGION IN THE WORLD TODAY?
Currently, my favorite is the Rhone Valley. The wines, both red and white, are
such great food wines.

WHAT LED YOU TO BECOME A SOMMELIER?
I have always loved wine and actually didn't intend to go into the restaurant
business until I started to work at the Angus Barn. I fell in love with the restaurant, its owners, and the wine list.

WHAT ARE THE BEST ASPECTS OF YOUR JOB?
Picking out the perfect wine for a guest that matches the food beautifully, getting a
guest to try a new wine, and keeping our wine list new and exciting for our customers.

IF YOU WERE NOT IN THE WINE PROFESSION, WHAT WOULD YOU BE DOING?
Working with mentally handicapped children.

Beef Barn
400 Saint Andrews Drive
Greenville, North Carolina 27834
phone 252-756-1161 fax 252-756-7655

Robert M. Simon
OWNER

WHAT ARE SOME OF YOUR ULTIMATE FOOD AND WINE PAIRINGS?
Smoked pork chops with big California Pinot Noir; our New York strip topped
with shallot sauce with California Meritage.

DESCRIBE YOUR WINE SELECTIONS.
The list has been developed over the last 18 years. We have more than 650
selections, with a focus on vertical selections of California Cabernet
Sauvignons.

WHAT IS YOUR FAVORITE WINE REGION IN THE WORLD TODAY?
California. I developed my taste for wine in the late 1970s and early 1980s and
grew up with the California explosion.

WHAT LED YOU TO YOUR CURRENT POSITION?
General interest, and desire to match food and wine at my restaurant.

WHAT ARE THE BEST ASPECTS OF YOUR JOB?
Educating the public about the fun of drinking wine.

IF YOU WERE NOT IN THIS PROFESSION, WHAT WOULD YOU BE DOING?
Running a golf resort.

Horizons

KEVIN SCHWARTZ, WINE BUYER

290 Macon Avenue, Asheville

828-252-2711

Liberty Oak Wine & Cheese

JOHN FANCORT, SOMMELIER

100 East Washington, Greensboro

336-273-7057

Lucky 32

JULIA LINGLE, BAR MANAGER

1421 Westover Terrace, Greensboro

336-370-0707

Second Empire at the Dodd-Hinsdale House

DANIEL SCHURR, EXECUTIVE CHEF
AND WINE BUYER

330 Hillsborough Street, Raleigh

919-829-3663

Giovanni's

25550 Chagrin Boulevard
Beachwood, Ohio 44122
phone 216-831-8625 fax 216-831-4338

Pierre Gregori

GENERAL MANAGER

WHAT ARE SOME OF YOUR ULTIMATE FOOD AND WINE PAIRINGS?
Veal chop with Barbera; lamb with Châteauneuf-du-Pape; pasta cavatelli and gnocchi with Chianti; halibut with Verdicchio; duck breast–stuffed foie gras with Burgundy; lamb shank with Nebbiolo.

DESCRIBE YOUR WINE SELECTIONS.
We have more than 600 selections from every great wine region in the world. We also offer thirty wines by the glass.

WHAT CATEGORY OF WINE IS THE BEST VALUE ON YOUR WINE LIST?
Italian wines, from varieties like Primitivo and Negroamaro, and producers like Falesco and Zardetto.

NAME RECENT WINE DISCOVERIES THAT HAVE EXCITED YOU.
Italian wines from Umbria, the south and the islands.

WHAT IS YOUR FAVORITE WINE REGION IN THE WORLD TODAY?
Italy. They have never been so good.

WHAT LED YOU TO YOUR CURRENT POSITION?
A passion for great food and wine.

WHAT IS THE BEST ASPECT OF YOUR JOB?
Pulling the cork of a great bottle of wine with the people who are going to enjoy it.

IF YOU WERE NOT IN THIS PROFESSION, WHAT WOULD YOU BE DOING?
I don't know. I love this industry and I love food and people.

Swingos on the Lake

12900 Lake Avenue
Lakewood, Ohio 44107
phone 216-221-6188 fax 216-221-9878

Matthew J. Swingos
PRESIDENT

WHAT ARE SOME OF YOUR ULTIMATE FOOD AND WINE PAIRINGS?
Cumin and garlic–blackened salmon over creamy curry risotto and citrus and cayenne coulis, red pepper and pineapple relish, with Pinot Gris or Pinot Noir; tarragon and goat cheese–crusted rack of lamb with a ten-year-old Bordeaux; hazelnut and chocolate mousse crêpes with Banyuls.

DESCRIBE YOUR WINE SELECTIONS.
We have a global selection, more than 1,880 selections from more than 26 countries, with great breadth and depth in wines from the Rhône Valley, Bordeaux and Burgundy.

WHAT CATEGORIES OF WINE ARE THE BEST VALUES ON YOUR WINE LIST?
Spain and Greece.

NAME RECENT WINE DISCOVERIES THAT HAVE EXCITED YOU.
The wines of Greece. New World style with Old World acidity.

WHAT ARE YOUR FAVORITE WINE REGIONS IN THE WORLD TODAY?
Burgundy, the pinnacle of Pinot Noir and Chardonnay with refined elegance. And the Wachau Valley, Austria, with its food-friendly whites with "sweet pea" aromas.

WHAT LED YOU TO YOUR CURRENT POSITION?
Passion for wine.

WHAT IS THE BEST ASPECT OF YOUR JOB?
Educating staff and guests.

IF YOU WERE NOT IN THIS PROFESSION, WHAT WOULD YOU BE DOING?
Building sailboats.

Alana's Food and Wine
KEVIN BERTSCHI, PROPRIETOR
AND WINE BUYER
2333 North High Street, Columbus
614-294-6783

Alberini's Restaurant
LISA BUNDY, WINE DIRECTOR
AND CELLAR MASTER
1201 Youngstown Warren Road, Niles
330-652-5895

L'Antibes
DALE GUSSETT, CO-OWNER
AND WINE BUYER
772 North High Street, Columbus
614-291-1666

Johnny's Bar
ANTHONY "BO" SANTOSUOSSO,
WINE BUYER
3164 Fulton Road, Cleveland
216-281-0055

Maisonette Restaurant
MICHAEL COMISAR, CO-OWNER
114 East Sixth Street, Cincinnati
513-721-2260

Palace Restaurant
DON LANYI, WINE BUYER
601 Vine Street, Cincinnati
513-381-3000

The Refectory
DAVID McMAHON, SOMMELIER
1092 Bethel Road, Columbus
614-451-9774

La Baguette Bistro
MICHEL BUTHION, OWNER
AND WINE BUYER
7408 North May Avenue, Oklahoma City
405-840-3047

Boulevard Steakhouse
SAGE SHURWADY, WINE BUYER
505 South Boulevard, Edmond
405-715-2333

Southpark Seafood Grill and Wine Bar

901 Southwest Salmon Street
Portland, Oregon 97205
phone 503-326-1300 fax 503-326-1301
website www.southpark.citysearch.com

David B. Holstrom
WINE CONSULTANT

WHAT ARE SOME OF YOUR ULTIMATE FOOD AND WINE PAIRINGS?
Braised beef or lamb with southern Rhône red; Catalan fish stew with Greek white wine.

DESCRIBE YOUR WINE SELECTIONS.
Our program specializes in varieties and wine regions that are not well-known to most Americans. We search out regions that offer wines with a great price-to-value ratio that taste good.

WHAT CATEGORIES OF WINE ARE THE BEST VALUES ON YOUR WINE LIST?
Mosel Riesling, and wines from southwestern France, the Languedoc and Austria.

NAME RECENT WINE DISCOVERIES THAT HAVE EXCITED YOU.
Greek white wines and German Sekt.

WHAT ARE YOUR FAVORITE WINE REGIONS IN THE WORLD TODAY?
The Mosel and Austria.

WHAT LED YOU TO YOUR CURRENT POSITION?
It was a way to meet women in college. It became evident (more times than not) that the wines were, over time, more interesting.

WHAT IS THE BEST ASPECT OF YOUR JOB?
Introducing a new wine, variety or region to guests that they have never experienced, and having them love it.

IF YOU WERE NOT IN THIS PROFESSION, WHAT WOULD YOU BE DOING?
Teaching or cooking.

Couvron Restaurant
MATTHEW MATHER, WINE BUYER
1126 Southwest 18th Avenue, Portland
503-225-1844

The Dining Room at The Westin Salishan Resort
MICHAL McGARY, WINE STEWARD
7760 North Highway 101,
Glenedon Beach
541-764-2371

The Heathman Restaurant
MS. TYSON PIERCE, SOMMELIER
1001 Southwest Broadway, Portland
503-790-7752

Morton's of Chicago
JOHN MITCHELL, BEVERAGE
DIRECTOR
213 Southwest Clay Street, Portland
503-248-2100

Wildwood Restaurant
RANDY GOODMAN, DIRECTOR
OF SERVICES AND WINE
1221 Northwest 21st Avenue, Portland
503-248-9663

The Fountain at Four Seasons

1 Logan Square
Philadelphia, Pennsylvania 19103
phone 215-963-1500 fax 215-963-2748
website www.fourseasons.com/philadelphia

Melissa B. Monosoff

SOMMELIER

Team: Stephane Castera, Sommelier; Cherie Vallance, Sommelier

WHAT ARE SOME OF YOUR ULTIMATE FOOD AND WINE PAIRINGS?
Roasted halibut with sweetbreads, morels, baby white asparagus and veal jus paired with Meursault or Puligny-Montrachet; smoked salmon and caviar crème fraîche with Savennières; and chèvre with Sancerre or Pouilly-Fumé.

DESCRIBE YOUR WINE SELECTIONS.
We are known for depth in the heavy-hitting French and California wines, but I balance the rest of the list with wines from under-recognized regions and from smaller, lesser-known producers.

WHAT CATEGORIES OF WINE ARE THE BEST VALUES ON YOUR WINE LIST?
Southern Italy, southern France and Australia.

NAME RECENT WINE DISCOVERIES THAT HAVE EXCITED YOU.
Pinot Noirs and Sauvignon Blancs from South Africa.

WHAT IS YOUR FAVORITE WINE REGION IN THE WORLD TODAY?
I have several: Alsace and the Loire for elegance, the Rhône for intensity and value, and southern Italy for great new wines that show a huge improvement in quality.

WHAT LED YOU TO BECOME A SOMMELIER?
When I was at the Striped Bass, Marnie Old, the sommelier, took me under her wing while I was a cook. I have followed this path ever since.

WHAT ARE THE BEST ASPECTS OF YOUR JOB?
Teaching the staff and interacting with the guests. It's fun opening people's eyes to new things, teaching and sharing information.

IF YOU WERE NOT IN YOUR CURRENT POSITION, WHAT WOULD YOU BE DOING?
In the kitchen, cooking.

Savona Cucina Della Costa

100 Old Gulph Road
Gulph Mills, Pennsylvania 19428
phone 610-520-1200 fax 610-520-2045
website www.savonarestaurant.com

Brice Y. Del Clos

PARTNER AND WINE DIRECTOR
Team: Thomas Comdescot-Lepere, Sommelier

PENNSYLVANIA

WHAT ARE SOME OF YOUR ULTIMATE FOOD AND WINE PAIRINGS?
Dover sole, lightly sautéed and filleted, topped with pinenuts, sweet peas, shaved artichokes, scallions and asparagus tips in a lemon butter sauce with Chardonnay; roasted free-range chicken with Condrieu "Les Terasses de l'Empire" from Georges Vernay; roasted rack of lamb with Château de Pez, St. Estèphe 1995.

DESCRIBE YOUR WINE SELECTIONS.
We are known for the diversity, scope and complexity of our wine program, which features wines from many different countries and a range of prices, styles, producers and varietals, accented by several vertical selections.

WHAT CATEGORY OF WINE IS THE BEST VALUE ON YOUR WINE LIST?
German Riesling.

WHAT IS YOUR FAVORITE WINE REGION IN THE WORLD TODAY?
Bordeaux. The soil, the climate and the history can all be tasted in the wine.

WHAT LED YOU TO YOUR CURRENT POSITION?
Working with talented people who were very involved with wine. It made me want to learn and participate.

WHAT ARE THE BEST ASPECTS OF YOUR JOB?
The contact with the guests is the high point. Showing them something new and different is gratifying.

IF YOU WERE NOT IN YOUR CURRENT POSITION, WHAT WOULD YOU BE DOING?
I would have to be in the restaurant business in some capacity.

Wooden Angel Restaurant

308 Leopard Lane
Beaver, Pennsylvania 15009
phone 724-774-7880 fax 724-774-7994
website www.wooden-angel.com

Alex E. Sebastian
RESTAURATEUR

DESCRIBE YOUR WINE SELECTIONS.

Having fun and taking the snobbishness out of wine selection and drinking is what we're known for. I work the floor and I say to guests, "If you don't like the wine, I'll drink it!" Our monthly by-the-glass program is very user-friendly. Our selections are affordable. Beginning this year, I have cut back purchasing bottles of expensive (over $30 retail) wine. I downplay the tired trilogy of Chardonnay, Merlot and Cabernet Sauvignon and encourage Pinot Noir, Zinfandel, Viognier, etc.

WHAT CATEGORY OF WINE IS THE BEST VALUE ON YOUR WINE LIST?

Our wines by the glass. For special occasions, the older vintages, which have been aged in our cellars for many years.

NAME RECENT WINE DISCOVERIES THAT HAVE EXCITED YOU.

Better bottlings of Rhône blends, Zinfandel blends and proprietary blends, as well as wines from Ohio, Lake Erie, New York, Virginia and Missouri.

WHAT IS YOUR FAVORITE WINE REGION IN THE WORLD TODAY?

America, of course. But I like the Sauvignon Blancs of New Zealand and the wines of Alsace and the Rhône.

WHAT LED YOU TO YOUR CURRENT POSITION?

I was born into the restaurant business. Early on, I decided to challenge the American, misplaced preference for French wines.

WHAT ARE THE BEST ASPECTS OF YOUR JOB?

Teaching at the table and converting a snobbish or uninformed Francophile to the True Faith of American wines.

Yangming
1051 Conestoga Road
Bryn Mawr, Pennsylvania 19010
phone 610-527-3200 fax 610-527-0229

James T. Mullen, III
SOMMELIER AND BEVERAGE MANAGER

DESCRIBE YOUR WINE SELECTIONS.

We have an extensive wine list featuring California Chardonnays and Cabernet Sauvignons, and wines from France, Italy, Australia, Germany, New Zealand, Spain, Chile and Japan.

WHAT IS YOUR FAVORITE WINE REGION IN THE WORLD TODAY?

California. I believe California produces the best wines in the world. Some of my favorites come from the Carneros region.

WHAT LED YOU TO BECOME A SOMMELIER?

I started with the company as a bartender and worked my way up the "corporate ladder."

WHAT IS THE BIGGEST CHALLENGE IN YOUR JOB?

Trying to get guests from always thinking "mainstream." Everybody knows Chardonnay and Merlot. I want them to try Chenin Blanc and Syrah.

IF YOU WERE NOT IN YOUR CURRENT POSITION, WHAT WOULD YOU BE DOING?

Bartending.

Le Bec-Fin

GREGORY CASTELLS, SOMMELIER

1523 Walnut Street, Philadelphia

215-567-1000

La Bonne Auberge

LINO FUENTES, SOMMELIER

Gerard Caronello, Wine Buyer

Village 2, Mechanic Street, New Hope

215-862-2462

The Carlton

KEVIN JOYCE, WINE BUYER

500 Grant Street, Pittsburgh

412-391-4099

Deux Cheminées

JIM PETRIE, WINE BUYER

1221 Locust Street, Philadelphia

215-790-0200

Dilworthtown Inn

JACQ MARC, SOMMELIER

1390 Old Wilmington Pike, West Chester

610-399-1390

Evermay on the Delaware

BILL MOFFLY, WINE BUYER

889 River Road, Erwinna

610-294-9100

La Famiglia Restaurant

GUSIPPE SENA, WINE BUYER

Mario Fattorini, Sommelier

8 South Front Street, Philadelphia

215-922-2803

Founders Restaurant

ERIC SIMONIS, SOMMELIER

Broad and Walnut Streets, Philadelphia

215-790-2814

Hayden Zug's Restaurant

TERRY LEE, WINE BUYER

1987 State Street, East Petersburg

717-569-5747

Hyeholde Restaurant

JAMES BRINKMAN, DINING ROOM MANAGER

190 Hyeholde Drive, Moon Township

412-264-3116

Jake's

RYRAN MARGOLIS, SOMMELIER

4365 Main Street, Manayunk

215-483-0444

The Palm

KEVIN FRANKLIN, SOMMELIER

200 South Broad Street, Philadelphia

215-546-7256

Passerelle

BRIAN SABARESE, MANAGER AND WINE BUYER

175 King of Prussia Road, Radnor

610-293-9411

The Prime Rib at the Warwick

DREW MONTESANO, BEVERAGE MANAGER AND SOMMELIER

1701 Locus Street, Philadelphia

215-735-6000

Sign of The Sorrel Horse

CHRISTIAN GAUMONT, SOMMELIER

4424 Old Easton Road, Doylestown

215-230-9999

Smith & Wollensky

PAUL DUMONT, BEVERAGE MANAGER

210 West Rittenhouse Square, Philadelphia

215-545-1700

Strawberry Hill
DENNIS C. KEREK, PROPRIETOR
128 West Strawberry Street, Lancaster
717-393-5544

Striped Bass
EDWARD MURRAY, SOMMELIER
1500 Walnut Street, Philadelphia
215-732-4444

Vallozzi's
JIM MANONALKIS, WINE BUYER
Route 30 East, Greensburg
724-836-7663

Boathouse II Restaurant

397 Squire Pope Road
Hilton Head Island, South Carolina 29926
phone 843-681-3663 fax 843-342-2288
website www.celebrationusa.com

David A. Smith
WINE DIRECTOR AND SOMMELIER

WHAT ARE SOME OF YOUR ULTIMATE FOOD AND WINE PAIRINGS?
Crispy, seared flounder with an apricot shallot glaze with Pinot Blanc; steak
frites topped with béarnaise sauce with Syrah; potato-crusted salmon with garlic
sour cream sauce with Viognier.

DESCRIBE YOUR WINE SELECTIONS.
We have about 130 items on our list, predominantly from California, with ten
to fifteen featured wines.

WHAT CATEGORY OF WINE IS THE BEST VALUE ON YOUR WINE LIST?
Rhône varietals from around the world.

NAME RECENT WINE DISCOVERIES THAT HAVE EXCITED YOU.
Tempranillo from Spain. Great wine, great value.

WHAT IS YOUR FAVORITE WINE REGION IN THE WORLD TODAY?
Santa Barbara. Great wines and unique producers.

WHAT LED YOU TO BECOME A SOMMELIER?
I was bartending at a fine dining restaurant and fell in love with wine with my
first sip.

WHAT ARE THE BEST ASPECTS OF YOUR JOB?
Tasting and selling wine for a living; selecting the wines on the list; and having
someone say, "Thank you. What a wonderful suggestion."

IF YOU WERE NOT IN THIS PROFESSION, WHAT WOULD YOU BE DOING?
Something in the golf industry.

Charleston Grill at the Charleston Place Hotel

224 King Street
Charleston, South Carolina 29401
phone 843-577-4522 fax 843-724-8405
website www.charlestongrill.com

Roberto Fuschi
SOMMELIER

WHAT ARE SOME OF YOUR ULTIMATE FOOD AND WINE PAIRINGS?
Maine lobster tempura over lemon grits and fried mini green tomatoes in a yellow tomato tarragon butter paired with white Burgundy; poached fresh turbot filet over caramelized fennel and Vidalia onions with Maine lobster in Dijon mustard and thyme sauce with Santa Barbara Pinot Noir; chilled duck breast with a citrus truffle oil dressing with spinach and duck crackling paired with Tocai Friulano from Collio.

DESCRIBE YOUR WINE SELECTIONS.
Our selection is extensive (1,200) and includes a strong representation of California Chardonnay and Cabernet Sauvignon, Burgundy and Bordeaux. We also have fifty wines by the glass.

WHAT CATEGORY OF WINE IS THE BEST VALUE ON YOUR WINE LIST?
Italian reds.

NAME RECENT WINE DISCOVERIES THAT HAVE EXCITED YOU.
White wines from the Collio region and Sangiovese from Napa Valley.

WHAT IS YOUR FAVORITE WINE REGION IN THE WORLD TODAY?
The Rhône Valley, for the character of the wines.

WHAT LED YOU TO BECOME A SOMMELIER?
The search for the ultimate wine and food pairings; the love of dining room service; the desire to work with a great chef.

WHAT ARE THE BEST ASPECTS OF YOUR JOB?
Satisfying guests and creating a perfect tasting menu with wine pairings.

IF YOU WERE NOT A SOMMELIER, WHAT WOULD YOU BE DOING?
Cooking again.

CQ's Restaurant

140 Lighthouse Road
Hilton Head Island, South Carolina 29928
phone 843-671-2779 fax 843-671-6787
website www.celebrationusa.com

Scott E. Entrup
WINE DIRECTOR

WHAT ARE SOME OF YOUR ULTIMATE FOOD AND WINE PAIRINGS?
Our version of a grilled cheese sandwich: house brioche slices, Boursin cheese, chunks of filet mignon all made into a sandwich then sautéed in duck fat and served with a tomato jam paired with a Napa Valley Cabernet; any blue-veined, hearty cheese and a flight of Ports from around the world.

DESCRIBE YOUR WINE SELECTIONS.
We select wines that complement our cuisine. We feature American cuisine with a French influence. Two-thirds of our list is American, the other third is international.

WHAT CATEGORY OF WINE IS THE BEST VALUE ON YOUR WINE LIST?
California Chardonnay.

NAME RECENT WINE DISCOVERIES THAT HAVE EXCITED YOU.
South African wines. The quality has improved over the last five years and there are a number of great values.

WHAT IS YOUR FAVORITE WINE REGION IN THE WORLD TODAY?
Oregon. The wines reveal terroir more so than California wines.

WHAT LED YOU TO YOUR CURRENT POSITION?
An interest in learning more about wine.

WHAT IS THE BEST ASPECT OF YOUR JOB?
Seeing the guests enjoy a wine I've suggested.

IF YOU WERE NOT IN YOUR CURRENT POSITION, WHAT WOULD YOU BE DOING?
Anything in food and beverage.

Old Fort Pub at Hilton Head Plantation

65 Skull Creek Drive
Hilton Head Island, South Carolina 29926
phone 843-681-2386 fax 843-681-9287
website www.celebrationusa.com

Christopher L. Tassone
VICE PRESIDENT OF OPERATIONS
AND SOMMELIER

WHAT ARE SOME OF YOUR ULTIMATE FOOD AND WINE PAIRINGS?
New Zealand rack of lamb with Shiraz; crab cakes with buttery Chardonnay; filet mignon with a Cabernet Sauvignon; grilled Atlantic salmon with brie crêpes and sweet corn velouté with Chardonnay.

DESCRIBE YOUR WINE SELECTIONS.
We have an award-winning list with more then 275 selections. Our wine list was created to complement the cuisine of the Old Fort Pub, which is American with a global influence.

WHAT CATEGORY OF WINE IS THE BEST VALUE ON YOUR WINE LIST?
Chardonnay from Australia and California.

NAME RECENT WINE DISCOVERIES THAT HAVE EXCITED YOU.
Italian wines.

WHAT IS YOUR FAVORITE WINE REGION IN THE WORLD TODAY?
Bordeaux.

WHAT LED YOU TO BECOME A SOMMELIER?
The appreciation of food and wine with respect to creating a complete dining experience.

WHAT ARE THE BEST ASPECTS OF YOUR JOB?
Exceeding guest expectations and making the experience memorable.

IF YOU WERE NOT IN THIS PROFESSION, WHAT WOULD YOU BE?
A fine art and antiques dealer.

Woodlands Resort & Inn

125 Parsons Road
Summerville, South Carolina 29438
phone 800-774-9999 fax 843-875-2603
website www.woodlandsinn.com

Stephane Peltier
SOMMELIER

WHAT ARE SOME OF YOUR ULTIMATE FOOD AND WINE PAIRINGS?
Butter-poached Maine lobster, maiitake "egg foo yong," Chinese black bean
sauce with Pinot Noir from New Zealand; seared foie gras, apricot vinegar
sauce with vanilla-poached Texas sweet onions and spiced pecans with
Gewürztraminer from Zind-Humbrecht, Alsace; roast breast of duck, noodles
scallion galette, oyster sauce scented with ginger and cilantro paired with Shiraz
from Australia.

DESCRIBE YOUR WINE SELECTIONS.
We have more than 900 selections, including more than ninety half-bottles,
that cover mainstream as well as obscure varietals and regions, such as Vernaccia
and Tannat, Lebanon and South Africa.

WHAT CATEGORIES OF WINE ARE THE BEST VALUES ON YOUR WINE LIST?
Spanish white wines and southern Italian reds.

NAME RECENT WINE DISCOVERIES THAT HAVE EXCITED YOU.
Albariño from Spain; Pinot Noir from New Zealand.

WHAT ARE YOUR FAVORITE WINE REGIONS IN THE WORLD TODAY?
Piedmont, Italy, and the Côte de Beaune in France because there is magic in
both areas as well as artisanal winemakers who are passionate about their craft.

WHAT LED YOU TO BECOME A SOMMELIER?
At school, I became fascinated with various wine regions and how they could
produce distinctive wine styles.

WHAT ARE THE BEST ASPECTS OF YOUR JOB?
Meeting people and helping them enjoy the pleasures of wine and food.

IF YOU WERE NOT IN THIS PROFESSION, WHAT WOULD YOU BE DOING?
A carpenter.

Boat House on East Bay

MONIQUE BAILEY, WINE BUYER

549 East Bay Street, Charleston

843-577-7171

Cypress Low
Country Grille

TRAY STEVENSON, WINE DIRECTOR

167 East Bay Street, Charleston

843-727-0111

Magnolia's Restaurant

TRAY STEVENSON, WINE DIRECTOR

185 East Bay Street, Charleston

843-577-7771

Peninsula Grill

STEVE PALMER, SOMMELIER

112 North Market Street, Charleston

843-723-0700

Mario's

2005 Broadway Street
Nashville, Tennessee 37203
phone 615-327-3232 fax 615-321-2675
website www.mariosfinedining.com

Daniel Mora
PART OWNER AND SOMMELIER

WHAT ARE SOME OF YOUR ULTIMATE FOOD AND WINE PAIRINGS?
Rack of lamb with heavy Cabernet or Zinfandel; veal piccata with Pinot Noir;
sea bass with Chardonnay or Italian white.

DESCRIBE YOUR WINE SELECTIONS.
We have 392 selections on our wine list, plus additional rare wines that I sell
verbally. Sixty percent of our wines are Italian and the remainder are from
California and the rest of the world.

WHAT ARE YOUR FAVORITE WINE REGIONS IN THE WORLD TODAY?
Piedmont and Tuscany. They make outstanding wines.

WHAT LED YOU TO BECOME A SOMMELIER?
I was born in San Remo, Italy, and was stomping grapes by the time I was ten
years old. My love of wine started there.

WHAT IS THE BEST ASPECT OF YOUR JOB?
Every day is exciting with so many new wines in the market. As soon as I learn
about one, it seems that another one comes along.

IF YOU WERE NOT IN YOUR CURRENT POSITION, WHAT WOULD YOU BE?
A chef.

Opryland Hotel

2800 Opryland Drive
Nashville, Tennessee 37214
phone 615-871-6000 fax 615-871-7872

Gina R. Hendrix
BEVERAGE MANAGER AND WINE BUYER

WHAT ARE SOME OF YOUR ULTIMATE FOOD AND WINE PAIRINGS?

Chocolate desserts with late-harvest Zinfandel; blue cheese–stuffed filet mignon with Petite Sirahs; game with bold Zinfandel; pistachio-crusted salmon with Pinot Noir.

DESCRIBE YOUR WINE SELECTIONS.

We specialize in user-friendly, approachable, progressive wine lists with many options and, of course, a few gems of quality and grandeur. I want people at every level of wine appreciation to feel comfortable with the wines we offer.

WHAT CATEGORY OF WINE IS THE BEST VALUE ON YOUR WINE LISTS?

Creative red varieties. Interest in them is growing and interest in Merlot is shrinking.

NAME RECENT WINE DISCOVERIES THAT HAVE EXCITED YOU.

Malbecs from Argentina (especially from Catena) and Chilean wines in general, which offer both great value and great quality.

WHAT IS YOUR FAVORITE WINE REGION IN THE WORLD TODAY?

Paso Robles, California. I really love the Zinfandels, Syrahs and Petite Sirahs from this region. They taste wild to me.

WHAT LED YOU TO YOUR CURRENT POSITION?

My love for wine and an interest in educating restaurant staff about wine in a way that makes wine simple and approachable, not "snotty."

WHAT IS THE BEST ASPECT OF YOUR JOB?

The creativity I am allowed with all of the great new concepts going on in Gaylord Opryland. We are a large corporation, but I have tremendous freedom.

IF YOU WERE NOT IN THIS PROFESSION, WHAT WOULD YOU BE DOING?

Teaching preschool.

Chez Philippe
Chris Hue, Wine Buyer
149 Union Avenue, Memphis
901-529-4188

The Orangery
Stewart Kendrick, Wine Buyer
5412 Kingston Pike, Knoxville
865-588-2964

Stock-Yard Restaurant
Andrew Penland, Wine Buyer
901 Second Avenue North, Nashville
615-255-6464

Sunset Grill
Craig Clifft, General Manage
and Wine Buyer
2001-A Belcourt Avenue, Nashville
615-386-3663

La Tourelle
Glen Hayes, Wine Buyer
2146 Monroe Avenue, Memphis
901-726-5771

The Wild Boar Restaurant
Brett Allen, Sommelier
2014 Broadway, Nashville
615-329-1313

The Green Room

2715 Elm Street
Dallas, Texas 75226
phone 214-748-7666 fax 214-748-7704

R. Whitney Meyers, Jr.
PROPRIETOR AND WINE BUYER

WHAT ARE SOME OF YOUR ULTIMATE FOOD AND WINE PAIRINGS?
Swiss Chasselas and lobster rolls; red Zinfandel and Texas barbecue; Savennières and pâté de foie gras.

DESCRIBE YOUR WINE SELECTIONS.
An eclectic, award-winning list, featuring wines from fifteen countries.

WHAT IS YOUR FAVORITE WINE COUNTRY?
Lebanon. Chateau Musar is my favorite wine.

WHAT LED YOU TO YOUR CURRENT POSITION?
Chef laziness.

WHAT IS THE MOST CHALLENGING ASPECT OF YOUR JOB?
Time management. Trying to juggle responsibilities for each business while making time for staff training, product selection and wine list updates at each restaurant.

IF YOU WERE NOT IN THIS PROFESSION, WHAT WOULD YOU BE DOING?
Litigating ACLU cases or running political campaigns.

Mansion on Turtle Creek

2821 Turtle Creek Boulevard
Dallas, Texas 75219
phone 214-559-2100 fax 214-526-5345

Kent Rice
SOMMELIER

WHAT IS ONE OF YOUR ULTIMATE FOOD AND WINE PAIRINGS?
A simple roasted chicken with great California Cabernet Sauvignon or Château Haut-Brion.

DESCRIBE YOUR WINE SELECTIONS.
Our list is one of the best in the nation. It is fairly evenly divided between French and California wines, with representations from many other regions and countries as well. The selections include many unusual and rare vintages and a large number from small, boutique producers.

WHAT IS YOUR FAVORITE WINE REGION IN THE WORLD TODAY?
Napa Valley, because of the quality of wines and the natural beauty of the region.

WHAT LED YOU TO BECOME A SOMMELIER?
As a youngster, I lived in a Texas vineyard. I was always curious about wines and vineyards. Eventually, I began to study wine and dreamed of going to Paris by way of Dallas—but in Dallas he stays!

WHAT ARE THE MOST CHALLENGING ASPECTS OF YOUR JOB?
First, overcoming the "fear factor" that some guests have about consulting a sommelier. Second, matching the food to the appropriate wine, within the guest's budget.

IF YOU WERE NOT IN THIS PROFESSION, WHAT WOULD YOU BE?
A playwright.

Café Pacific
DAVID KNOUSE, WINE BUYER
24 Highland Park Village, Dallas
214-526-1170

Chaparral Club in the Adams Mark Hotel
WES HARRELL, BEVERAGE DIRECTOR
400 North Olive Street, Dallas
214-777-6539

Del Frisco's Double Eagle Steak House
BRIAN SOLOWAY, WINE DIRECTOR
5251 Spring Valley Road, Dallas
972-490-9000

The French Room at Hotel Adolphus
AUGUSTINE YBARRA, SOMMELIER
1321 Commerce Street, Dallas
214-742-8200

Nick & Sam's
NATE BIDDICK, SOMMELIER
3008 Maple Avenue, Dallas
214-871-7444

Pappas Brothers Steakhouse Dallas
ROBERT SMITH, WINE BUYER
10477 Lombardy Lane, Dallas
214-366-2000

The Riviera
JOSEPH ICHO, SOMMELIER
7709 Inwood Road, Dallas
214-351-0094

Brennan's of Houston

3300 Smith Street
Houston, Texas 77006
phone 713-522-9711 fax 713-522-9142
website www.brennanshouston.com

Martin W. Korson
THE WINE GUY

WHAT ARE SOME OF YOUR ULTIMATE FOOD AND WINE PAIRINGS?
Our spicy shrimp remoulade with German Riesling; house-smoked salmon with California Zinfandel.

DESCRIBE YOUR WINE SELECTIONS.
Our wine list has more than 370 wines from major wine-producing regions. We offer many classic, well-known wines as well as new, interesting wines that help me to educate and "wow" guests. We also feature twenty-seven dessert wines on our dessert list.

WHAT CATEGORY OF WINE IS THE BEST VALUE ON YOUR WINE LIST?
"Martin's Affordable Alternatives," a section where I provide a range of good-value wines for guests seeking new, affordable wines.

NAME RECENT WINE DISCOVERIES THAT HAVE EXCITED YOU.
Argentina Malbec and whites from Austria. They are great with our food and can be great values.

WHAT IS YOUR FAVORITE WINE REGION IN THE WORLD TODAY?
Germany. Its Rieslings have low alcohol and crisp acidity, and are amazing when matched with our rich, spicy cuisine.

WHAT LED YOU TO BECOME A SOMMELIER?
A love of wine and a desire to stay in the restaurant business.

WHAT ARE THE BEST ASPECTS OF YOUR JOB?
Writing our wine list, helping guests choose wine for their meals and educating people about wine and food. I enjoy demonstrating that wine is not as mysterious as they think.

IF YOU WERE NOT IN YOUR CURRENT POSITION, WHAT WOULD YOU BE?
An executive chef and, ultimately, a chef instructor at the CIA.

Café Annie

1728 Post Oak Boulevard
Houston, Texas 77056
phone 713-840-1111 fax 713-840-1558

Paul N. Roberts

<small>MASTER SOMMELIER AND WINE DIRECTOR</small>

WHAT IS ONE OF YOUR ULTIMATE FOOD AND WINE PAIRINGS?
Brundlmeyer 1999 Grüner Veltliner Loiser Berg with fresh crabmeat and avocado salad on corn chips.

DESCRIBE YOUR WINE PROGRAM.
Eclectic and educational, based on a desire to explore the unknown and to open the minds and palates of our diners. Lots of high-acid, low-wood whites and a big emphasis on red and white Burgundy.

WHAT IS YOUR FAVORITE WINE REGION IN THE WORLD TODAY?
Burgundy. The sheer talent that the producers display in overcoming tough climatic conditions is amazing. Year in and year out, the wines of Burgundy continue to fascinate and enchant me.

WHAT LED YOU TO BECOME A SOMMELIER?
Love of wine and a desire to introduce more people to the extraordinary world of wine.

WHAT ARE THE MOST CHALLENGING ASPECTS OF YOUR JOB?
Staff training and trying to overcome customers' beliefs that they must drink only certain types of wines.

IF YOU WERE NOT IN THIS PROFESSION, WHAT WOULD YOU BE DOING?
Hanging out with sommeliers.

Lynn's Steakhouse
955 Dairy Ashford Road
Houston, Texas 77079
phone 281-870-0807 fax 281-870-0888

Loic Carbonnier
PROPRIETOR AND WINE BUYER
Team: Lynn Foreman, Proprietor and Wine Buyer

WHAT ARE SOME OF YOUR ULTIMATE FOOD AND WINE PAIRINGS?
Prime beef Châteaubriand with Napa Cabernet (especially from the Stag's Leap District); Cajun snapper étouffée with Alsatian Riesling.

DESCRIBE YOUR WINE SELECTIONS.
Our wine list is focused on reds, since we're a steakhouse. We have a great selection of red Burgundies, and at reasonable prices.

WHAT CATEGORY OF WINE IS THE BEST VALUE ON YOUR WINE LIST?
Burgundy.

NAME RECENT WINE DISCOVERIES THAT HAVE EXCITED YOU.
New Zealand Sauvignon Blancs, for their bouquets and crispness.

WHAT IS YOUR FAVORITE WINE REGION IN THE WORLD TODAY?
Burgundy, for the challenge it represents. (Who could stay married to a Pinot Noir wife!)

WHAT LED YOU TO YOUR CURRENT POSITION?
When I started cooking, I soon discovered my love for wine. I was fortunate to meet the right people and was given the opportunity to pursue it.

WHAT IS THE MOST CHALLENGING ASPECT OF YOUR JOB?
Finding the right wines and making customers happy, whether it is with a twenty-dollar or two thousand–dollar bottle of wine.

IF YOU WERE NOT IN YOUR CURRENT POSITION, WHAT WOULD YOU BE DOING?
Cooking or fly fishing.

Mark's American Cuisine

1658 Westheimer Road
Houston, Texas 77006
phone 713-523-3800 fax 713-523-9292
website www.marks1658.com

Matthew T. Pridgen
MANAGER AND WINE STEWARD

WHAT ARE SOME OF YOUR ULTIMATE FOOD AND WINE PAIRINGS?
Hearth-roasted Mapleleaf duck over wild rice and pearl pasta, with raspberry and blackberry sauce, paired with 1997 Amarone; heirloom tomatoes with Sancerre; hearth-roasted oysters with white Burgundy; Copper River salmon with Oregon Pinot Noir; seared escolar with Alsace Riesling.

DESCRIBE YOUR WINE SELECTIONS.
We have a selection of approximately 250 wines, and a focus on California, France and Italy. The majority of our selections are from small estates.

WHAT CATEGORY OF WINE IS THE BEST VALUE ON YOUR WINE LIST?
New Zealand Sauvignon Blanc. It is by far the best value at the moment.

NAME RECENT WINE DISCOVERIES THAT HAVE EXCITED YOU.
South African Syrahs and New Zealand Sauvignon Blancs, unpretentious wines and extraordinary values.

WHAT IS YOUR FAVORITE WINE REGION IN THE WORLD TODAY?
Italy. The vast number of native grape varieties and its many terroirs are eminently appealing to me.

WHAT LED YOU TO BECOME A SOMMELIER?
Tasting a 1938 Château Palmer. It fascinated and inspired me.

WHAT IS THE MOST CHALLENGING ASPECT OF YOUR JOB?
The flexibility and creativity involved in putting together a wine list and conveying that to the consumer.

IF YOU WERE NOT IN THIS PROFESSION, WHAT WOULD YOU BE DOING?
Art. Photography has always been a great passion of mine.

Pappas Brothers Steakhouse
5839 Westheimer Road
Houston, Texas 77057
phone 713-780-7352 fax 713-780-8119

Scotti A. Stark
SOMMELIER AND WINE DIRECTOR

WHAT ARE SOME OF YOUR ULTIMATE FOOD AND WINE PAIRINGS?
Gooey pecan pie with Fonseca twenty-year-old tawny Port; pizza and big Zinfandel.

DESCRIBE YOUR WINE SELECTIONS.
Very extensive. We have more than 1,700 wines from around the world on our list.

WHAT ARE YOUR FAVORITE WINE REGIONS IN THE WORLD TODAY?
Napa Valley and Sonoma County, where the weather is spectacular year-round and the wines are consistently great.

WHAT LED YOU TO BECOME A SOMMELIER?
I started here as a server and had never worked in a restaurant with sommeliers. I was fascinated!

WHAT ARE THE MOST CHALLENGING ASPECTS OF YOUR JOB?
Keeping the wine list updated and making enough time for training, tasting and traveling.

IF YOU WERE NOT IN THIS PROFESSION, WHAT WOULD YOU BE DOING?
Probably something similar, selling and/or educating.

Rainbow Lodge

1 Birdsall Street
Houston, Texas 77007
phone 713-861-8666 fax 713-861-8405
website www.rainbow-lodge.com

William D. Orchard
WINE DIRECTOR

WHAT ARE SOME OF YOUR ULTIMATE FOOD AND WINE PAIRINGS?
Grilled south Texas fallow chop in a natural reduction with northern Rhône red; braised rabbit with red oak lettuce and roasted tomato with Pinot Noir.

DESCRIBE YOUR WINE SELECTIONS.
We have an ever-changing wine program with a variety of wines from around the world. We specialize in wines from new regions and varieties. Our focus at the moment is on Pinot Noir and Cabernet Sauvignon.

WHAT CATEGORY OF WINE IS THE BEST VALUE ON YOUR WINE LIST?
Red Australian.

NAME RECENT WINE DISCOVERIES THAT HAVE EXCITED YOU.
Several South African Chardonnays—with an excellent quality-to-value ratio; a New Zealand Pinot Noir (Rowland), which was outstanding and had unique characteristics.

WHAT IS YOUR FAVORITE WINE REGION IN THE WORLD TODAY?
Burgundy. The wines show so much craftsmanship and character.

WHAT LED YOU TO YOUR CURRENT POSITION?
I worked for a restaurant that had a nice wine list, but no sommelier. As a waiter, I needed to know more in order to sell the wines. That's where the passion began.

WHAT IS YOUR BIGGEST CHALLENGE IN YOUR JOB?
Delivering a wine that is exactly what the guest wants in style, flavor and characteristics.

IF YOU WERE NOT A WINE DIRECTOR, WHAT WOULD YOU BE DOING?
Managing a restaurant.

Rotisserie for Beef & Bird

2200 Wilcrest Drive
Houston, Texas 77042
phone 713-977-9524 fax 713-977-9568
website www.rotisserie-beef-bird.com

Vincent S. Baker
CELLAR MASTER AND SOMMELIER

WHAT ARE SOME OF YOUR ULTIMATE FOOD AND WINE PAIRINGS?
Our Texas tortilla soup with New World Sauvignon Blanc; our Texas wild game dinner (with wild boar, venison, duck, quail, etc.) paired with Petite Sirah or Syrah.

DESCRIBE YOUR WINE SELECTIONS.
We offer great-value, interesting selections from around the world. We want wine to be fun and inviting as opposed to intimidating or boring.

WHAT CATEGORIES OF WINE ARE THE BEST VALUES ON YOUR WINE LIST?
California Petite Sirah and Australian Shiraz blends. Both offer a great range of flavors, styles and values.

NAME A RECENT WINE DISCOVERY THAT EXCITED YOU.
Montes, 2000 Cabernet/Carmenère from Chile. Unusual blend at a great price, with great New World style.

WHAT IS YOUR FAVORITE WINE REGION IN THE WORLD TODAY?
Sonoma County, California. Its many microclimates allow for better and more specialized wines.

WHAT LED YOU TO BECOME A SOMMELIER?
I filled in for a sommelier one time. I found I enjoyed the challenge and grew to love it.

WHAT ARE THE BEST ASPECTS OF YOUR JOB?
Associating with wineries; making guests happy and excited about their dinner wines; being able to relay something new or special to guests about wine.

IF YOU WERE NOT IN THIS PROFESSION, WHAT WOULD YOU BE DOING?
Something service-oriented.

America's
RIGO ROMERO, WINE BUYER
1800 South Post Oak, Houston
713-961-1492

Arcodoro Ristorante Italiano
ELFISIO FARRIS, SOMMELIER
5000 Westheimer Road, Houston
713-621-6888

Ibiza Food and Wine Bar
GRANT COOPER, CO-OWNER
AND WINE BUYER
2450 Louisiana, Houston
713-524-0004

The Palm
MARK LARUE, SOMMELIER
6100 Westheimer Road, Houston
713-977-2544

Quattro
MICHAEL SAVINO, WINE BUYER
1300 Lamar Street, Houston
713-652-6250

La Reserve
IVO NIKIC, SOMMELIER
4 Riverway Drive, Houston
713-871-8177

River Oaks Grill
JOHN O'ROURKE, MANAGER
AND SOMMELIER
2630 Westheimer Road, Houston
713-520-1738

Sierra Grill
ROBERT COVINGTON, SOMMELIER
4704 Montrose, Houston
713-942-7757

Tony's
ARMANDO DAWDY, SOMMELIER
1801 Post Oak Boulevard, Houston
713-622-6778

La Tour d'Argent
BASSAM DODIN, SOMMELIER
2011 Ella Boulevard, Houston
713-864-9864

Bohanan's
219 East Houston Street, Suite 275
San Antonio, Texas 78205
phone 210-472-2600 fax 210-472-2276

Andre H. Mack
SOMMELIER

WHAT ARE SOME OF YOUR ULTIMATE FOOD AND WINE PAIRINGS?
Candied, pickled jalapeños with cream cheese paired with Crozes-Hermitage blanc; fresh grilled oysters with Grand Cru Chablis.

DESCRIBE YOUR WINE SELECTIONS.
An international wine list with all major regions represented. We have a strong emphasis on California wines, and feature several Texas wines.

WHAT CATEGORIES OF WINE ARE THE BEST VALUES ON YOUR WINE LIST?
California Zinfandel and Texas wines.

WHAT IS YOUR FAVORITE REGION OR AREA IN THE WORLD TODAY?
Burgundy. It's complex and elegant.

WHAT LED YOU TO BECOME A SOMMELIER?
A passion for food and wine.

WHAT IS THE MOST REWARDING ASPECT OF YOUR JOB?
Introducing guests to new wines.

IF YOU WERE NOT IN THE WINE PROFESSION, WHAT WOULD YOU BE DOING?
Playing trumpet in a jazz band.

The Grille at the Westin La Cantera Resort

16641 La Cantera Parkway
San Antonio, Texas 78256
phone 210-558-6500 fax 210-558-2400
website www.westinlacantera.com

Steven A. Krueger
RESORT SOMMELIER

WHAT IS ONE OF YOUR ULTIMATE FOOD AND WINE PAIRINGS?
Cowboy-cut ribeye with 1997 California Cabernet Sauvignon.

DESCRIBE YOUR WINE SELECTIONS.
Our list is predominantly California wine with a broad foundation of wines from around the world.

WHAT CATEGORY OF WINE IS THE BEST VALUE ON YOUR WINE LIST?
Every category has at least two great wine values.

NAME RECENT WINE DISCOVERIES THAT HAVE EXCITED YOU.
Texas wines! Improving every year by leaps and bounds. Watch for the "Super Texans" as vineyards begin bottling the warm-climate varietals like Sangiovese, Tempranillo and Syrah.

WHAT IS YOUR FAVORITE WINE?
Syrah, from the Rhône, California, Washington, Australia, South Africa and South America. The variety of styles and character of Syrah is dazzling!

WHAT LED YOU TO BECOME A SOMMELIER?
A love of wine, lots of wine training over a nine-year period in fine dining restaurants and repeated encouragement from supervisors and associates.

WHAT IS THE BEST ASPECT OF YOUR JOB?
The rigorous study, tasting and evaluation of wines from around the world. The most challenging part is deciding which few of the countless great wines of the world are best for this resort.

IF YOU WERE NOT IN THIS PROFESSION, WHAT WOULD YOU BE DOING?
There is not a better career in the world!

Ruth's Chris Steak House

7720 Jones-Maltsberger Road
San Antonio, Texas 78216
phone 210-821-5051 fax 210-821-5095
website www.ruthchris-sanantonio.com

Janet Easterling
SOMMELIER
Team: James Pate, Manager of Wines

WHAT ARE SOME OF YOUR ULTIMATE FOOD AND WINE PAIRINGS?
Filet mignon with red Bordeaux; cowboy ribeye with California Cabernet
Sauvignon; Southern pecan pie à la mode with Port; crème brûlée with German
Auslese; veal chop with Pinot Noir; lamb chops with Syrah or Barolo; lobster
with Chardonnay.

DESCRIBE YOUR WINE SELECTIONS.
With nearly 500 selections, our wine list features high -quality wines from
every major wine region, and includes many rare, limited-production wines.
We specialize in hearty red wines, since we have a steakhouse menu.

WHAT CATEGORIES OF WINE ARE THE BEST VALUES ON YOUR WINE LIST?
California Zinfandel, Sauvignon Blanc and Chilean reds.

NAME RECENT WINE DISCOVERIES THAT HAVE EXCITED YOU.
California Zinfandel. Delicious, high-quality wines at affordable prices.

WHAT IS YOUR FAVORITE WINE REGION IN THE WORLD TODAY?
California. It has so much diversity in terms of climate and soil and an extraordinary ability to express power and richnesss. I love big, lush California wines.

WHAT LED YOU TO BECOME A SOMMELIER?
Early exposure to French food and wine pairing sparked my passion for wine.

WHAT IS THE MOST REWARDING ASPECT OF YOUR JOB?
Sharing my enthusiasm and knowledge about wine with dinner guests and staff.

IF YOU WERE NOT IN THIS PROFESSION, WHAT WOULD YOU BE DOING?
Some type of work dealing with plants and animals.

Ruth's Chris Steak House

1170 East Commerce Street
San Antonio, Texas 78205
phone 210-227-8847 fax 210-227-7447
website www.ruthschris-sanantonio.com

Sandra L. Waldhelm
SALES MANAGER AND SOMMELIER

WHAT ARE SOME OF YOUR ULTIMATE FOOD AND WINE PAIRINGS?
Steak with Cabernet Sauvignon or Syrah; ribeye with Hermitage.

DESCRIBE YOUR WINE PROGRAM.
We strive to offer the best selections the world of wine has to offer and to educate the staff as well as the clientele about those wines as thoroughly as possible.

WHAT CATEGORIES OF WINE ARE THE BEST VALUES ON YOUR WINE LIST?
California Cabernet Sauvignons and Chilean wines.

WHAT IS YOUR FAVORITE WINE REGION IN THE WORLD TODAY?
Burgundy. The region is intriguing and complex, and produces some of the finest wines in the world.

WHAT LED YOU TO BECOME A SOMMELIER?
I developed a passion for wine after working in the industry for nineteen years.

WHAT ARE THE MOST CHALLENGING ASPECTS OF YOUR JOB?
Keeping up with new vintages as well as new producers from around the world. Training the staff regularly.

IF YOU WERE NOT IN THIS PROFESSION, WHAT WOULD YOU BE?
A stay-at-home mom and a wine consultant on the side.

Market Street Broiler

260 South 1300 East
Salt Lake City, Utah 84102
phone 801-583-8808
website www.gastronomyinc.com

Patrick T. LeBras
GENERAL MANAGER, WINE BUYER AND
SOMMELIER

WHAT ARE SOME OF YOUR ULTIMATE FOOD AND WINE PAIRINGS?
Fresh halibut, shrimp and scallop skewers with Sauvignon Blanc; fresh, broiled
Atlantic salmon with Pinot Noir.

DESCRIBE YOUR WINE SELECTIONS.
We have a wide range of white wines, rosés and light reds for our mostly
seafood menu. We are attempting to introduce more varietals to the
Chardonnay and Merlot crowd.

WHAT CATEGORIES OF WINE ARE THE BEST VALUES ON YOUR WINE LIST?
Rosé and miscellaneous whites like Grüner Veltliner, Riesling, Pinot Blanc,
Gewürztraminer and Pinot Grigio.

NAME A RECENT WINE DISCOVERY THAT EXCITED YOU.
Bonny Doon Pacific Rim Dry Riesling. A great food wine at a great price.

WHAT IS YOUR FAVORITE WINE REGION IN THE WORLD TODAY?
Sonoma County. It is underrated when compared to Napa Valley, and produces
great wines at reasonable prices.

WHAT LED YOU TO BECOME A SOMMELIER?
I was raised by French parents. My love of food and wine led me to this profession.

WHAT ARE THE BEST ASPECTS OF YOUR JOB?
I enjoy pairing food and wine, introducing guests to new wines (that they love),
and teaching my staff about wine.

IF YOU WERE NOT IN THIS PROFESSION, WHAT WOULD YOU BE DOING?
I could not do anything else. It's my passion.

Stein Eriksen Lodge

7700 Stein Way
Park City, Utah 84060
phone 435-649-3700 fax 435-645-6465
website www.steinlodge.com

Cara Schwindt

BEVERAGE MANAGER AND SOMMELIER

WHAT ARE SOME OF YOUR ULTIMATE FOOD AND WINE PAIRINGS?
Caribou tenderloin and northern red Rhône; salmon chowder and dry Alsace
Riesling.

DESCRIBE YOUR WINE SELECTIONS.
A broad range of wines with a worldwide view.

WHAT CATEGORY OF WINE IS THE BEST VALUE ON YOUR WINE LIST?
I try to have good values in every category.

NAME A RECENT WINE DISCOVERY THAT EXCITED YOU.
A simple Merlot with a vibrant blueberry nose, a rich, lush texture, and an
easy-to-drink nature; a wine our customers will love.

WHAT IS YOUR FAVORITE WINE REGION IN THE WORLD TODAY?
Italy. I love the vast array of flavors, textures and styles in Italian wines.

WHAT LED YOU TO BECOME A SOMMELIER?
The job of being a sommelier chose me.

WHAT ARE THE BEST ASPECTS OF YOUR JOB?
Food, wine and people.

IF YOU WERE NOT IN THIS PROFESSION, WHAT WOULD YOU BE DOING?
Teaching Pilates.

Deer Valley Resort
SYNDEY KEEL, WINE BUYER
2250 Deer Valley Drive South, Park City
435-649-1000

Goldener Hirsch Inn
MICHAEL SCHMIDT, DINING ROOM
MANAGER AND WINE BUYER
7570 Royal Street East, Park City
435-649-7770

Sai-Sommet at the Deer Valley Club
PETE BARQUIN, WINE BUYER
7720 Royal Street East, Park City
435-645-9909

Hemingway's Restaurant
TIM BRISCOLL, SOMMELIER
Route 4, Killington
802-422-3886

The Hermitage Inn
JIM McGOVERN, WINE BUYER
Cold Brook Road, Wilmington
802-464-3511

The Inn at Sawmill Farm
BRILL WILLIAMS, WINE BUYER
Mount Snow Valley #100, West Dover
802-464-8131

Inn at Little Washington

Middle and Main Street
Washington, Virginia 22747
phone 540-675-3800 fax 540-675-3100

William E. Lee
WINE DIRECTOR AND SOMMELIER

WHAT IS ONE OF YOUR ULTIMATE FOOD AND WINE PAIRINGS?
Pistachio-crusted baby rack of lamb with ginger-infused carrot sauce and 1990 Brunello di Montalcino Riserva, Soldera.

DESCRIBE YOUR WINE SELECTIONS.
Our list focuses on the wines of Bordeaux, Burgundy and California, and includes enough diversity to complement Chef Patrick O'Connell's complex, flavorful dishes. We also have many verticals from renowned producers (Chateau Montelena back to 1982).

WHAT IS YOUR FAVORITE WINE REGION IN THE WORLD TODAY?
Burgundy. No other area is so complex and dynamic, consistent and indicative of terroir. The Holy Grail of wine.

WHAT LED YOU TO BECOME A SOMMELIER?
An intense love of wine, wine service, and wine with food pairings.

WHAT ARE THE MOST CHALLENGING ASPECTS OF YOUR JOB?
Time management and getting great wines in Virginia.

IF YOU WERE NOT IN THIS PROFESSION, WHAT WOULD YOU BE?
The most awesome house-husband in the world!

Lansdowne Grille at Lansdowne Resort

44050 Woodridge Parkway
Leesburg, Virginia 20176
phone 703-729-4073 fax 703-729-4096
website www.lansdowneresort.com

Mary L. Watson-DeLauder
RESORT SOMMELIER

WHAT ARE SOME OF YOUR ULTIMATE FOOD AND WINE PAIRINGS?
Pinot Noir with filet mignon; big Cabernet Sauvignon with ribeye; Zinfandel with New York strip; Champagne with caviar or smoked salmon; big, ripe Zinfandel with lamb.

DESCRIBE YOUR WINE SELECTIONS.
The wine list is predominantly American. I am very proud of the wines we are making in the United States.

WHAT CATEGORIES OF WINE ARE THE BEST VALUES ON YOUR WINE LIST?
Zinfandel, Syrah/Shiraz and Meritage.

NAME RECENT WINE DISCOVERIES THAT HAVE EXCITED YOU.
Austrian Grüner Veltliner, Ribera del Duero reds from Spain.

WHAT IS YOUR FAVORITE WINE REGION IN THE WORLD TODAY?
California, especially Napa Valley, Sonoma County and Mendocino County. Every year, we see more quality wines and new producers and innovators from here.

WHAT LED YOU TO BECOME A SOMMELIER?
I love wine. I love everything about it, from grape growing all the way to making it, aging it, serving it and enjoying it with food.

WHAT ARE THE BEST ASPECTS OF YOUR JOB?
I especially enjoy staff wine training and guest interaction. Hearing one of the servers relate something we have talked about to a guest is incredibly satisfying.

IF YOU WERE NOT IN THIS PROFESSION, WHAT WOULD YOU BE?
A chef, a gardener or landscaper. Maybe even a farmer or grape grower.

Maestro at the Ritz-Carlton Tysons Corner

1700 Tysons Boulevard
McLean, Virginia 22102
phone 703-506-4300 fax 703-917-5499
website www.ritzcarlton.com

Vincent Feraud
SOMMELIER

WHAT ARE SOME OF YOUR ULTIMATE FOOD AND WINE PAIRINGS?
Trio of tartan fish with Venica Sauvignon Blanc from Collio; roasted potatoes wrapped around John Dory with Chalk Hill Chardonnay.

DESCRIBE YOUR WINE SELECTIONS.
Our wine list is French, Italian and American and includes a number of producers from Virginia.

WHAT CATEGORY OF WINE IS THE BEST VALUE ON YOUR WINE LIST?
Italian white wines.

NAME RECENT WINE DISCOVERIES THAT HAVE EXCITED YOU.
Valpolicella Ripasso from Zenato and 2000 Tocai Friulano from Venica.

WHAT IS YOUR FAVORITE WINE REGION IN THE WORLD TODAY?
Burgundy. I enjoy its flavors and terroir. I also enjoy Amarone.

WHAT LED YOU TO BECOME A SOMMELIER?
When I was an apprentice waiter at sixteen years old, one of the sommeliers in the restaurant in which I worked broke too many glasses. They fired him and I started my sommelier training.

WHAT ARE THE BEST ASPECTS OF YOUR JOB?
Having a good time at night in the restaurant and selling the right wine to the right person.

IF YOU WERE NOT IN THIS PROFESSION, WHAT WOULD YOU BE DOING?
I'd live on a windy island and try to make a living off the water.

Palm Court Restaurant at the Westfield Conference Center

14750 Conference Center Drive
Chantilly, Virginia 20151
phone 703-818-3522 fax 703-818-0363

David J. Pennell
MAÎTRE D'HOTEL AND SOMMELIER

WHAT ARE SOME OF YOUR ULTIMATE FOOD AND WINE PAIRINGS?
Red snapper with Caymus Conundrum; lobster bisque with California or Alsace Pinot Blanc; abalone with Chardonnay; lamb shank with Rioja Reserva; peppered tenderloin with Santa Barbara Rhône-style blend.

DESCRIBE YOUR WINE SELECTIONS.
We offer a range of international selections, and strive for a balance between known vineyards and the lesser-known ones. Our markups are moderate, which allows guests to try better wines without taking out a loan.

WHAT CATEGORY OF WINE IS THE BEST VALUE ON YOUR WINE LIST?
California reds.

NAME RECENT WINE DISCOVERIES THAT HAVE EXCITED YOU.
Portuguese red wines, which are great values, and Austrian white wines, which are excellent food wines at moderate prices.

WHAT IS YOUR FAVORITE WINE REGION IN THE WORLD TODAY?
Santa Barbara County. I like the ripeness and rich flavors of its wines.

WHAT LED YOU TO BECOME A SOMMELIER?
The property had no sommelier and I was very interested in wines and wine education.

WHAT ARE THE BEST ASPECTS OF YOUR JOB?
Finding a new wine, then sharing it with guests—and watching their smiles as they taste it.

IF YOU WERE NOT IN THIS PROFESSION, WHAT WOULD YOU BE DOING?
Teaching.

Williamsburg Inn Regency Dining Room

136 Francis Street
Williamsburg, Virginia 23187-1776
phone 757-229-2141 fax 757-220-7096
website www.colonialwilliamsburg.com

Paul B. Austin
SOMMELIER

WHAT ARE SOME OF YOUR ULTIMATE FOOD AND WINE PAIRINGS?
Foie gras with Sauternes; lobster with Loire Valley white; crab Randolph with white Burgundy; roast rack of lamb with Syrah or Shiraz; cheese samplers after dinner with vintage Port; Iranian Beluga caviar with huge white Burgundy (Montrachet, Corton-Charlemagne).

DESCRIBE YOUR WINE SELECTIONS.
We have an international selection of 400 wines. To help guide customers through the list, we have a sommelier and wine stewards on the floor at dinner and brunch.

WHAT CATEGORIES OF WINE ARE THE BEST VALUES ON YOUR WINE LIST?
Wines in the international section from Chile, Argentina, Australia, New Zealand, South Africa and other regions, and from California's Central Coast.

NAME RECENT WINE DISCOVERIES THAT HAVE EXCITED YOU.
Jurançon (Petit Manseng varietal) and Mendocino Charbono.

WHAT IS YOUR FAVORITE WINE REGION IN THE WORLD TODAY?
Burgundy. The whites and reds range from light as a feather to full and earthy.

WHAT LED YOU TO BECOME A SOMMELIER?
A chance meeting with a publisher and wine journalist who was a customer at a restaurant I ran. He let me taste wonderful wines and complimented my palate. I was hooked.

WHAT ARE THE BEST ASPECTS OF YOUR JOB?
Making people feel at home with wine; seeing the child of a guest I first met when he was eight years old, now old enough to order wine.

IF YOU WERE NOT A SOMMELIER, WHAT WOULD YOU BE DOING?
Designing and building restaurants.

L'Auberge Chez Francois
ADRIANO ROSSI, WINE BUYER
332 Springvale Road, Great Falls
703-759-3800

Clifton Inn
DAVID MORGAN, GENERAL MANAGER
AND WINE BUYER
1296 Clifton Inn Drive, Charlottesville
434-971-1800

Colvin Run Tavern
RICHARD MAHAN, SOMMELIER
8045 Leesburg Pike, Vienna
703-356-9500

The Dining Room at Ford's Colony
ADAM STEELY, MANAGER
AND WINE BUYER
240 Ford's Colony Drive, Williamsburg
757-258-4107

Elysium
EDWARD BERRIMAN, FOOD
AND BEVERAGE DIRECTOR
116 South Alfred Street, Alexandria
703-838-8000

Brasa

2107 Third Avenue
Seattle, Washington 98121
phone 206-728-4220 fax 206-728-8061

Bryan Hill
OWNER AND WINE GUY

WHAT ARE SOME OF YOUR ULTIMATE FOOD AND WINE PAIRINGS?
Albariño with squid ink risotto; Fiano di Avellino with beef carpaccio with truffle oil, Reggiano and arugula.

DESCRIBE YOUR WINE SELECTIONS.
I list wine by the occasion it was meant to be enjoyed: daily wines, which are kept in the fridge or on the kitchen in ample supply; wines meant to enlighten, made from unusual grapes or visionaries; and wines for special occasions, the wines we keep in our cellars.

WHAT IS YOUR FAVORITE WINE REGION IN THE WORLD TODAY?
Willamette Valley, Oregon, mostly because the people are so unassuming and gracious.

WHAT LED YOU TO YOUR CURRENT POSITION?
Fate. I have always been in the restaurant business. When I moved to Seattle, I worked at Chateau Ste. Michelle, where much of my technical knowledge came from.

WHAT IS THE MOST CHALLENGING ASPECT OF YOUR JOB?
Finding the time to adequately inform and educate the staff, given a list that changes weekly and an entire restaurant to oversee.

IF YOU WERE NOT IN THIS PROFESSION, WHAT WOULD YOU BE?
A landscape architect or winemaker.

Café Juanita

9702 Northeast 120th Place
Kirkland, Washington 98034
phone 425-823-1505 fax 425-823-8500
website www.cafejuanita.com

Judith E. Ham

GENERAL MANAGER AND WINE DIRECTOR

WHAT ARE SOME OF YOUR ULTIMATE FOOD AND WINE PAIRINGS?
Octopus and Vermentino; rabbit and Teroldego Rotaliano; pork agro-dolce with Barolo; a selection of Italian cheeses with Tocai Friulano; veal sweetbreads with blended Barbera.

DESCRIBE YOUR WINE SELECTIONS.
We are known for our Italian wines, specifically our large selection of Piemonte wines. Eighty percent of our list is Italian wines.

WHAT CATEGORY OF WINE IS THE BEST VALUE ON YOUR WINE LIST?
Italian blended varietals from small wineries.

NAME RECENT WINE DISCOVERIES THAT HAVE EXCITED YOU.
Friggiali Brunello di Montalcino 1997—the texture is incredible; Pieve di Santa Restituta Rosso 1999, for its complexity and richness.

WHAT IS YOUR FAVORITE WINE REGION IN THE WORLD TODAY?
Italy. I love the complexity of the wines.

WHAT LED YOU TO YOUR CURRENT POSITION?
I was selling Italian wines to Café Juanita and was approached with an offer.

WHAT IS THE BEST ASPECT OF YOUR JOB?
Introducing our guests to Italian wines.

WASHINGTON

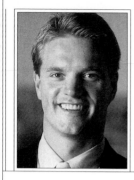

Canlis Restaurant

2576 Aurora Avenue North
Seattle, Washington 98119
phone 206-283-3313 fax 206-283-1766
website www.canlis.com

Shayn E. Bjornholm
WINE DIRECTOR

WHAT ARE SOME OF YOUR ULTIMATE FOOD AND WINE PAIRINGS?
Canlis salad with Loire Valley Sauvignon Blanc; Wasyugyu tenderloin steaks
with Northwest Syrah; crab cakes with white Burgundy.

DESCRIBE YOUR WINE SELECTIONS.
We have an extensive, global representation of the world's finest producers, with
a focus on California Cabernet Sauvignon, red Bordeaux, red and white
Burgundy and Northwest wines.

WHAT CATEGORY OF WINE IS THE BEST VALUE ON YOUR WINE LIST?
Our high-end offerings, where prices are sometimes below retail levels!

NAME RECENT WINE DISCOVERIES THAT HAVE EXCITED YOU.
Aged Champagne, for its finesse and complexity; Washington Syrah for its
potential.

WHAT IS YOUR FAVORITE WINE REGION IN THE WORLD TODAY?
Burgundy. At its best, it leaves you speechless!

WHAT LED YOU TO YOUR CURRENT POSITION?
One great incident with Sauternes, and one great experience with fellow professionals learning about the sommelier profession.

WHAT IS THE BEST ASPECT OF YOUR JOB?
Watching the light go on in a person's head when he makes a great food and
wine connection, and knowing that that moment will be an important part of
his taste memory.

IF YOU WERE NOT IN THIS PROFESSION, WHAT WOULD YOU BE?
A special designer.

Cascadia Restaurant

2328 First Avenue
Seattle, Washington 98109
phone 206-448-8884 fax 206-448-2242
website www.cascadiarestaurant.com

Jake Kosseff
SOMMELIER

WHAT ARE SOME OF YOUR ULTIMATE FOOD AND WINE PAIRINGS?
Oregon white truffle bisque with Willamette Valley Dijon clone Chardonnay;
mature tête-de-cuvée Champagne and movie theater popcorn; ice wine or
Eiswein with salty, creamy cheeses.

DESCRIBE YOUR WINE SELECTIONS.
We specialize in handcrafted wines from very small producers. In keeping with
our food, we also try to keep at least 60 percent of the list from the Cascadia
region (Pacific Northwest).

WHAT CATEGORY OF WINE IS THE BEST VALUE ON YOUR WINE LIST?
Cascadia whites (Pacific Northwest).

NAME RECENT WINE DISCOVERIES THAT HAVE EXCITED YOU.
1998 Strangeland "Silver Leaf" Pinot Noir: complex, earthy, perfect balance.
2000 Buty Semillon/Sauvignon Blanc from the Columbia Valley: rich, crisp
and intense.

WHAT IS YOUR FAVORITE WINE REGION IN THE WORLD TODAY?
Willamette Valley. It has great farming practices and small producers who make
fabulous, handcrafted wines.

WHAT LED YOU TO BECOME A SOMMELIER?
A fascination with and love for wine, food and restaurants.

WHAT ARE THE BEST ASPECTS OF YOUR JOB?
Making people truly happy and showing them new things. Also, putting
together the wine list. I believe that there is such a thing as a perfect wine list.

IF YOU WERE NOT IN THIS PROFESSION, WHAT WOULD YOU BE?
Smoke jumper or something intellectual like professor of classical philosophy.

El Gaucho

2505 First Avenue
Seattle, Washington 98121
phone 206-728-1337 fax 206-728-4477
website www.elgaucho.com

Michael R. Kaminski
WINE CAPTAIN

WHAT ARE SOME OF YOUR ULTIMATE FOOD AND WINE PAIRINGS?
Châteaubriand with red Burgundy, especially Pommard; porterhouse steak with
big Napa Cabernet Sauvignon; crisp Provence rosé with salad (in Marseilles); a
ripe white peach with Viognier.

DESCRIBE YOUR WINE SELECTIONS.
Our list is constantly evolving. As a steakhouse, we specialize in big red wines
from regions all over the world, from those with solid reputations to those with
cult followings, and from the obscure to the offbeat.

WHAT CATEGORY OF WINE IS THE BEST VALUE ON YOUR WINE LIST?
Spanish red.

NAME A RECENT WINE DISCOVERY THAT EXCITED YOU.
Betz Family Cabernet Sauvignon, from the Columbia Valley, Washington. It is
rich and elegant with a supple, long finish, at a great price.

WHAT IS YOUR FAVORITE WINE REGION IN THE WORLD TODAY?
Spain. Wines from Rioja, Ribera del Duero and Priorat offer real quality and
value.

WHAT LED YOU TO BECOME A SOMMELIER?
A B.A. in Film Studies guaranteed me a career in the restaurant industry. Wine
became a tool, hobby and passion.

WHAT IS THE BEST ASPECT OF YOUR JOB?
Seeing the wine program evolve and have a favorable impact on my customers
and the local marketplace.

IF YOU WERE NOT IN THIS PROFESSION, WHAT WOULD YOU BE?
Rock star.

Flying Fish Restaurant

2234 First Avenue
Seattle, Washington 98121
phone 206-728-8595 fax 206-728-1551

Brian K. Huse

GENERAL MANAGER AND WINE BUYER

WHAT ARE SOME OF YOUR ULTIMATE FOOD AND WINE PAIRINGS?
Salt-and-pepper crab with Alsace Gewürztraminer; oysters and Champagne;
lamb and Rhône red.

DESCRIBE YOUR WINE SELECTIONS.
We offer wines in a variety of styles, from a range of regions, and at multiple
price levels. We seek out wines that match our food and that are a sheer pleasure to drink.

WHAT CATEGORY OF WINE IS THE BEST VALUE ON YOUR WINE LIST?
Sauvignon Blanc from New Zealand and the Loire Valley.

WHAT ARE YOUR FAVORITE WINE REGIONS IN THE WORLD TODAY?
France, all of it, and New Zealand.

WHAT LED YOU TO YOUR CURRENT POSITION?
I love the stuff.

WHAT IS THE BEST ASPECT OF YOUR JOB?
Seeing that our customers enjoy their entire restaurant experience.

IF YOU WERE NOT IN THIS PROFESSION, WHAT WOULD YOU BE DOING?
A stay-at-home dad.

The Herbfarm

14590 Northeast 145th Street
Woodinville, Washington 98072
phone 425-485-5300 fax 206-789-2279
website www.theherbfarm.com

Christine Mayo
SOMMELIER

WHAT ARE SOME OF YOUR ULTIMATE FOOD AND WINE PAIRINGS?
Seared sea scallops and spiced carrot sauce with Riesling; duck with Oregon black truffles and mature Pinot Noir; foie gras and Sauternes.

DESCRIBE YOUR WINE SELECTIONS.
We have 1,400 selections, specializing in the wines of the Pacific Northwest, including very deep selections of Oregon Pinot Noir. Our nightly, nine-course prix fixe dinner includes six paired wines.

WHAT CATEGORY OF WINE IS THE BEST VALUE ON YOUR WINE LIST?
The wines of the Pacific Northwest.

NAME RECENT WINE DISCOVERIES THAT HAVE EXCITED YOU.
Austrian white wines. They are precise and expressive wines with great character and flavor.

WHAT IS YOUR FAVORITE WINE REGION IN THE WORLD TODAY?
The Pacific Northwest. Its pioneering spirit, camaraderie and potential greatness make it a very exciting place to be.

WHAT LED YOU TO BECOME A SOMMELIER?
Dumb luck. I was just out of grad school and was very lucky to be working at a restaurant that had an outstanding wine program.

WHAT ARE THE BEST ASPECTS OF YOUR JOB?
With our nine-course, fixed menu we do precise pairings of five or six wines each night. It is wonderful to see our guests' faces when they hit the "ah-ha" moment, when they realize that the wine is not incidental to their meal.

IF YOU WERE NOT IN THIS PROFESSION, WHAT WOULD YOU BE DOING?
More painting.

Metropolitan Grill

820 Second Avenue
Seattle, Washington 98104
phone 206-624-3287 fax 206-389-0042

David Coyle

HEAD SOMMELIER AND WINE BUYER

WHAT ARE SOME OF YOUR ULTIMATE FOOD AND WINE PAIRINGS?
Met Grill Châteaubriand with soft, velvety Washington Merlot; parmesan cheese–crusted halibut cheeks with Semillon or Sauvignon Blanc/Semillon blend.

DESCRIBE YOUR WINE SELECTIONS.
Our focus is on West Coast reds, but includes wines from around the world, all served in Reidel stemware.

WHAT CATEGORY OF WINE IS THE BEST VALUE ON YOUR WINE LIST?
Australian reds, particularly Shiraz.

NAME A RECENT WINE DISCOVERY THAT EXCITED YOU.
The difference that proper stemware makes in a wine program. Proper stemware has brought our wine service to a world-class level.

WHAT IS YOUR FAVORITE WINE REGION IN THE WORLD TODAY?
Washington. Great wines and very consistent vintages.

WHAT LED YOU TO BECOME A SOMMELIER?
I was given the chance to join the sommelier team here twelve years ago. I loved the job from day one.

WHAT IS THE MOST REWARDING PART OF YOUR JOB?
Having guests from around the world take my advice on food and wine pairing and thank me for it.

IF YOU WERE NOT IN YOUR CURRENT POSITION, WHAT WOULD YOU BE DOING?
Maître d' or floor manager.

Metropolitan Grill

820 Second Avenue
Seattle, Washington 98104
phone 206-624-3287 fax 206-389-0042

William Dave Prigmore
SOMMELIER AND CAPTAIN

WHAT ARE SOME OF YOUR ULTIMATE FOOD AND WINE PAIRINGS?
Porterhouse steak with 1996 Alexander Valley Silver Oak Cabernet Sauvignon; Delmonico steak with 1999 Januik Winery Cabernet Sauvignon; peppercorn New York steak with Petite Sirah; mesquite-grilled salmon with Yakima Valley Syrah.

DESCRIBE YOUR WINE SELECTIONS.
We offer principally Bordelais varietals from the classic regions, including Bordeaux, California and Washington. However, we feature wines from all classic wine regions worldwide, from Hungary to Argentina and from South Africa to British Columbia.

WHAT CATEGORY OF WINE IS THE BEST VALUE ON YOUR WINE LIST?
California Cabernet Sauvignon.

NAME A RECENT WINE DISCOVERY THAT EXCITED YOU.
Vega Sicilia. One of the best red wines I've tasted.

WHAT IS YOUR FAVORITE WINE REGION IN THE WORLD TODAY?
Washington. Cabernet Sauvignon and Merlot from the Columbia Valley and Syrah from the Yakima Valley are outstanding.

WHAT LED YOU TO BECOME A SOMMELIER?
I worked as a sous-chef with a CIA graduate on over forty winemaker dinners.

WHAT ARE THE BEST ASPECTS OF YOUR JOB?
Every day I meet fifty to one hundred diners and wine enthusiasts who are interesting, engaging and full of curiosity about the kaleidoscopic world of wines.

IF YOU WERE NOT IN THIS PROFESSION, WHAT WOULD YOU BE DOING?
More winemaking; greater involvement in a wholesale nursery, featuring perennials, alpine plants and conifers.

Rover's

2808 East Madison Street
Seattle, Washington 98112
phone 206-325-7442 fax 206-325-1092

Cyril R. Frechier
MANAGER AND SOMMELIER

WHAT IS ONE OF YOUR ULTIMATE FOOD AND WINE PAIRINGS?
Seared Hudson Valley foie gras and a foie gras nage with Zind-Humbrecht
1997 Pinot Gris, Clos Windsbuhl.

DESCRIBE YOUR WINE SELECTIONS.
An extensive coverage of French, Californian and Pacific Northwestern
vineyards.

WHAT IS YOUR FAVORITE WINE REGION IN THE WORLD TODAY?
Burgundy. No other region gives me that toe-curling sensation that I get when
I taste a truly great Burgundy.

WHAT LED YOU TO BECOME A SOMMELIER?
My love of food and wine and the restaurant world. It's a great industry.

WHAT IS THE MOST CHALLENGING ASPECT OF YOUR JOB?
Staying current with the ever-expanding wine world. All these great new wine
regions and winemakers; too many wines, too little time!

IF YOU WERE NOT IN THIS PROFESSION, WHAT WOULD YOU BE DOING?
Working the vineyard, making wine.

Salish Lodge & Spa Dining Room

6501 Railroad Avenue Southeast
Snoqualmie, Washington 98065
phone 425-888-2556 fax 425-888-2533
website www.salishlodge.com

Randall L. Austin
CELLAR MASTER

WHAT ARE SOME OF YOUR ULTIMATE FOOD AND WINE PAIRINGS?
Warm salad of Maine lobster, mango and avocado with Pinot Gris; Douglas
fir–roasted, wild northwest salmon with Pinot Noir; mustard nut-crusted lamb
rack with Merlot or Petite Sirah; salmon with Pinot Noir or Grenache; venison
with Cabernet, Syrah, Bordeaux, Meritage or Zinfandel.

DESCRIBE YOUR WINE SELECTIONS.
We offer 1,200 wines from all over the world, but we are best known for our
selection of Washington wines.

WHAT CATEGORY OF WINE IS THE BEST VALUE ON YOUR WINE LIST?
Australian Shiraz.

NAME RECENT WINE DISCOVERIES THAT HAVE EXCITED YOU.
Washington Syrah. It is dramatic, not just for value, but for power, intensity
and purity of fruit.

WHAT IS YOUR FAVORITE WINE REGION IN THE WORLD TODAY?
Washington. It is a truly great wine-producing region and a rising star. The
wines have great complexity, fruit and power.

WHAT LED YOU TO YOUR CURRENT POSITION?
Someone gave me a wine book years ago and it changed my career.

WHAT IS THE BEST ASPECT OF YOUR JOB?
Performing on the floor as a sommelier.

IF YOU WERE NOT IN THIS PROFESSION, WHAT WOULD YOU BE DOING?
Writing and playing music.

Salish Lodge & Spa Dining Room

6501 Railroad Avenue Southeast
Snoqualmie, Washington 98065
phone 425-888-2556 fax 425-888-2533
website www.salishlodge.com

Jennifer L. Bushman
SOMMELIER AND CELLAR KEEPER

WHAT ARE SOME OF YOUR ULTIMATE FOOD AND WINE PAIRINGS?
Warm salad of lobster, mango and avocado with Riesling; fennel-seared loin of rabbit with dried fruit couscous with Pinot Noir; squab with Grenache; wild boar with Nebbiolo.

DESCRIBE YOUR WINE SELECTIONS.
Our selection is 1,200 strong and honors all parts of the world. Our focus is on Washington and the Pacific Northwest.

WHAT CATEGORY OF WINE IS THE BEST VALUE ON YOUR WINE LIST?
Australian Shiraz and Italian wines.

NAME RECENT WINE DISCOVERIES THAT HAVE EXCITED YOU.
Washington Syrah. It is exciting, powerful, intense, and a good value.

WHAT IS YOUR FAVORITE WINE REGION IN THE WORLD TODAY?
Alsace. It's intriguing, mysterious and surprising.

WHAT LED YOU TO BECOME A SOMMELIER?
I'm completely passionate about wine.

WHAT IS THE BEST ASPECT OF YOUR JOB?
The magic that emerges with a great food and wine pairing.

IF YOU WERE NOT IN THIS PROFESSION, WHAT WOULD YOU BE DOING?
Chiropractic medicine.

Sun Mountain Lodge
Patterson Lake Road
Winthrop, Washington 98862
phone 509-996-2211 fax 509-996-4711

Hector A. Garibay
FOOD AND BEVERAGE MANAGER

DESCRIBE YOUR WINE SELECTIONS.
Our wine list is very strong on Washington wines.

WHAT IS YOUR FAVORITE WINE REGION IN THE WORLD TODAY?
Spain. The Basque region has great wines that now compare with the quality of French wines.

WHAT IS THE MOST CHALLENGING ASPECT OF YOUR JOB?
Following all the new wines from all over the world.

IF YOU WERE NOT IN THE WINE PROFESSION, WHAT WOULD YOU BE DOING?
Enjoying a full bottle of wine.

Tulio Ristorante

1100 Fifth Avenue
Seattle, Washington 98101
phone 206-624-5500 fax 206-623-0568

Michael Degano
GENERAL MANAGER AND SOMMELIER

WHAT ARE SOME OF YOUR ULTIMATE FOOD AND WINE PAIRINGS?
Roasted salmon with spinach, mascarpone and grilled lemons paired with
Piedmont Barbera; foie gras with late-harvest Semillon; venison with Australian
Shiraz; asparagus with Sauvignon Blanc.

DESCRIBE YOUR WINE SELECTIONS.
We have wines from every wine region in Italy and the Northwest. Our wine
by-the-glass program shows off the best of Washington.

WHAT CATEGORY OF WINE IS THE BEST VALUE ON YOUR WINE LIST?
Southern Italian reds (Primitivo, Nero d'Avola, Salento).

NAME RECENT WINE DISCOVERIES THAT HAVE EXCITED YOU.
Washington Syrahs from 1998. They are unbelievable, with balance and fruit.
Excellent juice.

WHAT IS YOUR FAVORITE WINE REGION IN THE WORLD TODAY?
Piedmont. I love the wines. Winemakers combine a passion for tradition and
the desire to make drinkable wine.

WHAT LED YOU TO BECOME A SOMMELIER?
My passion for wine and knowledge. It was the natural progression in my
career.

WHAT IS THE MOST CHALLENGING ASPECT OF YOUR JOB?
Wine list maintenance. Keeping it balanced and inspired.

IF YOU WERE NOT IN THIS PROFESSION, WHAT WOULD YOU BE?
A physical therapist.

Campagne
SHAWN MEAD, WINE BUYER
86 Pine Street, Seattle
206-728-2800

Place Pigalle
BILL FRANK, PROPRIETOR
AND WINE BUYER
81 Pike Street, Seattle
206-624-1756

Ray's Boathouse
DAVID CARREON, WINE DIRECTOR
AND SOMMELIER
6049 Seaview Avenue Northwest, Seattle
206-789-3770

Serafina
JOHN NEUMARK, CHEF
AND WINE BUYER
2043 Eastlake Avenue East, Seattle
206-323-0807

Ten Mercer
BRIAN CURRY, GENERAL MANAGER
AND WINE BUYER
10 Mercer Street, Seattle
206-691-3723

W Hotel
DAWNIEL GEIBEL, BEVERAGE MANAGER
1112 Fourth Avenue, Seattle
206-264-6000

Wild Ginger
BRUCE STURGEON, GENERAL MANAGER
AND WINE BUYER
1401 Third Avenue, Seattle
206-623-4450

The Greenbrier Dining Room at the Greenbriar Hotel

KEVIN DOTT, BEVERAGE DIRECTOR
AND SOMMELIER
300 West Main Street, White Sulphur
Springs
304-536-1110

Red Fox Restaurant

JOHN BETZ, DIRECTOR
OF WINE SERVICE
1 Whistlepunk Village, Showshoe
304-572-1111

Bartolotta's Lake Park Bistro

PETER DONAHUE, CORPORATE
WINE DIRECTOR
3133 East Newberry Boulevard,
Milwaukee
414-962-6300

The Immigrant Room at The American Club

DEAN SCHAAP, BEVERAGE
COORDINATOR
Highland Drive, Kohler
800-344-2838

Karl Ratzsch's

TOMAS ANDERO, WINE BUYER
320 East Mason Street, Milwaukee
414-276-2720

Blue Lion Restaurant

KYLE THOMPSON, WINE BUYER

160 North Millward Street, Jackson

307-733-3912

Snake River

BOB MERRIMAN, GENERAL MANAGER

AND WINE BUYER

84 East Broadway Street, Jackson

307-733-0557

Chapter Five
Resources

Confrérie de la Chaîne des Rôtisseurs

444 Park Avenue South, Suite 301
New York, New York 10016–7321
phone 212-683-3770 fax (212) 683–3882
email chaine@chaineus.org
website www.chaineus.org

The Chaîne des Rôtisseurs is an international gastronomic society founded in Paris in 1950. It is devoted to promoting fine dining and "les arts de la table" (the arts of the table) in the broadest sense. The Chaîne is based on the traditions and practices of the old French Royal Guild of Geese Roasters, "les Ayeurs" (geese were particularly appreciated in those days). Its authority gradually expanded to the roasting of all poultry, meat and game. The written history of "les Ayeurs" has been traced back to the year 1248.

Today, the society has members in more than 100 countries around the world. Each chapter, called a "bailliage" (in English, bailiwick) is headed by a "bailli" (bailiff) and other officers who plan the individual chapter's activities. All bailliages offer fine dining events, often black tie, in the best local restaurants and hotels. The menus and dishes are created exclusively for these dinners by the chefs, many of whom are also members of the confrérie. Each bailliage also holds one grand gala event each year to celebrate the induction of new members. Members receive a distinctive ribbon that is worn at Chaîne gatherings.

The Chaîne des Rôtisseurs is an active supporter and organizer of educational programs and events, and annually sponsors a national Sommelier competition, open to Chaîne members between the ages of 23 and 32. The competition allows participants an opportunity to display their knowledge of wine, tasting expertise, and wine service proficiency. For information about the 2003 event, to be held in May 2003 in Miami, Florida, please contact Dan Gulbronsen, Echanson des États-Unis, at dan4wines@aol.com.

Ten years ago a sommelier in North America had very few resources with which to further his or her education and career. Today there are numerous wine training and certification programs available across the nation. The following includes the significant professional wine training programs, consumer-oriented programs and a list of wine education-related resources.

I. ASSOCIATION DE LA SOMMELLERIE INTERNATIONALE MEMBERS

Every three years, A.S.I. hosts the Meilleur Sommelier du Monde Competition, or "Concours Mondiale." Giuseppe Vaccarini is President of the Milan-based organization. Only one sommelier association in each nation is recognized by A.S.I.

AUSTRIA
AUSTRIAN SOMMELIERS
ASSOCIATION
Siegfried Brudermann, President
Skilftstrasse 315, A-5753
Saalbach
phone +43-6541-6284
fax +43-6541-6284-20

BELGIUM
BELGIUM SOMMELIERS GUILD
Alain de Mol, President
B.P. 129, B-1400 Nivelles
phone 067-21-51-55
fax 067-22-05-81

BRAZIL
BRAZILIAN SOMMELIERS
ASSOCIATION
Danio Braga, President
Pr. Do Flamengo, 66, Bloco B, 307
Rio de Janeiro RJ CEP : 22228-900
phone 55-21-285-0497
fax 55-21-265-2157

CANADA
CANADIAN ASSOCIATION OF
PROFESSIONAL SOMMELIERS
Jacques Orhon, President
150, rue Lesage, Sainte-Adèle,
Quebec J8B 2R4
phone 450-229-7604
fax 450-229-5771
email: orhon@cqocable.ca

CHILE
CHILEAN SOMMELIERS
ASSOCIATION
Héctor Vergara F., President
Bernardo O'Higgins Avenue, No.
816, Santiago
phone 56-2-758-5800
fax 56-2-758-5808

CHINA
HONG KONG SOMMELIERS
ASSOCIATION
Nelson Chow, President
22/F, 447-449 Lockhart Road,
Causeway Bay, Hong Kong
phone 852-28363938
fax 852-28362316

CHAPTER FIVE

CROATIA
CROATIAN SOMMELIERS
ASSOCIATION
Ninoslav Dusper, President
Hotel Intercontinental,
Krsnjavoga 1, 10000 Zagreb
phone 385-1-48-36-572
or 385-98-322-534
fax 385-48-36-572

THE CZECH REPUBLIC
THE CZECH REPUBLIC
SOMMELIER ASSOCIATION
Martin Pastyrík, President
Rest. Palac Kinski,
Staromëstské nám. 12,
110 00 Praha 1
phone 420-2-2481-0750
fax 420-2-232-61-37

DENMARK
DANISH SOMMELIERS
ASSOCIATION
Tim Vollerslev, President
Radisson SAS Hotels Worldwide,
Engvej 171, 2300 Copenhagen S.
phone 45-23-60-31-09
fax 45-32-87-04-05

FINLAND
FINNISH SOMMELIERS
ASSOCIATION
Kristiina Laitinen, President
Pengerkatu 19 A 15,
00500 Helsinki
phone +358-9-726-0386

FRANCE
FRANCE SOMMELIERS
ASSOCIATION
Georges Pertuiset, President
Les Hameaux du Suzon, 12 rue
Paul Delouvrier, 21000 Dijon
phone 03-80-70-92-10
fax 03-80-71-62-11
website www.wine-waiters.com

GREAT BRITAIN
THE ACADEMY OF FOOD AND
WINE SERVICE
Richard Edwards, President
Burgoine House, 8 Lower
Teddington Road Hampton
Wick, Surrey KT1 4ER
phone 020-8943-1011
fax 020-8977-5519

GERMANY
GERMAN SOMMELIERS
ASSOCIATION
Bernd Glauben, President
Romantik-Hotel, Goldene
Traube, Am Viktoriabrunnen
2D-96450 Coburg
phone 0-95-61/87-60
fax 0-95-61/87-62-22

GREECE
GREEK SOMMELIERS
ASSOCIATION
Kostas Touloumtzis, President
33 Avenue Pentelis, 15235,
Vrilissia
phone +30-1-6138651
fax +30-1-61-39696

ICELAND
ICELANDIC SOMMELIERS
ASSOCIATION
Haraldur Halldørsson, President
Hàaleitisbraut 24, 108 Reykjavik
phone +354-588-3071

364   CHALK HILL WINERY SOMMELIER GUIDE TO RESTAURANTS IN AMERICA

IRELAND

THE IRISH GUILD OF
SOMMELIERS
Oliver J. Murtagh, President
22 Cherry Court, Terenure,
Dublin 6W
phone/fax 353-1-4900156

ITALY

ITALIAN SOMMELIERS
ASSOCIATION
Giuseppe Vaccarini, President
20125 Milano, V.le Monza, 9
phone 02-28-46-237 (r.a.)
fax 02-26-11-23-28
email p.simonetti@sommelier.it
(Paola Simonetti)
website www.sommelier.it

JAPAN

JAPAN SOMMELIERS
ASSOCIATION
Takashi Atsuta, President
JC Bldg 5F 3-6-22, Shibakoen
Minato-Ku, Tokyo
phone 81-3-5473-7831
fax 81-3-5473-7822

KOREA

KOREAN SOMMELIERS
ASSOCIATION — IN VINO
VERITAS
Sun-Tschu Lie, President
724-35, Yedksamdong,
Kangnam-Gu, Seoul, 135-082
phone 822-555-8158
fax 822-569-8158

LUXEMBURG

LUXEMBURG SOMMELIERS
ASSOCIATION
Claude Phal, President
B.P. 2524 (Horesca), L-1025
Luxembourg
phone 46-03-11 fax 46-52-07

MEXICO

MEXICAN SOMMELIERS
ASSOCIATION
Victor Absalon Lopez
Callao No. 802, Col. Lindavista,
C.P. 07300, Mexico, D.F.
phone 52-53-94-03-85
fax 52-52-54-55-87

MONACO

MONACO SOMMELIERS
ASSOCIATION
Jean Pallanca, President
3, passage St-Michel,
MC 98000 Monaco
phone/fax 377-93-30-75-00

NETHERLANDS

DUTCH SOMMELIERS
ASSOCIATION
Cees Vos, President
Vianenstraat 12, 4861 TJ Chaam
phone 0161-492070
fax 0161-492780

NORWAY

NORWEGIAN SOMMELIERS
ASSOCIATION
Knut Aanonsen, President
DNVF c/o Aperitif, Furuveien
39 C, 0678 Oslo
phone +47-22-19-00-75
fax +47-22-67-14-77

POLAND

POLISH SOMMELIERS
ASSOCIATION
Wojciech Gogolinski, President
Ul. Litewska 24/64, 30-014
Krakow
phone 48-12-423-40-69
fax 48-12-429-18-56

PORTUGAL

PORTUGUESE SOMMELIERS
ASSOCIATION
Joaquim Santos, President
Av. Almirante Reis, 58 r/c - Dto.
1150-019 Lisboa
phone/fax +351-21-813-25-42

ROMANIA

NATIONAL SOMMELIER CLUB
OF ROMANIA
Prof. Radu Nicolescu, President
CNSR, CP 1-234, Bucarest
phone/fax +401/313-52-88

SLOVAKIA

SLOVAK SOMMELIERS
ASSOCIATION
Christophe Mondorowicz,
President
Timravina 13, 811 06 Bratislava 1
phone +421-7-54-41-23-07
fax +421-7-54-41-82-39

SLOVENIA

SLOVENIAN SOMMELIER
ASSOCIATION
Franko Rutar, President
Delpinova 7A, 5000 Nova Gorica
phone +386-65-12640 fax +386-
65-1264270

SPAIN

SPANISH SOMMELIERS
ASSOCIATION
Juan Muñoz Ramos, President
Riera Bonet, 5, At. 3.a, 08750
Molins de Rei, Barcelona
phone/fax 93-668-65-86

SWEDEN

SWEDISH SOMMELIERS
ASSOCIATION
Mischa Billing, President
Stora Fiskaregatan 7, Lund,
S-222-24
phone +46-46-33-50-65
fax +46-46-33-50-63

SWITZERLAND

SWISS ASSOCIATION OF
PROFESSIONAL SOMMELIERS
Myriam Broggi, President
Champ-Pallet 2, 1801
Le Mont-Pélerin
phone/fax 41-21-921-18-91

TURKEY

TURKISH SOMMELIER
ASSOCIATION
Randolph Ward Mays, President
Göktürk Köyü, Kumlugeçit
Mevkii No. 2
Kemerburgaz, Istanbul
phone 90-212-239-9350
fax 90-212-239-9359

USA

AMERICAN SOMMELIERS
ASSOCIATION
Andrew Bell, President
100 Old Gulph Road, Gulph
Mills, PA 19428
phone 610-520-1200
fax 610-520-2045
email: asasommelier@aol.com

VENEZUELA

VENEZUELAN SOMMELIERS
ASSOCIATION
Leonardo D'Addazio, President
Avd. Las Americas, Edf. SADA
Planta Baja, Puerto Ordaz
phone 58-86-23-47-15
fax 58-86-23-23-14

II. THE BRITISH MASTER PROGRAMS

The Master Sommelier and the Master of Wine are professional titles earned after several years of examinations and tastings. Both the Court of Master Sommeliers and the Institute of Masters of Wine are based in the U.K., and are modeled on the trade guilds of the 19th century. As the titles imply, the Master Sommelier program emphasizes wine service skills while the Master of Wine program requires a broad understanding of all aspects of the industry, from viticulture and vinification to finance, marketing and contemporary issues. Both programs examine the wine world at large, from a British standpoint. North America is important, but takes a backseat to Old World areas such as France, and to New World areas such as Australia. Only 105 have earned the M.S. (ten women) and 250 the M.W. (forty-six women). Three men—North America's Ronn Wiegand and Doug Frost, and France's Gerard Basset— have earned both titles.

Master Sommelier

Established in 1969 "to encourage improved standards of beverage knowledge and service in hotels and restaurants," and internationally recognized in 1977, the Court of Master Sommeliers is an educational body. The Court explains: "In the service of wine, spirits and other alcoholic beverages, the Master Sommelier Diploma is the ultimate professional credential that anyone can attain worldwide." The M.S. syllabus includes production methods of wines and spirits, international wine laws, harmony of food and wine, wine tasting skills, and practical service and salesmanship, including service of liqueurs, brandies, ports and cigars. In a blind tasting of six wines in twenty-five minutes, candidates must correctly identify grape varieties, country and region of origin, age and quality.

All exams after the Basic Introductory Course are verbal and in the presence of a panel of judges. Prerequisites to sitting for the M.S. Diploma are successful completion of the Introductory Sommelier Course and the Advanced Sommelier Course, which require several years of practical experience in the restaurant industry. After passing the Advanced level you are invited to sit for the M.S. Diploma. You will have three years or three tries to pass all three sections at the Master's level—Theory, Tasting and Practical Service. If your clock runs out without passing all of the three parts you may start again. Once you pass all three, you are invited to join the Court as a Master Sommelier.

Court of Master Sommeliers
North American Chapter, Kathleen Lewis
1200 Jefferson Street
Napa, California 94559
phone 707-255-7667 fax 707-255-1119
email courtofms@aol.com
website www.mastersommeliers.org

American Master Sommeliers

Nunzio Alioto, Alioto's Restaurant & Valhalla Restaurant,
San Francisco, CA

Robert Bath, The RLB Wine Group, St. Helena, CA

Wayne Belding, Boulder Wine Merchant, Boulder, CO

Michael Bonaccorsi, Bonaccorsi Wine Company, Santa Monica, CA

Scott Carney, Glazier Group, New York, NY

Roger Dagorn, Chanterelle, New York, NY

Fred Dame, Paterno Imports, San Francisco, CA

Gilles de Chambure, Robert Mondavi Winery, Oakville, CA

Richard Dean, The Mark Hotel, Long Island City, NY

Catherine Fallis, Planet Grape, Pacific Grove, CA

Jay Fletcher, Southern Wine & Spirits of CO & Aspen Wine Sense
Consulting, Aspen, CO

Kenneth Fredrickson, Denver, CO

Doug Frost, Kansas City, MO

Chuck Furuya, Fine Wine Imports, Honolulu, HI

Tim Gaiser, Consultant, San Francisco, CA

Steven Geddes, Vintage Consultants, Las Vegas, NV

Evan Goldstein, Allied Domecq, Santa Rosa, CA

Keith Goldston, Las Vegas, NV

Peter Granoff, Napa, CA

Ira Harmon, Southern Wine & Sprits, Las Vegas, NV

Greg Harrington, BR Guest, New York, NY

Andrea Immer, French Culinary Institute of New York City, Stamford, CT

Jay James, Bellagio, Food & Beverage, Las Vegas, NV

Robert Jones, Kysela Pere et Fils Ltd., Richmond, VA

Emmanuel Kemiji, Miura Vineyards, Napa, CA

Fran Kysela, Kysela Pere et Fils Ltd., Winchester, VA

Michael McNeill, Ritz Carlton-Buckhead, Atlanta, GA

Sally Mohr, Boulder Wine Merchant, Boulder, CO

Steve Morey, Diageo Chateau & Estate Wines, San Francisco, CA

Ron Mumford, Southern Wine & Spirits, Las Vegas, NV

Lawrence O'Brien, Augustan Wine Imports, Orlando, FL

David O'Connor, McCall Associates-Events Management, Inc.,
San Francisco, CA

Damon Ornowski, Rudd, Oakville, CA

Ed Osterland, Osterland Enterprises, San Diego, CA

William Sherer, Ritz Carlton, New York, NY

Cameron Sisk, International Wine Shop, Las Vegas, NV

Joseph Spellman, Paterno Imports, Chicago, IL

Larry Stone, Rubicon, San Francisco, CA

Elizabeth Schweitzer, Beverly Hills, CA

Angelo Tavernaro, Wine and Service Consultant, Las Vegas, NV

Greg Tresner, Mary Elaine's at the Phoenician Resort, Phoenix, AZ

Madeline Triffon, Unique Restaurant Corp., Bingham Farms, MI

Claudia Tyagi, Las Vegas, NV

John Unger, Lockkeppers at Thornburg Station, Parma, OH

Kevin Vogt, Delmonico Steak House at the Venetian Resort,
Las Vegas, NV

Barbara Werley, Four Seasons Resort, Scottsdale, AZ

Ronn Wiegand, Restaurant Wine, Napa, CA

III. OTHER PROFESSIONAL RESOURCES

Master of Wine

Like the Court of Master Sommeliers, the Institute of Masters of Wine
is an educational body. The first examination was held in 1953. The
M.W. syllabus includes three units of theory— Production of Wine,
Business of Wine and Contemporary Issues, plus one wine analysis unit,
the Practical, or blind, tasting.

A separate U.K. organization, the Wine and Spirit Education Trust, offers three courses to educate and train the trade and public, the Certificate, Higher Certificate and Diploma. Successful completion of these courses is highly recommended for anyone wishing to begin the M.W. program. WSET courses are currently available in Boston, New York City and Philadelphia, or by correspondence course. Mary Ewing-Mulligan M.W. at NYC's International Wine Center has arranged a Home Study Program in conjunction with the WSET.

The Institute of Masters of Wine North America Ltd.
Roger Bomrich, M.W., President
phone 212-355-0700
Mary Ewing-Mulligan, M.W., North America Advisory Board
phone 212-627-7170
website www.masters-of-wine.org

Wine and Spirit Education Trust North America Offered at:
New York:
Mary Ewing-Mulligan, M.W., President
Linda G. Lawry, Director
May Matta-Aliah, Wine Program Coordinator
International Wine Center
1133 Broadway, #520
New York, New York 10010
phone 212-627-7170 fax: 212-627-7116
email iwcny@aol.com
website www.learnwine.com

Boston:
Sandy Block, M.W., Bill Nesto, M.W., Boston University,
Special Programs
Elizabeth Bishop Wine Resource Center
808 Commonwealth Avenue Boston, Massachusetts 02215
phone 617-353-9852 fax: 617-353-4130
email boswine@aol.com

Philadelphia:
Neal Ewing
Independent Wine Club of Delaware Valley
P.O. Box 1478, Havertown, Pennsylvania 19083
phone 610-649-9936 fax 610-649-9936
email: IWCwine@aol.com